MADDEN & SUMMERALL

MADDEN & SUMMERALL

HOW THEY REVOLUTIONIZED NFL BROADCASTING

RICH PODOLSKY

FOREWORDS BY JOE BUCK AND TROY AIKMAN

LYONS PRESS

Essex, Connecticut

LYONS PRESS

An imprint of The Globe Pequot Publishing Group, Inc.
64 South Main Street
Essex, CT 06426
www.globepequot.com

Copyright © 2025 by Rich Podolsky

All rights reserved. No part of this book may be reproduced in any form or by any electronic or mechanical means, including information storage and retrieval systems, without written permission from the publisher, except by a reviewer who may quote passages in a review.

British Library Cataloguing in Publication Information available

Library of Congress Cataloging-in-Publication Data available

ISBN 9781493091980 (cloth) | ISBN 9781493091997 (epub)

For Diana

Contents

Foreword *Joe Buck* ix
Foreword *Troy Aikman* xiii
Author's Note xvii
Introduction: How NFL Broadcasting Has Changed
   Throughout the Years xxiii

CHAPTER 1: Will the Real John Madden Please Stand Up 1
CHAPTER 2: Summerall: Right Place, Right Time 13
CHAPTER 3: Masterclass by the Dutchman 23
CHAPTER 4: It's "Super Summerall" 31
CHAPTER 5: Madden and Summerall Rise to New Heights 43
CHAPTER 6: The Rise and Fall of Brookshier—and Summerall . . . 59
CHAPTER 7: For John Madden, 1980 "Tasted Great!" 71
CHAPTER 8: The Contest: Would It Be Summerall or Scully? 83
CHAPTER 9: What Made Them Great 103
CHAPTER 10: The Train, the Bus, the Game, the All-Madden
   Team, and the Matchmaker 125
CHAPTER 11: Disaster: How CBS Lost the NFL Contract 141
CHAPTER 12: The Intervention 157
CHAPTER 13: It Was the Perfect Marriage—Until It Wasn't 169
CHAPTER 14: Saying Good-Bye to Pat 179
CHAPTER 15: An All Madden Farewell 187

Afterword 199
Acknowledgments 201
Notes 203
Index 211

Foreword

By Joe Buck

When I was a kid my dad, Jack Buck, took me to see *The NFL Today* show. He also took me to see the Monday night games when my dad was doing MNF radio with Hank Stram. I got to see the pomp and circumstance of what was going on two booths down, in ABC's booth—the yellow blazers and the lights. Those are indelible images on my memory that kind of shaped what I wanted to do as I was growing up.

I've always heard that John Madden and Pat Summerall were friends but living in separate silos off the air—and when they came together, it was just beautiful. The fact that they weren't tight friends, like Pat was with [Tom] Brookshier, worked to their advantage on the air. Nothing was over-rehearsed. Nothing was planned out. And I think Pat legitimately was just reacting to whatever John was doing, whether it was the bombastic style or the Telestrator. They were basically doing the Miller Lite commercials on the air. And I think Pat was amused by it. There was nothing staged, nothing fake. It was all just natural reaction for Pat, which was just beautiful to hear.

Anybody who had a reverence for my father and could make my father laugh, they automatically had an impact on me. I wanted to be around them, and I wanted to know what made them tick. I just know the love my dad had for Pat was reciprocated, and there was a respect level my dad had for Pat that I didn't see elsewhere over the years.

There are very few that could do what Pat did, go from on the field to in the booth to changing roles being a traffic cop. It's a very different skill set. I think Pat is one of the most underrated broadcasters we have ever had. It's probably the way he wanted it.

I don't think Pat craved attention. He would kind of glide into a room and keep to himself, from what I saw. I wasn't around him when he was running with Brookshier, but I saw him later in life. I saw his face light up when he saw my dad, and I saw my dad's face light up when he walked in. So as a young kid, I was aware that something special was in this package of Pat Summerall. So I paid attention to him. I didn't see a guy who was gathering crowds; I didn't see a guy who was desirous of attention and telling stories. He was just subtle. He had a subtle sense of humor, and a very dry sense of humor. He would interject and have the perfect line at the perfect time that was hilarious but wasn't some long drawn-out joke. It was just an observation.

The Pat I knew wasn't overly dramatic about anything. He was very understated. That's the way he broadcast, and that's the way he was when I was around him. He and my dad were buddies. Pat didn't try to lead or steer John into a corner that he didn't want to be in. That left John with a blank canvas to go anywhere he wanted to.

He chose his words very carefully. Most people just flood a microphone in a broadcast with words. The fact that he didn't, that he just found the right words to punctuate the moment at the right time, that's who he was.

When I took over for him at Fox, with Troy [Aikman] and Chris [Collinsworth], it took three people to fill the shoes of two people, and those shoes were never filled and still haven't been, and in my estimation never will be.

I fell into the trap of trying to sound like Pat. When I took over for Pat at Fox, the shadow was so long, and the shoes were so big, I was trying to be Patish, and I found myself doing a knockoff of that—being as minimalist as I could. It worked for Pat, but for me it came off as boring.

There was a gentleness to Pat. He played in the NFL, but if you didn't know that you'd be hard-pressed to believe it. He was so quiet. Most ex-players are the kind of guys that give you a forearm shiver. When they walk into a room, they're loud. And there was plenty for Pat to boast about, but he didn't do it. He was very gentle on the air and off the air.

FOREWORD: JOE BUCK

And he had the most melodic voice that worked as much for football as it did for golf as it did for tennis. Pat had that gentle soul, and I think it came out with the way he spoke.

The lesson is that there is only one. There's only one that came along at the perfect time with the perfect partner, who was the exact complement he needed to allow room for his brilliance, and yet Pat still carved out his own area on the broadcast. He made his words count.

Joe Buck, September 2024

Foreword

By Troy Aikman

I GOT TO KNOW PAT AND JOHN BECAUSE THEY WERE COVERING SO MANY of our games throughout my career. In 1994 and '95, I did a weekly TV show with Pat in Dallas. He was great to work with and made me feel so comfortable, but I never thought I'd go into broadcasting.

Pat spent 21 years allowing the guy next to him, John Madden, to be the star. One thing I know is that Pat had a lot of pride in what he did, but he's not a guy who had to be in the middle of the spotlight. I knew him first as a friend before I knew him professionally, and I don't know if there's a finer human being.

After a while, John would invite me up to Northern California over the Fourth of July, and we'd play golf and have dinner. So whenever I went up to Carmel, I called him.

Then John and I went into the Hall of Fame together in 2006. The following year, we were in Canton for a lunch and they left three different-colored golf shirts. Because I had flown in a day late, I wasn't sure which to wear for the lunch, so I texted John.

A little later, I got a message from him. When I got to the luncheon, he was laughing. He said, "That was the first time I ever texted." You can only imagine how John goes into the whole thing about his text and he then goes on the NFL Network, and he starts in, as only John can, that he got this text from me—and now he's a texter. Only John can pull it off.

When I went into broadcasting at Fox in the No. 2 booth, John was really helpful. I'd call him from time to time when I wasn't sure about something, and he was great. Then at the end of that season, I got a call

When Troy Aikman was broadcasting a 49ers game, there was always time to visit with John. COURTESY OF TROY AIKMAN

from him, and he said, "I didn't want you to read this in the paper—I wanted to let you know that I'm leaving [Fox] for *Monday Night Football*." I gave it no thought at the time to what that might mean for my career.

When John retired from broadcasting, whenever we were in San Francisco, Fox producer Richie Zyontz and I, and sometimes some others, would go pay a visit to John. Earlier, he would come into San Francisco. He had a place at the St. Regis across from the Four Seasons, or we'd drive out to see him at his place in Pleasanton. We'd have dinner

Foreword: Troy Aikman

Friday night and lunch Saturday at California Pizza Kitchen, which was right below the St. Regis.

I remember one time a few years ago, this was on a Friday, that Richie Z came to me with a request.

Richie Zyontz: "You're going to go with me tomorrow to see John, aren't you?"

Troy: "Gee, Z, I don't know if I can do it. I'm a little behind on my preparation for our game. I just don't know if I have time to drive out there to visit with John and come back. I've got a lot of work to do."

Zyontz: "I don't even care if you call the worst game of your career. This will be time that you won't get back."

I thought, "He's right." And I was so glad I did.

Troy Aikman, September 2024

Author's Note

It's funny how one event early in your life or career can send you in a totally new direction. One such event happened to me 54 years ago when I met a young editor named Mike Sisak.

In 1971, I was a raw rookie reporter in Wilmington, Delaware, working for *The Morning News* and *The Evening Journal* out of their Dover, Delaware, bureau. My beat included 13 high schools from the Henlopen Conference, three colleges, and Dover Downs racetrack. One of the sports I was covering was wrestling, which was new to me. One day I got a call from someone in the Wilmington office about a possible feature story. Caesar Rodney High School, the caller said, had a blind wrestler on its team.

After calling around and visiting the team practice, I confirmed that Ed Bordley indeed was blind since the age of seven and was a freshman, who not only was on the varsity, but also was undefeated in the 159-pound weight class, as mid-season approached. Bordley was from a large African American family and had mastered several languages. He could also play the piano and a few other instruments and was a straight-A student. The story practically wrote itself.

After interviewing Bordley and his coach, I wrote the feature story and sent it to Sisak, the night copy desk editor for *The Morning News*. After a few days went by and I hadn't seen the story in the paper, I called and asked if there was a problem. Sisak, who was previously a terrific reporter for *The Philadelphia Bulletin*, assured me the story was fine and that it would run soon.

On Wednesday, January 19, the day Caesar Rodney was to compete at Sussex Central High, the story finally ran. Sussex Central was coached by Herm Bastianelli, who had won multiple state championships before arriving there. Sisak had assigned photographer John Flanagan to photograph Bordley at home and at school. The story ran across the center of the first sports page, with the photos filling up the rest of the page. Nothing else appeared on the page except the word "Sports" in big black typeface at the top. I had never seen the first sports page laid out like that before.

Bordley won his match that night despite being taken down twice by his opponent who circled around and took him down from behind each time for two points. Both times Bordley reversed the takedowns to win. Bordley became an all-state wrestler and received a scholarship to Harvard. After the match I asked Bastianelli, the Sussex Central coach, who was a god of sorts in that area, if it was his idea to take Bordley down from behind or his wrestler's. Obviously perturbed, he turned toward me and blurted out, "What did you want my kid to do, tap him on the shoulder?" I used the quote in my story on the match the next day. The coach denied that he said it and tried unsuccessfully to get me fired. He settled for writing a letter to the sports editor and tracking me down at my Dover residence to yell at me for 20 minutes.

Sisak, I soon learned, was not only a terrific editor, but also a wonderful mentor for young writers. With a few small tweaks, he had improved my story, and he went over those tweaks with me as a learning experience. Later that year, without my knowledge, he entered the Bordley story in the Pennsylvania Newspaper Publishers Association contest for best sports story of the year, against entries from the Philadelphia and Pittsburgh newspapers. Delaware's only major papers were *The News* and *The Journal*, so it had no such contest. When the call came that I had won the Keystone Award for the story, I had no idea how or why it happened.

Mike Sisak had also introduced me to his previous sports editor at *The St. Petersburg Times*, Tom Kelly, who had become the executive editor of *The Palm Beach Post*. When Kelly learned of my Keystone Award, he asked me if I wanted to cover the Miami Dolphins for his paper. The Dolphins were coming off a perfect 17-0 Super Bowl season, so I jumped at the chance, which was all thanks to Mike Sisak's generosity on so many counts.

Author's Note

While covering the Dolphins I met Mike Pearl, a sports producer for WTVJ-TV in Miami, and I also became friends with the Dolphins' public-relations man, Beano Cook. Beano regaled me with stories of the decade he worked for Roone Arledge at ABC Sports. A few years later, when Beano took a similar job at CBS Sports, he managed to get me an interview there. Luckily, Mike Pearl had moved up and was the producer for CBS's new pregame football show, *The NFL Today*. He was happy to hire me as the writer for that show. That was 1977.

In 1979, CBS hired John Madden on a tryout basis. I was one of the only people at CBS that John knew when he arrived, since I had interviewed him several times previously. Before CBS hired me, I had worked briefly for the ABC show *The Superstars* doing a public-relations job that Beano had arranged. When the Raiders won the Super Bowl that year, Madden and 10 of his players were invited to compete in the year-end version of *The Superteams*, which took place in Hawaii. That week John and I spent every night talking pro football on his hotel porch. It is truly a small world. Thanks to Mike Sisak, I met and worked for Tom Kelly at *The Palm Beach Post*, and then I got to know Mike Pearl and Beano Cook. That took me to New York to work for CBS and to work again with John Madden.

It's now 54 years later, and it's been a great ride getting to write this book about Madden and Pat Summerall. I always enjoyed being with Pat at CBS. And like my last book, *You Are Looking Live!*, I have reconnected with Mike Sisak, and I'm very fortunate to have him as my editor again for this project.

❧

In December 2023, I was having lunch with former CBS colleague Janis Delson, who was a key contributor to *You Are Looking Live!* She said she had some good stories about her many years working with Madden and Summerall at both CBS and Fox that she wanted to journal. One thing led to another, and I started to think that a Pat and John story would be great book material.

They had such different lifestyles. Summerall liked to carouse every night while Madden was content at a deli with his young worker bees,

Full-page treatment for story of blind high-school wrestler Ed Bordley. COURTESY OF MIKE SISAK

Author's Note

the broadcast associates. Madden liked to talk; Summerall majored in listening. After years at CBS, they were paired together in a way that made for an incredible story in the history of NFL broadcasting. I thought I could still contact many of the people, young and old, who worked with them. A few hard-to-reach folks would be Van Gordon Sauter and Terry O'Neil, who were the ones who put them together. Luckily, I found them. Dozens of ex-colleagues followed, willing to share their stories. And Janis Delson's stories were both fabulous and hilarious.

Unlike Summerall's relationship with his former partner, Tom Brookshier, Pat and John rarely spent any time together off the air. But the relationship worked. As John's son Mike Madden told me, "It was like peanut butter meeting jelly for the first time." The result was the greatest NFL broadcasting team in history. And two personalities that shaped the history of the game we love.

Rich Podolsky, March 2025

INTRODUCTION

How NFL Broadcasting Has Changed Throughout the Years

It took television more than four decades of broadcasting the NFL before it found the perfect broadcast team in Pat Summerall and John Madden. For 21 years Madden and Summerall were more fun and entertaining, and taught us more about the game, than anyone for decades before or since. It is why they have been recognized as the greatest NFL broadcasting team in history.

The first televised NFL game was in 1939 between the now defunct Brooklyn Dodgers and the Philadelphia Eagles, on NBC's experimental station in New York. After World War II, NFL games became more prevalent on TV. From Harry Wismer and Red Grange to Chris Schenkel and Ray Scott, various sportscasters and otherwise uninspiring combinations tried to describe the action. The networks that covered the games in those years included the DuMont Network, NBC, and ABC, before CBS came up with the dream pairing of Summerall and Madden.

When radio and then television began broadcasting football, broadcasters preferred to call the games without a sidekick. Occasionally that led to mistakes. In the 1940s, NBC Radio's Bill Stern sometimes realized late in a touchdown run that he had identified the wrong player with the ball. Stern was known to correct himself at the last minute by saying that player Smith then laterals to player Jones for the touchdown.

The bluffing caught up with Stern in 1948 when he chided announcer Clem McCarthy for misidentifying the winner of the Preakness Triple Crown race. McCarthy retorted, "You can't lateral a horse, Bill."

Thirty-five-year-old Wismer called the first nationally televised NFL championship game in 1948 for ABC, in a blizzard at Philadelphia's Shibe Park (later renamed Connie Mack Stadium). The Eagles defeated the Chicago Cardinals, 7–0. Wismer, who had called games for the Detroit Lions radio network, worked by himself. He was an egotistical glad-hander who had the habit of saying celebrities were in the crowd when in fact they were not even close by.

In 1960, Wismer became the owner of the New York Titans in the new American Football League (AFL), but he couldn't raise the funds to run it successfully. He wound up selling the team in 1963 to a group led by Sonny Werblin who changed the team's name to the New York Jets and then drafted Joe Namath. In 1969, Namath led the Jets to his famous predicted victory over the Baltimore Colts in Super Bowl III.

The DuMont Network rivaled ABC, NBC, and CBS in the early 1950s pioneer years of television. DuMont purchased the rights to broadcast the NFL championship game for five years, beginning in 1951, with Scott doing play-by-play. He worked with Grange, who had called the game the year before for ABC.

DuMont owned stations in New York, Pittsburgh, and Washington, DC, and developed programming for Jackie Gleason, one of the early TV stars. But DuMont's inability to entice other stations around the country to carry its programming led to its downfall, and it eventually folded, allowing CBS to step in, in 1956, as the NFL's broadcaster of choice for regular-season games.

In the early '50s, broadcasting combinations for the NFL title game included Scott and Grange, and in 1954, 31-year-old Chris Schenkel called the championship game, along with Ken Coleman for DuMont. The following year Coleman did the game with Bob Kelley.

With DuMont close to folding, in 1955 NBC was able to buy the rights to broadcast the championship game for $100,000, which indicated not only an increase in interest but a rise in the number of television sets sold in America. After DuMont's demise, NBC signed a five-year agreement with the league to broadcast the championship game for $1 million, or double the previous annual price.

INTRODUCTION

Schenkel became an important figure in not only NFL broadcasting but sports broadcasting in general. Born and raised in Indiana, he began in radio before serving in World War II. In 1947, he took a job with a television station in Providence, Rhode Island, and began announcing football games at Harvard. He was hired by DuMont to call the NFL title game in 1954 and continued doing so for NBC in 1956, 1958, and 1959. The game in 1958, in which the Baltimore Colts defeated the New York Giants in overtime, became known as "the greatest game ever played." It drew approximately 45 million viewers, indicating that the NFL had truly arrived.

Schenkel's partners included Jack Brickhouse ('56) and Baltimore Colts announcer Chuck Thompson ('58 and '59). Schenkel's suave, easygoing style made him a likable choice for networks and viewers. He became an important mentor for Summerall when CBS paired them later in his career.

In the 1960s, with CBS dominating regular-season NFL broadcasts, Scott and Summerall became the top team on the air. Scott had a style that Summerall later adopted when he switched to play-by-play, of a minimalist approach. Scott believed that the pictures and the crowd noise told much of the story. He was known to describe a touchdown pass from Bart Starr to Boyd Dowler with just three words: "Starr . . . Dowler . . . touchdown!"

With the emergence of the AFL in 1960 and NBC replacing ABC in '65 broadcasting its games, the team of Curt Gowdy and Paul Christman became a national favorite. Gowdy, who was known as the cowboy from Wyoming, and Christman, who was a former NFL star quarterback, were a pleasant combination.

The next broadcast team to emerge as a national favorite was Summerall, who had switched to doing play-by-play in 1974, and former Eagles defensive back Tom Brookshier. These two presented the game as if viewers were listening to old football pals discussing the game in their favorite saloon. Summerall and Brookshier called Super Bowls X, XII, and XIV for CBS before they were separated. CBS Sports president Van Gordon Sauter felt their reputation for partying the night before their broadcasts was going too far.

Along the way, the NFL kept raising the price for networks to broadcast their games. CBS paid the NFL $9.3 million to broadcast all the league's regular-season games in 1962. That year CBS started sending two sets of announcers to each game. One would broadcast only back to the home city and the other to the visitors' region. That was the year CBS first hired Summerall. A former star placekicker for the Giants, he worked exclusively with Schenkel doing New York Giants games.

In 1964, with Pete Rozelle firmly in control as commissioner, he put the NFL contract up for auction for the first time, in a two-year sealed-bid process, with all three networks bidding. CBS won in a close call with NBC by bidding $28.2 million. The following year NBC paid the AFL $35 million for five years, or about half what CBS was paying the NFL per season. The NFL's most recent contract with Fox, CBS, NBC, ESPN, and Amazon combined to equal approximately $10 billion per year over 11 years for a total of $111 billion. They've come a long way.

When the NFL and AFL merged, with Rozelle remaining as commissioner, he allowed both NBC and CBS to televise Super Bowl I. NBC's announcers remained Gowdy and Christman, but CBS added former New York Giants star Frank Gifford as the analyst working with Scott and Jack Whitaker, who shared play-by-play duties, while Summerall became the sideline reporter.

The big change in the announce booth came in 1970 when ABC won the rights to *Monday Night Football*. As explained in my prior book, *You Are Looking Live!*, neither CBS nor NBC would bid on it because their prime-time programming on Mondays had higher ratings. ABC wasn't going to bid either until it realized Rozelle was going to syndicate the games using mostly ABC affiliates. At that point, ABC felt it had no choice and went along and bought the rights.

Arledge wanted to make it into an entertainment extravaganza and added controversial Howard Cosell to the booth. Keith Jackson did the play-by-play, with "Dandy" Don Meredith doing the color. It was the first three-man booth in the game's history. Meredith would sing "The Party's Over" in his Texas twang late in a game. He also came up with some great one-liners. When asked what he thought of Cleveland wide receiver Fair Hooker, Meredith responded, "Never met one."

Introduction

In 1971, Gifford, who had been the host of CBS's NFL pregame show, left CBS for ABC to replace Keith Jackson as the play-by-play announcer in the Monday Night booth. At the time it seemed like a great move, but Gifford was forever tormented by Cosell. Regardless, Gifford remained the main cog in the MNF booth until Al Michaels took over in 1985.

Three men in a booth never felt comfortable to most viewers. They would always seem to battle for airtime, which exhausted the viewers. Just like a single announcer in the early '50s wasn't enough, two seemed like the Goldilocks solution.

While many of the announce teams through the years had their merits, none has come close to Summerall and Madden's work. For one thing, when they were thrown together in 1981, with Terry O'Neil producing, they changed the culture of how to prepare for a televised broadcast.

Previously no broadcast personnel would arrive until the day before the game. The producer, director, and two announcers would meet with the public-relations directors from each team to learn the pronunciation of difficult player names and the starting lineups. Then everyone was free to have a night on the town.

O'Neil, Madden, and Summerall changed all that. O'Neil had the entire crew arrive two days before. Then they would all meet with the coaches and star players from each team. This would give them insight into each team's strategy and more. In doing so, CBS promised not to reveal anything they learned before the game started. The meetings would take place Friday afternoon and Saturday morning. Saturday night, Madden would hold a lengthy film session tutorial in the producer's hotel suite, with dinner being brought in. The tutorial was for the cameramen and the rest of the crew so they could understand what would probably happen during the games. No other network was doing anything like this. By the time the other networks caught up, the entire culture of the way broadcasters prepared for a game had changed.

It's been more than 20 years since Summerall and Madden last worked together for Super Bowl XXXVI in January 2002. Since then, the team of Joe Buck and Troy Aikman has been recognized as the best in the business. They've been together for 23 years and still sound fresh.

NFL television had also come a long way until it finally found the perfect pair to broadcast its games. Pat and John were more than just announcers. They loved NFL football, and their work showed it. However, the road wasn't easy before they were united. It began with Madden nearly getting fired his first year with CBS and Summerall becoming a broadcaster by accident.

Chapter One

WILL THE REAL JOHN MADDEN PLEASE STAND UP

JOHN MADDEN, A HALL OF FAME, SUPER BOWL–WINNING COACH WITH the Oakland Raiders, retired at age 42 in 1978. Bleeding ulcers forced his decision. He went on, however, to have a great second act. He became the greatest pro football analyst of all time, winning an astounding 16 Emmy Awards.

But to be frank, when Madden began his broadcasting career at CBS, he was mediocre at best. When he agreed to try broadcasting in 1979, he had no idea what an NFL analyst was supposed to do. And it showed. He was so placid that several CBS executives were in favor of dumping him at season's end. Then something happened that became a turning point in his career, and a major turning point in his life.

Three years earlier he had won Super Bowl XI, but despite his young age and his sterling record of having won 103 games in 10 seasons, Madden felt he had given everything he had in him to coaching. In that time the jovial big man had earned the love and respect of his players. "I'm glad I knew him," said All-Pro Gene Upshaw. "I'm glad he touched my life."

On the first NFL Sunday after his retirement, John drove to the Oakland Coliseum, as he always had, and walked around. Being with the crowd seemed a little funny to him, and he realized he didn't fit in. So he got in the car and drove back home. He really didn't know what to do with himself.

He retired to a home and a family that had gotten used to not having him around. A few years before, his wife Virginia opened her own bar, the Village Saloon, in the oldest building in the nearby East Bay town of Dublin, California. "If you own a bar," she said, "your best customers drink too much."[1] Their sons, Joe and Mike, who were then in high school, weren't exactly waiting for him to retire. They were busy playing sports and hanging with their friends. So John Madden became a couch potato, watching soaps with his two bulldogs, Boss and Tug, alongside.

Gary Bender, who was one of Madden's first broadcast partners, had some insight into this. "Virginia was tough," Bender said. "She had her own bar. She had some toughness in her. She said one time she came back from working in the back of the bar and there was John sitting with his two bulldogs in the backyard drinking Tabs, and she said to him: 'John, is this what it's going to be like now? You're not coaching anymore, so you're just going to sit out in this backyard and never have anything worthwhile to do?' And I guess she called CBS and got the ball rolling."[2]

Actually, it was CBS that contacted John's agent, Barry Frank. But John wasn't that interested in doing TV at first. For one thing, he didn't think much of the people he saw on TV doing the games. They didn't prepare, he felt, and they often said things he thought weren't true. He didn't want to be lumped in with them.

> *I first met John Madden in 1973 when I was covering the Miami Dolphins for The Palm Beach Post. A few years later we renewed our friendship after the Raiders won the Super Bowl. I was then working for the ABC show* The Superstars *when John joined our private charter to Hawaii for a weeklong battle of* The Superteams. *Claustrophobic, John hated to fly but was more comfortable on charters where he could move around the plane. John sat across from me on the first row, and for the rest of the flight and every night that week we sat up and talked football. His thirst for insight into Dolphins coach Don Shula's success was insatiable. When he came to New York in 1979 to be an analyst for CBS Sports, I was already working there as a writer, and I was one of the few people he knew. We went to dinner at fun places like Runyon's [see photo] to watch* Monday Night Football *and also spent many a night with Jimmy the Greek.*

Author Rich Podolsky next to John Madden, with Runyon's proprietor Joe Healey looking on. COURTESY OF JOE HEALEY

In February 1977, after the Raiders won the Super Bowl, John and 10 stars from the team participated in the ABC show *The Superteams*, which also featured players from the New York Yankees, Cincinnati Reds, and Minnesota Vikings that year. They all flew on a private charter to Hawaii together. Yes, Madden was still flying in February '77.

The show was the season-ender for the series known as *The Superstars*, which was co-owned by Dick Button's Candid Productions and sports marketing powerhouse International Management Group (IMG). At the event Madden spoke with some IMG executives about possible marketing representation. He thought that they might get him a sponsor for his trademark short-sleeve shirts that he wore on the sidelines.

So when CBS had an interest in Madden after he retired, John wound up being represented by Frank, IMG's super-agent who had already spent a stint as president of CBS Sports. It's hard to believe that NBC didn't go after him first. After broadcasting Madden's games for a decade and seeing what a great personality he was, it didn't seem to move them.

During the mid-'70s, future NBC Sports executive producer Mike Weisman was an associate producer on games directed by Ted Nathanson. When contacted for this book, Weisman said: "It was Ted, after every meeting, who would say, 'This guy [Madden] is so entertaining. This guy's great.' It was Teddy, when Madden retired, who told NBC, whether it was Chet [Simmons] or Scotty [Connal] or talent relations, to hire Madden. And I'm sure we made him an offer." But apparently they didn't.

"Back then when you had an untested talent [like Madden]," Weisman continued, "you'd offer them four or five or six games at maybe $500 a game. We were confident he'd come with us because we were the AFC and he was more familiar with those teams. But he had Barry Frank [as his agent], and Barry then took him over to CBS and negotiated and got him more money and a better guarantee. Barry shopped the NBC offer and John took the better business deal."[3]

Here's what actually happened. Right after Madden retired he did some work on a syndicated program called *The Road to the Super Bowl*. The program's director, Jim Cross, raved about his work to NBC Sports executive Don Ohlmeyer.

"Madden told me he'd like to work for NBC," Cross told Ohlmeyer, who scoffed at the suggestion.

"Never," replied Ohlmeyer. "Have you seen what he looks like? He's a mess."

"I've not not only seen him," said Cross, "but worked with him and he's terrific."

"Not while I'm here," was Ohlmeyer's final word.[4]

And later Ohlmeyer bemoaned the omission. "We blew it," it was reported that Ohlmeyer said at the time. Instead, when Barry Frank told John of the CBS offer of $12,000 to do four games in 1979, John hesitated and told Frank he wasn't that interested. "Maybe in a few years," he said.

"You ought to do it," Frank told him. "We'll get a four- or five-game guarantee. If you like it, you can continue. If you don't you don't have to do it. But if you say no now and change your mind several years later, they may not be interested in you anymore."[5]

Madden thought Frank's suggestion made sense, but he had no idea how to be an analyst and insisted on CBS allowing him to do a mock practice game before his four regular-season games started. He was assigned to a preseason game in August 1979 between the Rams and the 49ers, with a very young Bob Costas as his play-by-play partner. When they met at the hotel, neither Madden nor Costas knew what to expect. At 6-foot-4 and 270, Madden was about twice as big as Costas, who was just 5-7, and at 27, looked much younger. The big man laughed out loud when they shook hands and walked to the car taking them to the game.

"I had never been in the booth in my life," Madden said. "But I knew the players and the coaches. So, when I met Bob Costas, and he got in the car he looked like a 12-year-old kid. And I thought, 'What am I going to do with this guy?'"

Although Costas had been calling games for CBS for several years by that time, Madden had no idea who he was. "Geez," Madden thought, "they put me in here with this kid."

If you thought Costas looked young then, you should have seen him five years earlier. At that time (in 1974), after studying communications at Syracuse, Costas sent an audition tape of a game he did to the Spirits of St. Louis from the old American Basketball Association (ABA). "I sent a tape of a game that I had done between Syracuse and Rutgers," Costas recalled. "I rerecorded it with the treble down and the bass up, to make myself sound a little older and more authoritative. And bingo, I got the job. It didn't hurt that I was willing to work cheap."

It was rumored that at CBS's first August NFL seminar, which Costas attended for talent and production people, Tom Brookshier mistook Costas for a runner and asked Bob to get him a cold drink.

"The 'Get me a Coke' thing never happened," Costas said when contacted for this book. "Anyway, the day Madden and I did the audition game, [Vin] Scully was doing the actual broadcast on CBS. By that time ['79], I had already done about 10 or 12 games that actually aired on CBS. That's why they had me do the 'audition' game with Madden. They knew I could provide a reasonably professional play-by-play framework so that they could evaluate John."[6]

Before the game, Madden was down on the field talking to all the players he knew, and he didn't realize it was getting a little late for him to get upstairs to the booth.

"I got up there and I thought holy shit we're in the LA Coliseum and it's like a mile away," Madden said, "and I'm looking, and I don't know what's going on here." This was despite Costas earlier talking to Madden about their opening. "So, Costas started," said Madden: "'We're here in LA in the beautiful sun of southern California,' and I look over and I thought, holy moly that's the little guy that I rode over with? He had a great voice, and he didn't read anything; he was just doing it. I thought holy moly this guy is really good. And he was!"

Costas helped John get through the opening and then tried to relax him a bit.

"I remember him being rather nervous and unsure of himself," Costas said, "but his anxiety was misplaced. From the start he was distinctive, and you could tell he could be really good once he got the hang of it. He was appreciative of the fact that I was solid enough with the basics, and that made him more comfortable."

Costas more than made him feel comfortable. He spent time with John before the game telling him what to expect. It was the first time anyone at CBS had offered Madden any advice of any kind.

He even attended a June seminar for broadcasters where he thought he would be shown tapes and get instruction on what an analyst was supposed to do. Instead, all they talked about, according to Madden, was how to fill out an expense report. That was followed by a cocktail party and a flight home. "I left New York," he said, "not knowing any more about television than before I came." And when the game started, Costas's big booming voice reassured John he wasn't working with any kid.

When Madden got home, he watched a copy of his mock tryout and realized he had a long way to go if he was going to be any good at this. "I just knew that I had to cut down," Madden explained. "I had to be more concise. You just can't talk when you want to. I didn't understand that part of it. You have to hit commercials, you have to have halftime, you have to do all of that. And I had to learn about putting the whole thing together."[7]

Three of Madden's four assigned games came and went, and in each game John tried to figure out more on his own. He knew he was getting the hang of it, but CBS wasn't so sure. For one thing, CBS tossed him around like a cue ball, assigning him to work with Frank Glieber, then Lindsey Nelson, and then Dick Stockton. All were solid play-by-play men, but that made it hard for Madden to get in a rhythm with one partner.

"I reviewed what he did," recalled the senior producer, Charles "Chuck" Milton III, "and I ran the audition for him. Most of the first year we stuck him out in the boondocks. Then I would get the tape and listen to him. He used to tell a lot of stories. They were good stories, but a lot of time they didn't fit. He had a hard time making things fit."

On November 25, 1979, John Madden was about to do his fourth and final game as an analyst for CBS Sports. Neither Madden nor CBS was sure it would work out when he signed. In effect, it was a tryout, an audition. He also never had the same producer and director. And his games only went back to two markets. For example, the Vikings against the Bucs was only seen in Minneapolis and Tampa Bay. No chance of it going back to New York. For Madden, this was probably a good thing because it gave him a little time to work things out.

One game was directed by Bob Fishman, who is now a member of the Sports Broadcasting Hall of Fame. "My first game with Madden, I had just come off directing *The NFL Today* [for five years]," Fishman said when interviewed for this book. "Madden was trying to be an announcer, and he was, frankly, very mediocre. He just didn't know what he was doing.

"Nobody gave him any coaching. He went in there with expectations that he didn't know what they wanted him to be. And I don't think either I or [producer] David Fox had the wherewithal or the intuitiveness to go to him and say, 'John, you suck at what you're doing. You've got to be the John Madden—the funny sideline guy—and teach us,' which is what he started doing later."[8]

CBS might not have been so sure about John at that point, but Madden didn't have any doubts. "I just felt this is it," he said. "I knew right away that I was going to keep doing it.... I didn't want to stay in football as a coach. I didn't want to be a general manager or an office guy. I didn't want to be a scout. But I wanted to broadcast. I didn't think I would, but I embraced it."

By his fourth and final game for CBS in 1979, Madden had begun to understand what to expect. By a quirk of luck, in that fourth game John got the biggest break of his fledgling broadcasting career when he was paired with CBS's No. 1 play-by-play man, Pat Summerall. This wasn't a reward. It happened because Summerall's regular partner, Tom Brookshier, took the weekend off to present his daughter at a debutante ball in Philadelphia. It left Pat without a partner.

To do the opening, Pat and John had to stand on a rickety platform the CBS crew had built so they could be seen high above Tampa Stadium. Madden, who was claustrophobic, was terrified of heights. Besides that, the wind was whipping around, and Madden's hair flew in all directions. He began sweating profusely, both visibly and through his shirt and coat.

"I thought he was nervous about being on the air," Summerall said. "I remember thinking, 'This guy is in the wrong business if he's nervous about being on television.'" After the opening, Madden confessed to Pat that he was terrified of heights. Summerall made sure that was the last time the two were out on the platform.[9]

The Bucs easily handled the Vikings that day and Madden's performance was okay, but nothing special, even though Summerall thought he showed promise. As I reviewed the game on YouTube, it became obvious that Madden seemed to be conservative and holding back the personality we had gotten to know of the fun-loving coach on the sidelines. He was quiet, his tone was low, unsure of himself. He was so drastically different from what we all came to know. Sound effects ["Boom!"] weren't part of his work yet. And it would be nearly two more years before Pat and John were working together in the same booth again.

CBS senior producer Chuck Milton recalled: "When he first started out with Summerall, he would state what he wanted to say, but it took him a long time and he was in Summerall's territory. So Summerall would usually take it when they were coming out of the huddle. He'd put the wide receivers on the right, and that sort of thing. On the first going, Madden had trouble editing himself, and he would run into Pat. But Pat was really gracious about it. He wouldn't say anything and just pick it up when Madden was through."

That was CBS's year to broadcast the Super Bowl. At that time, NBC and CBS alternated years doing it. In Super Bowl XIV, the Pittsburgh Steelers rallied to beat the Los Angeles Rams, 31–19. The game was played in the Rose Bowl in Pasadena, a half-hour drive from LA. Most of the CBS crew was headquartered at the beautiful Beverly Wilshire Hotel, just around the corner from the very posh Rodeo Drive, where a decade later the movie *Pretty Woman* was filmed.

> The Friday before Super Bowl XIV, I was at the Beverly Wilshire around 5 p.m. when John Madden invited me to join him in Hernando's Lounge, the equivalent of the more famous Polo Lounge at the Beverly Hills Hotel. "I'm meeting my oldest friend for a drink," he said, "and I want you to meet him too." The funny thing was that John didn't drink. I had no idea that his friend would turn out to be John Robinson, coach of the undefeated Southern Cal Trojans that year, who had just defeated Ohio State, 17–16, in the Rose Bowl. When Robinson joined us, Madden explained how they were boyhood pals in Daly City, California. "He was the left end, and I was the right end," said John. And they both laughed at that memory. As the hour wore on, it seemed like every celebrity in the lounge would stop by to say hello. I felt like I was living a dream.

Because it was CBS's year to televise the Super Bowl, the Television Academy of Arts & Sciences asked CBS Sports if it would host the academy's monthly luncheon that week at the Wilshire. CBS agreed, and just three days before the Super Bowl, on January 17, 1980, a packed house of over 500 television executives, advertisers, and media members crowded into tables in the spacious ballroom.

"There was a dais with Brent Musburger at one end acting as the emcee," said former CBS Sports executive Kevin O'Malley who was there. "Seated to Brent's right was NFL commissioner Pete Rozelle. Seated next to him were Hank Stram, George Allen, and John Madden, all Hall of Fame, Super Bowl–winning coaches. And they were all CBS analysts. It was a natural."[10]

There was no program, per se. Rozelle got up and said a few words, and then it was kind of quiet. Musburger threw the floor open to questions. No one volunteered. It looked like the luncheon would be a bust. Finally, Herb Gross raised his hand. Gross had been a top sales executive who helped run the CBS Sports division when former head Frank Smith departed. Apparently Smith was way overserved at a CBS cocktail party and embarrassed himself and the company by inappropriately complimenting and then fondling an advertiser's wife in a low-cut dress. Her husband proceeded to flatten Smith.[11]

Gross had a question for the three former Super Bowl coaches. It was something to the effect of whether any of them would ever consider going back to coaching if the right offer came along. George Allen went first and hemmed and hawed and danced around it but never really answered the question. Stram was next. He was already considered part of CBS's No. 2 team, so he professed how happy he was at CBS.

Then it was John Madden's turn. He had not worked a game for nearly two months, and few had seen him to that point anyway. This was even before Miller Lite had considered him for its national advertising campaign, so he wasn't exactly a household name yet. But what he was about to do would make everyone see him in a new light.

Madden got up from his seat and walked down the row of seats on the dais. Then, from behind, he leaned over and put his hand on Pete Rozelle's shoulder and said, "You know, people ask me all the time about officiating." He paused; Rozelle smiled. The combination of John's menacing size, impish grin, and the twinkle in his eye had the entire lunch crowd roaring with laughter. "And here's the problem," he continued, "from a coach's point of view, it's fourth and inches, and you go for it. The official [on the sideline] comes running in and raises his hand—it means he's got the spot. He flies to the middle of the field, and he's got the ball."

Madden is now as animated as he ever was on the sidelines, with his arms flying around and his shirttail slightly askew. He takes a step back and pretends to be charging forward and says, "If we're going from left to right, and that official is running in from the near sideline, it's a matter of inches. If his right foot hits the ground, you're short, and if his left hits the ground you've got it.

"So he's running, and then he stops. BOOM! And that last foot is his right. SHIT! You're four inches short. If he had taken one more stride, he would have put his left foot down and you would have made it by four inches. So, in my last season coaching, I just got 10 more right foots than left foots. You know, we [Raiders] were as good as we've ever been; we just got too many right foots."

He stands there grinning, with those massive arms outstretched in front of the commissioner. The audience explodes in laughter. Rozelle, red faced, is laughing. In five short minutes, John Madden now owns the room.

"That luncheon was a pivotal moment in Madden's life," said CBS Sports communications director Jay Rosenstein. "When he did that one-foot, two-foot thing—it may be more myth than reality—but the word I heard was that the Miller agency people took to that, and that begat what was the birth of Madden's Miller Lite commercials."[12]

More important, according to O'Malley: "That's how John Madden saved his job. There was no place for him coming back in 1980 if Herb Gross doesn't ask that question."

After the luncheon, dazzled by Madden's showmanship, CBS executives met in the lobby. His longtime agent Sandy Montag felt it struck a chord.

"I think the people at CBS saw something [in him] they hadn't seen before," he said.[13]

All of a sudden it hit them. In a few days they'll be broadcasting a two-and-a-half-hour Super Bowl pregame show, and John Madden isn't part of it. Something had to be done to remedy that, and it was immediately.

Management's whole attitude about Madden had changed. They no longer saw Madden as just another coach turned analyst.

They now saw him for what he could be!

CHAPTER TWO

SUMMERALL

Right Place, Right Time

HIS PARENTS, WHO DIVORCED BEFORE HE WAS BORN, DIDN'T WANT HIM. When he was three, he was destined for an orphanage in their tiny hometown of Lake City in northern Florida when an aunt and uncle intercepted.

They had a son named Mike the same age, so despite being named George Allen Summerall at birth in 1930, everyone called him "Pat," to match the popular fictional Irish buddies "Pat and Mike." From that point on, the rest of the world would forever know him as Pat Summerall.

As if things weren't tough enough for young Mr. Summerall, he was born with a club foot and a right leg—what turned out to be his kicking leg—that was twisted backward. Dr. Harry Bates then performed a new procedure that amazingly worked out better than anyone's hopes. Bates thought that with therapy Pat could later walk with only a slight limp. Instead, he could not only walk but could run as fast as any kid in the neighborhood.

At age three, another roadblock was thrown at him. His mother remarried and took him back, but there were beatings from his stepfather and they soon said that Pat no longer fit into their plans. This time his grandmother, Augusta Georgia Summerall, came to the rescue. Everyone called her "Aunt Georgia," and as a widow and a former teacher in a one-room schoolhouse, she provided the perfect atmosphere for him to grow up. Pat Summerall finally had a home.

"I never knew my grandfather," said Summerall, "but my grandmother often told me stories of him [Thomas Jefferson Summerall] and other ancestors while we sat on the open porch of her house, which served as my grandmother's neighborhood broadcast booth. I never got tired of her stories."[1]

He grew to be 6-foot-4 and an amazing athlete, and although he didn't play any organized sports until seventh grade, Pat wound up lettering in five sports. While it was no surprise that he was named All-State in football and basketball, it was another sport that shocked everyone that Pat excelled at: tennis!

Lake City's Columbia High School didn't have a tennis team and didn't have anyone who could coach it. But Summerall found the sport on his own at age 10 by hanging out at the two tennis courts at Young's Park near his grandmother's home. He'd watch the adults play, and they'd often let him hit with them after a while.

He became obsessed. "I read about Don Budge and Bobby Riggs and other top players of the day," he wrote in his autobiography, *Summerall: On and Off the Air*, "and I checked out books on tennis at the library to learn the finer points."

He wound up playing much older opponents and gave them everything they would ever want. He was fast and at 6-4 had a blistering serve. But other than his local park, Pat had nowhere to test his ability. He got so good that his school entered him as its only participant in a local conference tournament his junior year, and he breezed right through it.

That got his competitive juices flowing, and when he read about the Florida state tournament in Fort Lauderdale, he entered on his own and then proceeded to hitchhike 360 miles to find out just how good he was.

"Everybody thought I was nuts for even going," Summerall said, "because there were a lot of serious tennis players in southern Florida, but I was determined to go.... I packed up my stuff and stuck out my thumb with a tennis racket tucked under my arm."[2]

While most of his opponents were equipped with a bagful of the latest tennis rackets and stylish tennis attire, all Pat had was a single pair of old black sneakers and just the one racket he had under his arm.[3]

Hitchhiking was commonplace in the '40s, and some of the drivers who gave him a ride liked him so much that they also fed him. Summerall, who was 16 in 1946, made it to the 18-and-under finals, and according to a 1987 *Sports Illustrated* story, he defeated Herb Flam for the championship—the same Herb Flam who a few years later in 1950 made it to the finals at Forest Hills. It should be noted that in his own autobiography, Summerall wrote that he lost that match. Regardless, it was an amazing feat for a kid who was self-taught and never had a lesson.

The agility he learned playing tennis made him a better all-around athlete. He was his school's leading scorer in basketball, and with his speed and soft hands he was his football team's leading receiver. Because he never paid much attention to keeping his grades up, playing for colleges like Duke and Vanderbilt was out of the question.

Hoping for a chance to play both football and basketball, he did meet with Kentucky's famous basketball coach Adolph Rupp on a recruiting trip, but turned down a chance to play for him when Rupp said he wouldn't allow Pat to play both sports.

During his senior year in high school, his biological father reentered his life, possibly because of Pat's athletic achievements. His father campaigned hard for Pat to attend West Point. Even though Pat knew he didn't have the grades to get in, he went along with his father to see West Point and came home thinking it reminded him of the Florida State Penitentiary.

He also was hoping to play for the University of Florida, but his grades kept the recruiters away. However, his luck changed when the University of Arkansas sent recruiters to Lake City. They said they would allow him to play two sports, and Summerall felt right at home in Fayetteville, located near the Ozark Mountains.

Summerall was a two-way player, who played both offensive and defensive end, and was the team's leading receiver. And in his sophomore year, he became the Razorbacks' kicker as well when the coach held open tryouts where he boomed kicks 60 yards or more. They made him the primary kickoff man and the No. 1 option when a field goal was needed.

Punting and kicking a football is something he always fooled around doing as a kid, so it was no surprise to Pat that he could do it well at this stage of his life. In those days there weren't any soccer-style kickers, so Summerall just kicked them straight ahead. His most famous kick came in his senior year, on October 20, 1951, against fourth-ranked Texas in a home game at Fayetteville, where Arkansas had never beaten the Longhorns. His second-quarter 12-yard field goal was the difference in the Hogs' 16–14 victory. Actually, it gave them the lead at 9–7 that was never eclipsed.

One big influence on Pat at Arkansas was a young board member, Jackson T. "Jack" Stephens. When Pat didn't have a winter coat and threatened the coach that he'd go home if they couldn't get him one, Stephens, who had built one of the largest investment banking companies in the country and was a major benefactor to the university, was assigned the job.

"Jack took me to Dillard's and got me my first winter coat," Summerall wrote. "That began a friendship that covered many years and a lot of fairways. He became the fourth chairman of the board in the history of Augusta National and our friendship flourished in its later years."[4]

His one major regret was when he couldn't make it back to Lake City the winter that his grandmother died. He didn't have the money for the bus fare, and his father, who informed him of her passing, never offered to pay his way back. But it would be Augusta Georgia Summerall's soothing voice that would stay with him the rest of his life, and the memory of her voice would play a key role in his first broadcasting job.

Summerall was all set to return to the Arkansas basketball team in the spring of '52 when he learned that the Detroit Lions had drafted him in the fourth round. The Lions had a competitive team with the great Bobby Layne at quarterback.

When Pat joined the Lions they were one of the best teams in the NFL. Professional football was gaining popularity in America, although the salaries didn't really reflect that yet. Summerall was offered $5,000 a year to play but held out and got $6,000 plus a $500 signing bonus. Of the bonus, Summerall wrote in his book, *"At least it will pay for my bar tab."*

Summerall did not drink at all in high school, but once away from home with the good ol' boys in Fayetteville, it was an easy habit to pick up if you wanted to fit in. In his autobiography he wrote about several drinking adventures at Arkansas, but they didn't appear to be any worse than most young men in his position. The fact that he put the "*At least it will pay my bar tab*" in italics at the end of a chapter signified that he knew it was a forerunner of the horrors that would come.

Summerall caught on quickly with the Lions. Layne was a demanding quarterback on the field and a hard-drinking leader off the field. Pat found his way into Layne's circle, both on and off the field, with reliable play. He was also one of the backup kickers. Layne trusted him to make the blocks and catch the passes and be exactly in the right place. Just as the season was about to start, Pat pulled a hamstring. It was the first injury he'd ever endured, including college and high school, but it turned out to be just a mild hamstring strain.

After missing two weeks of practice, he was back in the defensive lineup in the season's second game against the Rams, which the Lions won by three points. On the last play of the game, Rams quarterback Norm Van Brocklin tried a desperation pass. Summerall rushed him from his defensive-end position but was taken out by a cut block and then flattened by Paul "Tank" Younger. Summerall had extended his arm, trying to break his fall just as Younger crushed him. His arm wound up being broken in a painful compound fracture. While the team flew home, Summerall spent two weeks in a Los Angeles hospital and the rest of the season recuperating.

The Lions were on their way to a championship season in 1952, but all Pat could do was watch. He did, however, get a share of the championship bonus check. Realizing that education might be the key to his future employment, during the off-season Summerall returned to Arkansas and studied Russian history while pursuing a graduate degree. The lectures from his favorite teacher, Mr. Dorsey Jones, may have inspired Pat to be a teacher himself, which he later did back in Lake City.

The following season he had a heart-to-heart with his coach, Buddy Parker, and confided that although his cast came off, he could no longer extend his arm as he could in the past and he couldn't reach all of

Layne's passes that he used to. The next thing he knew he was traded to the Chicago Cardinals, which was one of the worst teams in the league. According to Summerall, not only was the team bad, but the team was a direct reflection at how poorly the Bidwill family ran the organization.

Summerall wasn't very fond of his coach in Chicago, Joe Stydahar, either. "He was the only man I ever knew who could chew tobacco and drink whiskey at the same time, and I think he often did both while he was coaching."[5]

Unfortunately for Pat, he spent five mostly miserable seasons there before being traded to the New York Giants in 1958.

After his first season in Chicago, he took a part-time substitute-teaching job in his hometown of Lake City teaching eighth graders. He really enjoyed teaching and could see himself settling down doing that after his playing days were over. Then he and his principal got together and decided to invest in farmland. They bought 100 acres near Lake City and another 100 outside Ocala and planted watermelons, bell peppers, tomatoes, and squash. It was the hardest work he had ever done, but it turned into a very profitable venture, with each of them taking home $50,000—or nearly 10 times his NFL salary. In future off-seasons, the crop didn't pan out nearly as well, but Summerall kept his teaching job and enjoyed it more each year.

Along the way he met and got serious with Kathy Jacobs who was unlike any other woman he had dated. He wrote that "she was a very grounded and religious person," which he found most appealing. She wasn't much of a sports fan, and he thought she understood that he wanted to play at least one more season before they got married. That didn't stand well with her father. He decided they needed to get married sooner rather than later, which happened on July 5, 1955. Her dad gave Pat one piece of advice: "Don't let women screw up your life."[6]

When the Giants traded for him before the 1958 season, Summerall called their coach, Jim Lee Howell, whom he knew from when they both were at Arkansas. Howell was an administrator when Summerall played there. On the call, Howell told Pat they only planned to use him as a kicker and an occasional backup on offense. Summerall really enjoyed his time with the Giants. For one thing it was a very professional organization with some great players that included Southern Cal's Frank Gifford and Southern Methodist's great back Kyle Rote.

Not only were the Giants contenders, but they also had two of the greatest coaching coordinators in football. Vince Lombardi was the offensive coordinator, and Tom Landry ran the defense. They were assistants with the Giants from 1954 through 1958, and they both went on to win Super Bowls as head coaches, Lombardi with the Green Bay Packers and Landry with the Dallas Cowboys (who didn't exist until 1960). After winning five NFL championships including the first two Super Bowls, the Super Bowl trophy is now named for Lombardi.

"Their guidance grew into not just a model for playing, but also a model for living that anyone would be proud to aspire to," Summerall said. "They shaped me into the man I am."

That season the Giants were just one game behind the Cleveland Browns in the standings when they met on the final game of the season at Yankee Stadium. It was a cold, wind-blown snowy day, and the Giants knew they had to win that game to force a playoff with the Browns, and then win that game too, to make it to the championship game against Baltimore and Johnny Unitas.

Late in the fourth quarter the game was tied, 10–10, but a tie favored Cleveland, since there were no rules calling for overtime in regular-season games in 1958. When the Giants got the ball back in Cleveland territory, a decision had to be made on fourth down. With just under two minutes to go, Howell sent Summerall in to try a 49-yard field goal in the gusting snow.

Lombardi complained vehemently, lobbying to go for a first down. Maybe he was thinking about the 31-yard field-goal try Summerall had missed earlier in the game. When Pat joined the huddle, Giants quarterback Charlie Conerly revealed his surprise.

"What are you doing here?" asked the quarterback.

"They sent me to kick a field goal," Summerall responded.

"You're kidding!" said Conerly.

Despite Lombardi's doubts and Conerly's surprise, Summerall made the historic kick that sent the Giants into a playoff game with the Browns the following week. When Pat returned to the sideline, everyone congratulated him except one person. Lombardi grabbed him and shook him. "I thought he was going to hug me," Pat said, but above the excited crowd Lombardi screamed, "You son of a bitch. You know you can't kick it that far."

In explaining how he managed to stay so cool in that moment, Summerall told *Sports Illustrated*, "I've never been a very excitable person, and in many ways, I think that helped me as a kicker. You get all uptight and excited, full of adrenaline, jumping up and down, you forget what it is you need to do."[7]

And in his memoir, he explained: "I made the mistake of looking toward the distant goal shrouded in a heavy curtain of falling snow. The wind was howling. My breath was a vapor cloud hovering in front of my face. It was a good snap and a good hold. As soon as I kicked it, I knew it was going to be far enough, but the ball was on a very unpromising trajectory, knuckleballing like a missile gone awry. Yet somewhere it stayed on course and cleared the uprights by so much it would have been good from 65 yards out."

The following week, the Giants defeated the Browns, 10–0, in the playoff game and lined up against the Colts at Yankee Stadium on December 28, 1958, in what was recognized at the time as "the greatest game ever played." Pro football was becoming more popular, and the game, which was played on a Sunday afternoon and televised across the country by NBC, had record attendance and media coverage. It didn't hurt that it went into sudden-death overtime, which the NFL only allowed for the championship game. Baltimore won when Alan Ameche dove a yard into the end zone, 23–17.

Two years later, before the 1960 season, Summerall was in the right place at the right time when he answered a telephone in a hotel room he shared with Conerly. Summerall might not have realized it, but he had a great voice for broadcasting.

The caller was an executive from WCBS Radio. He asked for Conerly, and when Pat relayed that he wasn't there, the caller asked him to deliver the message to remind Conerly to be at CBS that afternoon to read a five-minute audition script.

Summerall said he'd be glad to tell him, and as he began to hang up, he thought he heard the caller say one more thing. So he picked the phone back up and the man asked, "What are you doing this afternoon?" When Pat said something to the effect of "not much," the caller said, "Well, why don't you come along with Charlie and give it a shot, too?"

"I felt like the starlet discovered by the Hollywood producer at the soda fountain," Summerall wrote in his autobiography. "So, I tagged

Summerall, looking young and handsome, in his blue Giants uniform and his famous number 88. COURTESY OF JAY SUMMERALL

along with Charlie. It turned out two other Giants, Alex Webster and Kyle Rote, were also there to try out."[8]

The reason CBS needed a New York Giant was because Frank Gifford, who had been doing the five-minute spots, was pulled off the show due to a sponsor conflict. Cigarette companies were huge sponsors of sports shows back then. Camel cigarettes (whose slogan was "I'd walk a mile for a Camel") sponsored Gifford's show, but Gifford had just signed a big personal promotional deal with Lucky Strike cigarettes. (Its slogan was "L.S.M.F.T.," which stood for "Lucky Strike Means Fine Tobacco.") So a new host was needed.

Summerall's rich voice and confident delivery won the job. His professional football career was almost over, and his days of farming were behind him. It turned out that his greatest gift came from his grandmother, who stayed with him all those years.

"I was surprisingly at home behind the microphone," Summerall recalled. "My grandmother read to me all the time when I was a boy, and reading aloud in a radio sound booth came naturally to me. It was as if her voice had trained mine."[9]

What followed a few years later in Summerall's career is so wild, it's almost not to be believed. It involved Pat getting two weeks of tutoring from LA disc jockey and game-show host Wink Martindale on how to be a morning radio man, teaching him how to do weather and traffic reports, spin records, and interview celebrities. No wonder WCBS began calling him "Super Summerall" in its ads.

Chapter Three
MASTERCLASS BY THE DUTCHMAN

Daly City, just 10 miles south of San Francisco, is probably best known for two things: (1) It's the home of the world-famous Cow Palace, which since 1941 has hosted the annual Grand National Rodeo, Horse & Livestock Show. It has also hosted the Beatles, the 1964 and '67 National Basketball Association Finals, and the 1956 and 1964 Republican Party conventions. And (2) it also happens to be the town where John Madden grew up.

The Madden family moved to Daly City in 1942, when John was six years old, from the farming community of Austin, Minnesota. His father, Earl, found a job as an auto mechanic at the Chevy dealership in town. His mother, Mary Margaret Flaherty, was a deeply religious Irish Catholic.

To young John, Daly City looked and smelled like heaven, with the Pacific Ocean just to the west and the San Francisco Bay to the east. There was a vacant lot next to the Maddens' home, and soon all the kids in the neighborhood called it "Madden's Lot," or just plain "Madden's." For years, John thought it was his.

One of those kids was John Robinson, who became John Madden's best friend.

They competed in almost every sport together, and they both excelled at football and baseball. Madden's Lot was all weeds, and if you pulled the ball while batting, it was even money that you'd break a dining room or kitchen window at Madden's house.

"We'd break windows all the time," Madden said, "but my mom didn't say a word. My dad didn't say a word either. That was a gift. I was lucky. It was never, 'You can't play anymore; don't break the window anymore.' He'd just fix it. Then he finally put chicken wire on the windows."[1]

Allowing John to play whenever he wanted to for as long as he wanted to was truly a gift his parents gave him. But when it came to schoolwork at the Our Lady of Perpetual Help parochial school, John wasn't that interested. "I always made fun of the people who sat in the front, who, when the nuns would ask questions, would be waving their hands," John recalled. "I never raised my hand. I just sat in the back and talked about other stuff until I got in trouble. You'd go to the principal's office and then whack!"[2]

All John ever thought about was lunch and recess and where he could play after school. And he and Robinson would do just about anything to see a game. They'd hop on streetcars or freights to see a minor league baseball game, and they'd hitchhike to Cal and Stanford football games together. They'd also hitchhike across the Bay to Moraga to the 49ers' training camp at Saint Mary's College. "We knew a lot of friends who went to games," said Robinson, "but John and I were the only ones who went to practices."

At Jefferson Union High School, John had grown to 6 feet 4 inches and well over 200 pounds. Despite his size, he was one of the fastest runners on the team. He anchored his team's offensive and defensive lines, and he was also an outstanding catcher on the school's baseball team. So much so that the New York Yankees and Boston Red Sox both offered Madden a minor league contract. Madden then decided that he'd rather play football.

It's not that John wasn't smart; it was just that he didn't care about his studies. In his quest to always find the next place to play, his grades suffered, which made it hard to get a football scholarship. When his buddy John Robinson went to Oregon on scholarship to catch passes, Madden enrolled in the tiny College of San Mateo. After a semester there, he was able to enroll at Oregon as a pre-law student. Despite Robinson's being there, Madden hated the constant rain in Oregon and the fraternity lifestyle, and he decided to transfer.

"I couldn't see myself wearing a suit and tie and sitting in an office all day," Madden said, "so I switched to education."[3]

His next stop was Aberdeen, Washington, a small fishing village where he spent a year at Grays Harbor College, another community college. Aberdeen's easygoing small-town-America feel fit John to a T. But, seeking a more competitive football program the following year, he transferred to California State Polytechnic University, otherwise known as Cal Poly–San Luis Obispo. His roommate at Cal Poly for the next two seasons was quarterback Bobby Beathard, who went on to a great career as an NFL personnel director, contributing to Super Bowl victories by both the Miami Dolphins and Washington Redskins. He was inducted into the Pro Football Hall of Fame in 2018.

"John was one of the fastest guys on the team," Beathard said. "Tall and big and fast. When we ran sprints after practice he was as fast as the wide receivers and defensive backs. He was also smart but didn't like to admit it."[4]

Those two seasons of 1957 and '58, Cal Poly went 18-2, with Madden anchoring the offensive line and receiving All-California Collegiate Athletic Association honors.[5]

In early 1958, Madden was shocked to read that he had been drafted by the Philadelphia Eagles in the 21st round, a year before he was eligible to play in the NFL. He was the 244th pick selected on January 28, 1958. It looked like his dream of playing 15 seasons of professional football was still alive despite being drafted in such a late round.

Before reporting to the Eagles' training camp in August '59, he happened to meet a young lady that changed his life. Virginia Fields was a feisty 5-foot-8 graduate student. She was teaching and taking night classes toward her master's in education. They met at Harry's Nightclub & Beach Bar, which 65 years later still stands out as one of the great dive bars on Pismo Beach. John and his friends were at a table listening to the live music when he spotted Virginia.

"I have no idea how he got up the courage to ask me to dance," she told *Cal Poly Magazine*, "because John couldn't dance." They did chat on the dance floor, and for the next few weeks Virginia noticed that John seemed to be wherever she went on campus.[6]

"Finally, after about the third week of this," she said, "he was hanging around outside the coffee shop, and I walked out and said, 'Do you want to talk to me?' And he said, 'Yes, I'd like to take you home.' Well, I lived 56 miles from campus, so I told him he probably didn't. But I let him drive me to my carpool pickup spot."

And so it began with Virginia and the big guy. Madden showed how much he cared about her when her father suddenly passed away by hitchhiking the 56 miles to her home in Los Alamos, California, to comfort her.

"He showed a lot of compassion and seemed to understand what I was going through," she said, "and that my first obligation was to my mom. It started there."[7]

⸻

After graduating with a bachelor's degree in education in 1959, Madden flew to the Eagles' training camp in Hershey, Pennsylvania, and reported in at 6-foot-4 and 263 pounds. Unfortunately, the dream didn't last long after he arrived. Disaster struck on a routine goal-line play. Madden was a guard on the left side, and the pile of bodies came up behind him and rolled over his leg. He had torn ligaments in his knee that required surgery. People didn't recover from those types of injuries as quickly as they do today. His season was over, and maybe his football career too.

With a Philadelphia dateline, here's how Madden's hometown paper, *The Redwood Tribune*, covered the story reporting the injury on August 5, 1959:

> *John Madden's professional career has ended almost before it started—for this year at least. . . . Team physicians said he may be hospitalized several weeks and will be in a cast for some time after that. He will definitely not play this season, they said. . . . Friends wishing to write him should address cards and letters to Madden in Room 1134 at Hahnemann Hospital.*

The possibility existed that he could play the next season, so the Eagles continued to pay him, and once the season began, he spent most of his early mornings rehabilitating his knee in the training room of Franklin Field on the campus of the University of Pennsylvania, where the Eagles played their regular-season games and practiced during the week. He'd get there early before everyone else so he wouldn't interfere with any of the players who needed the training room.

After his session in the Whirlpool was completed, he'd sit in the locker room where one morning he heard the whirring sound of a film projector. He thought he was alone, but he wasn't. In the front of the locker room was quarterback Norm Van Brocklin. The Dutchman was breaking down film of the Eagles' next opponent. Van Brocklin used one of the locker room walls of the crusty old building as his screen to watch the film.

Van Brocklin was one of the great quarterbacks in the NFL throughout the 1950s. In 1951, he led the Los Angeles Rams to the NFL championship, and in an early game that season he passed for a record 554 yards against the New York Yanks—a record that still stands. He was inducted into the College Football Hall of Fame in 1966 and Pro Football Hall of Fame in 1971.

Van Brocklin announced his retirement from the Rams after the 1957 season but came out of retirement in 1958 when he was traded to the Eagles. One major reason was that Eagles coach Buck Shaw told Van Brocklin he could have complete control of the offense. In effect, he became the offensive coordinator.

Here's how Madden described what happened as he sat quietly in the back of the locker room until Van Brocklin spotted him:

"Hey Red," Van Brocklin called out to John, who had reddish-blond hair. "Come on up."

"Now I'm not saying I had any input. I just sat there and listened as he broke the film down. He'd just talk out loud: 'Geez, I think I can get that post [pattern]. If I put Clarence Peaks out in the flat, I can get [Tommy] McDonald open . . .' And I'm watching and seeing how he's thinking how he's getting ready to attack a defense. That's where I learned pro football. Seeing from Norm Van Brocklin what it takes to prepare for a game."

"He was a great guy, a tough guy," Madden said of Van Brocklin. "He didn't take any crap from anyone. He was crusty outside, and he expected a lot out of everyone. He'd give everyone hell if they didn't give him everything they had. He was the coach of the Eagles."[8]

That season the Eagles improved to 7-5, and in 1960, they finished 10-2 and defeated Vince Lombardi's Green Bay Packers, 17–13, for the NFL championship. It was Lombardi's only postseason loss.

In 1980, while working for CBS Sports, I traveled to Atlanta for a Falcons game to spend time with Madden, who was calling the game that week. On Saturday night, John asked me to ride with him to Atlanta's new Superstation WTBS for an interview he agreed to do for Van Brocklin, a former coach of the Falcons who at that time was doing analysis for WTBS. To find Madden doing anything on the night before a game other than preparing was unusual. "You know I wouldn't do this for anybody else," he said to me on the car ride over. "If it wasn't for the Dutchman, I probably would have never become a coach."

What Van Brocklin accomplished in those early-morning sessions with Madden was teaching him to see the entire field. Until then, as an offensive lineman, John only cared about the guy who lined up across from him and the immediate area. After that 1959 season, the Eagles released John and he returned to Cal Poly to get his master's in education.

"By then I had a doctorate in football because of Van Brocklin," Madden said. "I couldn't have asked for anything better than that.... By then I knew I was going to be a coach. I should have known that all along, but I didn't."

There was another reason he wanted to go back to Cal Poly—to rejoin Virginia. He and Virginia got engaged shortly after he returned from training camp in August '59.

"I don't remember John ever saying, 'Will you marry me?' Virginia recalled. "But he did say that I was the type of girl that he wanted to marry. He kept showing up."

They were married December 26, 1959, at the St. Mary of the Assumption Church in Santa Maria, California. *The Santa Maria Times* reported that the bride "was radiant in an original gown of imported Chantilly lace over 'Deep Luster' ivory satin with Sabrina neckline edged with pearls."

The best man was John Robinson, who like Madden dreamed of playing in the NFL some day, but when it became obvious that they wouldn't, they both decided to become coaches. While Madden made it to the Pro Football Hall of Fame after coaching the Oakland Raiders 10 seasons, Robinson was elected to the College Football Hall of Fame for his years coaching the Southern Cal Trojans, who won four Rose Bowl titles under him and went undefeated in 1979. Robinson also had great success in the pros, coaching the Los Angeles Rams to four playoff victories.

Madden began his coaching career at Santa Maria's tiny Alan Hancock College in 1960, working his first two seasons as an assistant and then two more as the head coach, taking over in 1962 at age 25. His overall record was 12-6, going 8-1 his final year.

Madden knew that the road to becoming a head coach was through any networking he could do at the different coaching clinics he would attend. After attending a clinic one weekend, Virginia recalled that John came home all excited about his coaching prospects.

"'One day, Virginia,' he told me, 'football is gonna support us.' And I laughed like hell."

His next move happened in 1964 when San Diego State coach Don Coryell asked Madden to be his defensive coordinator. He met Coryell a few years earlier at a clinic where Southern Cal coach John McKay was diagramming his famous "I" formation offense. During the lecture, McKay introduced Coryell, his backfield coach, and mentioned that it was Coryell who installed the "I" formation. The "I" formation became college football's offense of choice for decades.

After the lecture, Madden was the only one who sought out Coryell. They became friends, and soon after, Coryell was named head coach at San Diego State. When Coryell's defensive coordinator, Tom Bass, left to join the coaching staff of the AFL's San Diego Chargers, Coryell's first call went to Madden.

Chapter Four

IT'S "SUPER SUMMERALL"

His years with the Chicago Cardinals were brutal ones for Summerall. The Cardinals' record those five years was 17-41-2, and Summerall couldn't have been any happier than when he was traded to the New York Giants before the 1958 season.

Despite his limited play, the 49-yard field goal he kicked that helped send the Giants to the 1958 championship game made Pat a semi-celebrity in town. When he won that 1960 audition to do the Giants insider reports for WCBS, it was a look into his future.

By 1962, Pat was thinking of retiring from pro football when another stroke of luck came his way. His pal Kyle Rote tipped Summerall off to an opening as an analyst on Giants games with CBS Sports. It happened because CBS's current announcer, former Notre Dame great Johnny Lujack, had a sponsor conflict. The opening was created when the Ford Motor Company became a primary sponsor of Giants games. When the automaker discovered that Lujack had married into the family that owned one of the most prominent Chevy dealerships in the country, Ford insisted on a new announcer.

In 1962, CBS was still sending two sets of announcers to each game—home and away. Summerall, who would be working next to play-by-play veteran Chris Schenkel, had been teaching eighth graders back home in Lake City. This would be a step up financially for him. There was just one thing he needed to do before CBS would even interview him—retire.

CBS Sports president Bill MacPhail was interested in hiring Pat, but the networks had an agreement with the NFL that they wouldn't poach any active players. So Summerall went straight to the Giants' headquarters to discuss it with team owner Wellington Mara.

"I don't want you to retire," Mara told Summerall, "and I don't think you can make this broadcasting business pay. But if that's what you want to do, I won't stand in your way."

"You won't have to retire first," Mara continued. "Just tell them that you're retired and see what they say. Then get back to me."[1]

It turned out that Mara was a better judge of football talent than broadcasting talent. Back at CBS, MacPhail got the okay to hire Pat, who started out getting $325 a game plus expenses for travel from Florida.

MacPhail and Summerall quickly became friends and drinking buddies as well. These were the '60s, the *Mad Men* days, when two- or three-martini lunches were standard. MacPhail and Summerall lunched regularly at La Grenouille, one of New York's classic French restaurants where celebrities like Elizabeth Taylor dined regularly. Just one block east of CBS, the mirrored, red-and-gold-drenched jewel box became a magnet for New York power players. The pair were also part of a regular four-man luncheon at Mike Manuche's that included NFL commissioner Pete Rozelle and Philip Morris's powerful marketing executive Jack Landry.

"Under MacPhail CBS was a blast, and everybody drank," said Ellen Beckwith, who was 21 years old when she was hired as an assistant in 1966. "We never knew how the shows would get on the air. On Thursdays we had cocktail hour [after work] at Kee Wah Yen, which was right down 52nd Street from CBS, and Pat usually joined us. Each week we'd give him a word he had to say on the air during the whip-around at the start of the pregame show [each Sunday]."[2] The "whip-around" was when CBS would go quickly from one game site to another, with the announcers each getting 30 seconds to talk about their game.

"One week," said Beckwith, "we gave him a word we never thought he'd work in. The word was 'geriatric.' But somehow he did while describing the Washington Redskins."[3]

It's "Super Summerall"

In those days, lunch was not only a business appointment but a social one, too. CBS's senior public-relations man Bill Brendle used to say, "I've been at CBS 18 years, but if you don't count lunches, seven."

Summerall was also smart enough to let Schenkel show him the ropes around Manhattan in the evenings. Schenkel was a dapper dresser who had been covering the Giants for 10 years and certainly knew his way around every top restaurant and nightclub in town. He also gave Pat some very good broadcasting advice: "If you're going to have to fill ten minutes on the air," he said, "prepare for a half hour."

In his autobiography, Summerall described Schenkel as someone who was "warm and engaging to everyone who approached him," with a "work ethic that was matched by a fondness for playing late into the night. His was a very civilized, very social, and very seductive lifestyle."[4]

It was 1962. Summerall had turned 32, and becoming a social drinker came easily to him. MacPhail, history has judged, had a pretty good eye for talent. Besides Summerall, he hired early television stars such as Schenkel, Frank Gifford, Jack Whitaker, Ray Scott, and Jim McKay.

Summerall was still teaching in Lake City weekdays when President Kennedy was assassinated on that dreary Friday in November 1963. The principal of the school asked Pat to make the announcement informing the students over the school's public address system. Even then Summerall's voice was comforting and perfect to announce such difficult news. Years later, CBS Sports publicist Beano Cook, attempting to emphasize how trusted Pat's delivery was, said, "If I ever get cancer, I want Pat Summerall to be the one to tell me."[5]

That weekend Pete Rozelle made possibly the only mistake in his tenure as commissioner. He decided to play the weekend's schedule of games while the whole country was mourning President Kennedy.

The teams may have played the games, but CBS chose not to broadcast them. Instead Schenkel and Summerall went to Yankee Stadium and sat in an executive's office and watched in horror as Jack Ruby shot and killed Kennedy's assassin, Lee Harvey Oswald, on live television.

In early 1964, Schenkel was offered the lucrative position of being the sports director for WCBS Radio in Manhattan but turned it down. Instead, he tipped off Pat about the job.

"He told me to call a sales guy at WCBS radio," Summerall said, "who invited me to audition by writing a brief sports show and then performing it on the air."

Despite talking a little too fast in the audition, Summerall was offered the job.

"How much is this gonna pay?" Summerall asked, "because I'm pretty happy with what's going on in my life now."

"We think you can move up pretty quickly," the radio executive said. "But the starting salary is seventy-five thousand dollars!"

"How soon do I start?" Summerall quickly responded.[6]

Despite the high salary, the new job was not a hit with Kathy Summerall, who was not thrilled about pulling up roots in Lake City, Florida, and moving to their new home in Connecticut with young daughter Susan and baby Jay. And the job had him much more involved than his previous weekend sports updates for the local station.

Now Pat was reporting sports all day long as part of the CBS Broadcast Group. He even bought a pocket tape recorder for interviews. He learned how to edit the interviews, write his own scripts, and even engineer his own broadcast—all that with just the help of a single researcher. He would take his tape recorder to team practices and interview stars like his old friend Mickey Mantle.

Mantle didn't like doing interviews, but because they knew each other back in Summerall's Arkansas days, he agreed to become Pat's first interview with the Yankees. Once the others saw that Mickey cooperated, most of them fell in line.

Longtime New York Islanders announcer Barry Landers was a young intern working for Summerall in 1966. One day Howard Cosell created a scene in the Yankee clubhouse. This is how Landers recalled the event when he retold it to David Halberstam of SportsBroadcastJournal.com:

"In his typical brash and loud (staccato) voice and for all to hear, Cosell announced 'Look who has arrived, old number 88 [Summerall's uniform number with the New York Giants], the greatest kicker in New York Football Giants history!'

"The reporters in the press room were startled by Howard's brashness," Landers said. "As Pat and I approached the table where Howard was sitting, Summerall, smiling, put his hand on Cosell's shoulder and leaned heavily on it as the blood drained from Cosell's face. Howard's face turned colors, from red to ashen. In less than a loud voice, Pat told Howard. 'If you ever pull that shit again, I will kick your ass from here to River Avenue,' which was the street right outside Yankee Stadium."[7]

Cosell recovered, and the two actually became drinking buddies after that. "Howard was a world class martini drinker," Summerall wrote in his autobiography, and the two often rode the train home together, drinking along the way. Cosell got off at Pound Ridge, New York, and Summerall a few stops later in Greenwich, Connecticut.

Summerall's four-minute sports capsules were played every hour during the afternoon on WCBS Radio. They were so successful that they were packed with commercials for national brands. Pat was even getting reviews from Frank Stanton, president of the CBS Network and the No. 2 man behind owner Bill Paley. Stanton would send Summerall little notes on brown paper. The notes only contained a hand-drawn smiley face or on occasion a frowny face. Stanton's notes seemed very strange. Regardless, Summerall's success was rewarded with a pay raise to $125,000 a year.

The job didn't come without its drawbacks. He was leaving mornings before his children were awake and coming home around 10 p.m. or later. He frequently would run into his old Giants teammate Kyle Rote who was doing sports radio for WNEW Radio, a New York independent station.

"One day," Summerall wrote, "he [Kyle] confided [to me] that he had divorced his wife. I noticed that Kyle was drinking more and figured it was how he coped with the loss. He may have noticed the same about me."[8]

⌘

Another amazing opportunity came Summerall's way when Arthur Godfrey left WCBS's morning variety show to do strictly television. Replacing Godfrey's popular show, management chose *The Jack Sterling Show*, a 5:30 a.m. "rise-and-shine" program that Sterling had been doing for the CBS radio network since 1948. Like Godfrey, Sterling had a folksy style and plenty of backup for his show. The backup included his personal writers for monologues, a studio band, and sometimes he even played records.

Sterling also did weather and traffic reports and welcomed in Summerall, whose sports reports increased from four minutes per hour to three minutes every half hour. Pat even taped some segments for the television network too.

After a few months with Sterling, the station manager shocked Summerall when he called him into his office and closed both the blinds and the door. "Pat," he said, "the more I listen to the morning show, it's apparent that it's becoming 'The Pat Summerall Show,' instead of 'The Jack Sterling Show.' I want you to take it over full time."

"You gotta be kidding," Summerall said. "I don't know anything about New York traffic. I don't know anything about New York weather. I don't know anything about music. I know sports—but that's all I know."[9]

Management was certain they could easily groom Pat for the job and give him help doing the traffic and the weather. In fact, they secretly sent him to Los Angeles for two weeks to learn the ropes from Wink Martindale, the morning deejay at CBS affiliate KFWB. This was before Martindale became known for hosting game shows.

Then on the morning of October 18, 1966, *The New York Times*' headline read:

Jack Sterling Spot on WCBS Is Taken by Pat Summerall

Jack Sterling (51) can sleep late this morning. Radio station WCBS announced last night that the "Jack Sterling Show," a 5:30 A.M. rise-and-shine program he had conducted for 18 years (since 1948), had been terminated by "amicable agreement."

The new host on WCBS's early morning program is Pat Summerall. . . . In recent months he had presented sports reports on the Sterling Show. *The announcement of the change was made by Thomas J. Swafford . . . who said: "It is with understandable regret that we announce this difficult decision. All of us at WCBS radio will feel a great sense of loss in view of the contribution Jack has made during the 18 years he has served as one of New York's foremost radio personalities."*[10]

It's "Super Summerall"

When Summerall returned, they surrounded him with staff and had someone pick the music for him. All Pat had to worry about was being personable on the air, and that was something that came easily to him. Besides his base salary, he was to get a piece of the profits from every commercial that ran during his show. All of a sudden, he was looking at an annual paycheck of nearly $500,000. (That would be equivalent to $4.8 million on today's Consumer Price Index calculator.)

Traffic reports were made much easier for him by the station's two helicopter pilots. And the station went all out with a new marketing campaign set around Summerall's traffic reports. They had him pose in a Superman outfit for a life-size poster that they called "Super Summerall," and they plastered the posters all over the city. They even had this crazy idea of distributing the "Super Summerall" posters to commuters, telling them if their car ever broke down to put the poster on top of the car. When the helicopter pilots would see a car with a "Super Summerall" poster, they'd radio for help.

Pat was becoming a full-fledged celebrity around town. At night he'd meet potential guests for his show at restaurants or clubs, and he'd interview the rich and famous actors, comedians, and singers on the morning show.

One of those interviews was with Sally Rand, the former fan dancer, who had seen her best years. Summerall apologized for getting her up so early to do the show, at which she responded, "Sweetheart, don't apologize. A few years ago, you could have just rolled over and nudged me."[11]

The good times and the sweet paycheck lasted less than a year. In August 1967, WCBS Radio went to an "all-the-news-all-the-time" format. Summerall's 3:30 a.m. wakeup calls were history, and probably no one was happier about it than Kathy Summerall.

Additionally, Summerall was working weekends as an NFL analyst on the TV side for CBS Sports. First with Chris Schenkel, then once CBS went to just one set of announcers for each game in 1968, Pat worked with Jack Buck and Ray Scott. MacPhail impressed upon Pat that it was a visual medium and told him, "I'll never criticize you for saying too little."[12]

WCBS Radio 88's fun cartoon promoting Pat as "Super Summerall."

It's "Super Summerall"

But working all those years as the Giants' home-team analyst, Summerall was not one to say anything negative about his former team. This was a problem for a few CBS executives.

"Summerall had been working with Schenkel, but he really wasn't very good," said Bill Fitts, who was the head of production in those years for CBS Sports. "Because he [Summerall] was good friends with MacPhail, he was protected. [CBS Sports programming director] Jack Dolph and I kept telling MacPhail that New York was too big a market to have an analyst who won't criticize anyone. He didn't want to say anything negative about anyone. Not the least bit negative. You can't really be an analyst that way."[13]

One of Pat's partners, Ray Scott, began his career calling the Green Bay Packers games in 1953 for the DuMont Network. DuMont was a television pioneer that eventually was absorbed by CBS. Scott was CBS's lead play-by-play announcer for the famous Ice Bowl game in 1967 between the Dallas Cowboys and the Green Bay Packers, played in sub-zero weather, and he also called Super Bowls I and II for CBS.

In 1970, Scott was paired with Summerall permanently. They were together one way or another for six and a half years. Many, including Summerall, believe this is where Pat learned his minimalist delivery style, which he became known for later in his career.

"In 6½ years with Ray, I never heard him [Scott] make a mistake," Summerall told Bill Lyon for Lyon's book *When the Clock Runs Out*. "That was because he wanted to make sure he was right before he spoke. He wasn't in a hurry, and he felt that often the pictures spoke for themselves, and all we did was get in the way."

Scott became known for the brevity of his touchdown calls on Packers games. Instead of going into detail to describe a pass play from quarterback Bart Starr to wide receiver Boyd Dowler, Scott simply said: "Starr . . . Dowler . . . Touchdown!"

Scott and Jack Buck became role models for Summerall.

"Ray in particular had great pipes, a real Cadillac of a voice," Summerall said. "His commentary was Spartan, very understated, but also filled with dramatic tones. I picked up on his pared-down style and adopted it."[14]

One thing Summerall learned doing sideline work for big games was how to deal with, or avoid dealing with, his former Giants coach Vince Lombardi. Super Bowl I was played in the Los Angeles Coliseum between the Kansas City Chiefs and the Packers. Both CBS and NBC were simultaneously broadcasting the game, in a decision made by Commissioner Rozelle to be fair to both networks.

At halftime NBC got caught in an interview with comedian Bob Hope and missed the second-half kickoff. CBS was shocked to hear that the officials had decided to re-kick. That's when Summerall got a request from CBS director Bob Dailey.

"Incredibly, my director's voice came over my headset as I stood on the Green Bay sidelines," Summerall said. "He asked me to ask Coach Lombardi if he would mind kicking off again.

"My answer was, 'Absolutely not.' There was no way I was going to get chewed out by Coach Lombardi on national television. 'You'll have to find someone else to tell him,' I said."[15]

In 1974, Scott did his last Super Bowl for CBS, Super Bowl VIII, when the Miami Dolphins defeated the Minnesota Vikings, 24–7. Summerall and Bart Starr worked alongside, but it was Scott's final game for CBS. Apparently he had gotten into a dispute with Bill Fitts, head of production.

The IFB or interruptible foldback earpiece was fairly new, and CBS had ordered all of its broadcasters to wear them during the games. The IFB allowed directors to give cues and one-way communication to the talent. It made it easier for the introduction of commercials, etc. The only problem was, Scott refused to wear his IFB. No matter how hard Fitts tried to get him to do so, Scott's old-school style made him way too uncomfortable with it.

"My only choice at that point," said Fitts, "was to fire him."

Later that year Summerall was working with Jack Buck. Bob Wussler had become the new president of CBS Sports, and one day he phoned Summerall at home and asked him to come into town to meet him for lunch. Pat wasn't sure if it was good news or bad.

Buck and Summerall were considered CBS's No. 1 NFL broadcast team. They met at Mike Manuche's restaurant at 152 West 52nd

Street, near CBS. Manuche's had a big circular bar when you walked in with plenty of beautiful leather-lined booths. It was a favorite meeting place for sports executives, including Pete Rozelle. At lunch Summerall ordered a drink followed by Manuche's famous special salad. Then Wussler dropped a bomb.

"I've got problems with you and Jack Buck," he said. "My problem is I can't tell which one of you is talking at any given time. You sound too much alike."[16]

This was not good news for Summerall, who had an especially close relationship with Buck, which was witnessed close up by Jack's son, Joe Buck.

"Anybody who had a reverence for my father and could make my father laugh, they automatically had an impact on me," Joe Buck recalled. "I wanted to be around them, and I wanted to know what made them tick. I just know the love my dad had for Pat was reciprocated and there was a respect level my dad had for Pat that I didn't see elsewhere over the years."[17]

Summerall realized he couldn't talk Wussler out of it because, indeed, they did have similar baritone voices. So instead of complaining, he made a suggestion:

"As long as I'm going to make a change," he said, "I'd like to try doing play-by-play."

Wussler liked the idea and wanted him to start right away. "Whom do you want to work with?" Wussler asked. Summerall gave him the name of a guy he used to hate playing against, Tom Brookshier. Three days later they worked the Cardinals-Giants game flawlessly. For several years they had been doing voice-overs together for *This Week in the NFL*. That was for NFL Films in Mount Laurel, New Jersey, just outside Philadelphia, and they really enjoyed working together. But the first time they met it was ugly.

That was in a 1959 game between the Giants and Brookshier's team, the Philadelphia Eagles. Brookshier was a defensive back known for his hard hitting. Late in the game, with the Giants way ahead, Summerall caught a short pass and then got walloped by Brookshier.

"He belted me so hard in the head," said Summerall, "that my helmet split open. We both hit the ground, and as I was trying to recover my senses, I lashed out at him."

"What's wrong with you?" Summerall said, firing back.

"You're pathetic," Brookshier shot back. "You shouldn't even be playing. You've got the game won."[18]

It was the making of a beautiful relationship that lasted for the rest of their lives together.

Chapter Five
MADDEN AND SUMMERALL RISE TO NEW HEIGHTS

Before John Madden was hired as defensive coordinator at San Diego State, Coach Don Coryell would stay with the Maddens whenever he was recruiting players from Northern California. Coryell wound up being one of college and pro football's great offensive minds. In his years at San Diego State (1961–1972), Coryell's teams went 104-19-2, including a 35-game unbeaten streak in the mid-'60s.

Coryell was nearly as successful in the NFL, coaching the St. Louis Cardinals and San Diego Chargers to the playoffs six different times. At the Chargers, Coryell's offense was nicknamed "Air Coryell," and with Dan Fouts passing to Charlie Joiner and Kellen Winslow, the Chargers set numerous offensive records. And all three players and Coach Coryell were elected to the NFL Hall of Fame.

"Don exploded the myth that if you threw the football, three things could happen and two of them were bad," Madden told *Sports Illustrated* for its August 1, 1996, issue. "All of a sudden it didn't matter the down or the distance. Just throw it."

The architect of Coryell's offense at San Diego State was coordinator Joe Gibbs. During the two years Madden was there, Gibbs coached the offense and Madden the defense. Though Coryell did not win a Super Bowl, his protégés Madden and Gibbs won a total of four.

The two assistant coaches got together often to discuss strategy, sometimes over a racquetball game. One day before Gibbs's offense was to scrimmage against John's defense, Madden asked Gibbs for a favor.

Madden: "Show me your plays."

Gibbs: "You're not seeing my plays."

Madden: "How am I going to call the defense if I don't know what you're running?"

Gibbs: "I don't know how you're gonna do it, but you're not seeing my plays."[1]

Madden was pissed, but Gibbs would not relent. It gave you an idea of the competitiveness the two had.

Gibbs was a college and NFL assistant for 17 years, but at age 40 he finally got his chance. Madden's old pal Bobby Beathard hired Gibbs in 1981 as the Washington Redskins head coach. Gibbs returned the favor by winning Super Bowl XVII in his second year with the team, then leading the Redskins to two more Super Bowl victories before retiring with a 171-101 record. He was elected to the Pro Football Hall of Fame in 1996.

Comparing strategy and ideas with Gibbs and Coryell at San Diego State turned out to be something impressive on John Madden's résumé when Al Davis was looking for someone to coach his Oakland Raiders defense.

Brought up in Brooklyn, New York, Al Davis was a fighter his whole life. He fought for every job he ever had, from assistant coach at The Citadel up to and including becoming the coach, general manager, and owner of the Oakland Raiders. In the '60s the Raiders were one of the more successful teams in the AFL, which was battling the NFL for the best eligible college players. With the AFL getting a TV contract with NBC and many new stadiums, a bidding war for players broke out between the two leagues. It was the type of battle that Al Davis loved.

Davis had taken on a somewhat tough-guy personality. He had slicked-back dark hair that often ended in a ducktail. He wore motorcycle sunglasses, and he spoke with a Brooklyn accent, calling his team the "Raiduhs." His motto was, "Just win, baby!"

In 1962, both the San Francisco 49ers and the San Diego Chargers (of the AFL) wanted the speedy Arkansas receiver Lance Alworth. Davis owned the AFL draft rights to Alworth and rushed onto the field and signed him under the goalpost after Alworth's final college game, as 49ers coach, Red Hickey, watched helplessly from the stands. Davis then traded Alworth to the Chargers for three players.

In 1966, Davis hired John Rauch to replace himself as head coach when the AFL owners voted Davis to be the league's commissioner. He continued as the Raiders general manager and owner and loved discovering great players at little-known colleges. One small college he liked to scout players at was San Diego State.

Davis liked and respected San Diego State head coach Don Coryell, but it was a former coach from the '50s to whom Al went for information. Paul Governali was the coach from 1956 (when the Aztecs went undefeated) through 1960, when he moved to the athletic department. In 1942, Governali was an All-American quarterback at Columbia University and finished second in the balloting for the Heisman Trophy behind Frank Sinkwich, who helped Georgia win the national championship that season.

Although Governali was no longer coaching, he was still a shrewd judge of talent. As a defensive coordinator at San Diego State, John Madden sought out Governali's counsel. Madden loved to talk strategy with the former coach. And Madden continued to seek information anywhere he could get it. One July weekend in 1963, he drove to Reno, Nevada, to listen to a lecture by Green Bay Packers coach Vince Lombardi.

"He spoke about one play—the Green Bay Power Sweep—for eight hours," Madden said. "Four hours before lunch, and four hours after lunch. One play! I thought I knew just about everything there was to know about offense. I didn't know anything. I couldn't even talk about any play for even 20 minutes."[2]

When Lombardi paused and took questions, the first one was from Sid Gillman, whose San Diego Chargers played for the AFL championship that year. That's how well respected Lombardi was among his fellow coaches.

"Vince Lombardi was my mentor," Madden said. "I always wanted to be like him, and I learned everything about him. So, whatever he wore is what I wore for a while. At one time it was a short-sleeve shirt and a tie. And that was the thing that you wore. And sometime later, it just got to be a short-sleeve shirt."[3]

Governali tipped off Davis that Madden was a coach on the rise. One day when Davis was watching San Diego State practice, he saw Madden writing some things down and asked him what it was. Madden explained he was trying to come up with a defense against their next opponent, small college powerhouse North Dakota State. Its offensive linemen usually lined up spread apart, or what Madden described as having "wide splits." He was looking to attack those open splits, and even Davis made a suggestion. Davis might not have known who Madden was when he first approached, but he sure knew who he was when he left.

On the practice field, Madden looked a little goofy. He wore high-top black shoes, baggy pants, a jacket, baseball cap, and a whistle. But that didn't slow Davis down. "When I talked to him," Davis said, "I felt an emotional love of football that was a little different than what you normally come across."

In 1966, the Raiders were looking for a linebackers coach. When asked for a recommendation, Governali reminded Davis about Madden, and then Davis had his head coach, John Rauch, call John and hire him. Madden accepted for a salary of $12,000 a year, which was a $2,000 pay cut.[4] Later that year after the leagues agreed to merge, Davis was back full time with Oakland, and Rauch didn't care for what he described as "Davis's constant interference."

The following year the Raiders went 13-1 with Madden coaching the linebackers and the special teams. After having won the AFL championship, they would be meeting Lombardi's mighty Green Bay Packers in Super Bowl II. Lombardi and Green Bay had easily defeated the Kansas City Chiefs in Super Bowl I the year before. Going up against Lombardi got Madden all revved up. The Raiders were still in the game at halftime, just trailing 16–7, but they couldn't come any closer, losing 33–14.

In 1968, the Raiders were again among the best in the NFL. They were involved in the famous "*Heidi* game" in November when they trailed the New York Jets by three points with 65 seconds to go, and all of a sudden TV screens across the country switched to the movie classic *Heidi*. It was 7 p.m. on the East Coast, and NBC technicians were programmed to run the movie at that time. The Raiders, however, scored two touchdowns in that final 65 seconds to win, but very few saw it. NBC executives, though they tried, were unable to reach the technician who flipped the switch.

Two weeks later, Joe Namath and the Jets got revenge on the Raiders in the AFL title game, winning 27–23, and earned the right to face Don Shula's heavily favored Baltimore Colts in Super Bowl III. Oddsmaker Jimmy "the Greek" Snyder had the Colts as a 17-point favorite. Despite that, Namath surprised the media by guaranteeing an outright victory for the Jets. He was right. He guided the Jets to an easy 16–7 victory to become the first AFL team to win a Super Bowl. Losing that chance to play in the Super Bowl did not sit well with Davis, and he let Rauch know it. While Davis traveled to Miami to see the game, Rauch had decided he'd had enough of Davis's second-guessing, and he secretly negotiated a deal to coach the Buffalo Bills instead.

When things settled back in Oakland, Davis announced to the staff that the head coaching job was open and that any assistant coach who was interested could come talk to him, but they'd have to wait until after the draft. Madden was the first to knock on his door. He was just 32 years old when he walked through that door, and he didn't wait for the draft to be over. He had all the confidence in the world.

When Davis reminded him how young he was, Madden snapped back: "What's that got to do with it? If I can be the head coach, I can be the head coach now. I either have it in me or I don't." Then Davis brought up his age again and asked, "What are your credentials?"

Madden replied, "What were your credentials to be the Raiders' [boss] at such a young age?"[5]

In the two years Madden had been with the Raiders, he and Davis talked almost every day, and they had gotten very comfortable with each other. What Madden was reminding Davis of was that Davis was pretty young himself—only seven years older than Madden—and that in 1963, when Davis coached Oakland to a surprise 10-4 season and was named AFL Coach of the Year, Davis was just 34.

The big difference between Rauch and Madden was that Rauch hated confrontation and hated debating with Davis when Al questioned him about strategy. Madden loved it.

"Al liked a good argument," Madden said. "He would say things just to see how you really felt about it. And I enjoyed arguing with him, too. All Al wanted to hear was what you thought. If you really believed in something bad enough to defend it."[6]

On the field, Madden was easy to spot, and if you were an official, even easier to hear. Here's how Raiders Hall of Fame tight end Dave Casper described him: "You'd see him on the sidelines with a mouth that could eat a watermelon. And he had the big hook nose and the flowing red hair. He was a cartoon character."[7]

One writer said he looked like "an unmade bed," which Madden didn't mind. "That's not bad," Madden decided. "I didn't have a lot of clothes, so if we won, that became my lucky outfit."[8]

On February 4, 1969, Davis introduced Madden as the new head coach. He said Madden had great relationships with his players. He compared his personality to that of Walter Alston, who managed the Brooklyn/Los Angeles Dodgers from 1953 to 1976. Davis also made Madden, at 32, the youngest head coach in the NFL. Although many in the news media thought Madden would be nothing more than a puppet for Davis, Madden soon proved that no one was pulling his strings. For the announcement, Madden wore a suit and tie and had his hair cut and neatly parted. It was probably the first time he wore a tie since his wedding day.

In his first season, Madden led the Raiders to a 12-1-1 record but lost the AFC title game to Kansas City, 17–7, partly due to an injured throwing hand sustained by Oakland quarterback Daryle Lamonica. The loss was especially disappointing because the Raiders had beaten the Chiefs twice in the regular season. The Chiefs went on to win Super Bowl IV, defeating the Minnesota Vikings, 23–7. Although the Raiders would continue to be one of the NFL's best teams, it would be another seven years before they won a Super Bowl.

In 1970, they came close again, losing the AFC championship game to the Baltimore Colts, 21–14, who also went on to win the Super Bowl. In Madden's 10 seasons coaching the Raiders, he took them to the playoffs nine times, the AFC championship game seven times, and the Super Bowl once. In that decade his team came up against some of the most dominating teams in NFL history. Among them were the Pittsburgh Steelers and Miami Dolphins. During Madden's tenure, the Steelers and the Miami Dolphins went to six Super Bowls, winning five.

That included 1972 when the Dolphins went 17-0. That year Oakland suffered possibly its toughest playoff loss ever. Playing the divisional round at Pittsburgh, the Raiders held a 7–6 lead late in the game after quarterback Kenny Stabler made a terrific 30-yard touchdown run.

The Steelers, playing at home in Three Rivers Stadium (which they shared with the Pirates), were desperate with just 22 seconds remaining, facing fourth down and 10 at their own 40-yard line. Quarterback Terry Bradshaw's pass bounced off defender Jack Tatum's shoulder pad and went back toward Bradshaw when it was scooped up by Pittsburgh's Franco Harris. He either caught the ball off his shoe tops or on a short hop off the ground. The catch was never verified because the TV replays didn't record it. Harris, meanwhile, ran into the end zone with the ball, which after a long delay was ruled a touchdown for the Steelers.

The late Myron Cope, Pittsburgh's colorful radio analyst and national sports journalist, labeled Harris's catch and touchdown run "the Immaculate Reception." It was a play that haunted Madden for the rest of his life.

Part of the delay was the result of referee Fred Swearingen using a telephone in the Pirates' dugout to call the press box and speak with Art McNally, the NFL's supervisor of officials. Years later, when Madden was working a Steelers game as an analyst for CBS, he was walking on the field before the game with producer Bob Stenner. John's assistant at the time, Mike Frank, described what happened.

"It was '88 or '89. It was the first time John was back in Pittsburgh since the Immaculate Reception," recalled Frank. "John and Stenner passed by the Pirates' dugout and John says, 'Stenner, that's the phone that [referee] Fred Swearingen used to call upstairs to Art McNally.'"

Madden: "Right there—that's the phone, right there, that the referee talked on and then decided the Immaculate Reception was a touchdown. So I just keep walking, boom, boom, boom. After practice, we're walking off the field, and Stenner goes up and grabs the phone, jerks it off the set, and he pulls it in and puts it in his briefcase and gives it to me later. And we've got that phone now."

Mike Frank: "They gave it to me, and we put it in the bus. At Christmas time, I took the phone to a trophy dealer and had it mounted on a special plaque for John. I think Virginia still has it. It had a gold engraving that said, 'Who did Fred Swearingen call?' John loved it."[9]

The handset of the phone the NFL used to decide the Immaculate Reception against the Raiders. CBS producer Bob Stenner appropriated it for Madden. COURTESY OF MIKE MADDEN

Madden and Summerall Rise to New Heights

For Madden, the 1974 and '75 seasons were very frustrating. His team was a combined 25-5 those years but did not reach the Super Bowl either season. Some critics said Madden couldn't win the big games.

"Yeah, I heard that stuff about how Madden couldn't win the big game," Madden said. "But I used to say . . . tell me when there's a little one. We won a lot of big games. A lot of regular-season big games, playoff games, games to get into the playoffs. We never lost to a bad team. We lost to some of the greatest teams in the history of the NFL."

Nineteen seventy-six changed all that. The Raiders were 13-1 in the regular season and looked like a lock to make the Super Bowl. But the New England Patriots had other ideas when they traveled to Oakland to play the divisional round. The Patriots looked like they were on their way to an upset, leading 21-17 in the fourth quarter, when they were called for a controversial roughing-the-quarterback penalty against Stabler. That gave Oakland new life, and with only seconds remaining, Stabler scored the winning touchdown from a yard out.

The Raiders easily handled the Steelers in the conference title game, 24-7, and went on to crush the Minnesota Vikings in the Super Bowl, 32-14. The day before the Super Bowl, running back Pete Banaszak remembers Madden ending practice after just 20 minutes. "Let's stop right now," Banaszak recalls Madden saying. "If we play like this, we're going to kill them."

And in the locker room before the game, Madden knew his team was ready. Not needing any Knute Rockne–type speech, all Madden said was, "Gentlemen take a knee. This will be the single biggest event of your whole life. As long as you win."

Madden was a players' coach. He only had three rules: (1) be on time, (2) pay attention, and (3) play like hell on Sunday. He often said, "The fewer rules a coach has, the fewer there are for the players to break."

Said Stabler: "No hair codes, no dress codes, no curfew. I always thought his strong suit was his style of coaching. John just had a great knack for letting us be what we wanted to be, on the field and off the field. . . . How do you repay him for being that way? You win for him."

Other players were just as grateful. "John helped raise us. He loved us," said Art Shell. "I loved John Madden. He was for the players. He would do anything for the players."[10]

In his blog, author Pat Toomay, who was a Raiders defensive end during Madden's last two seasons, gave some perspective on the type of man John was:

"During film sessions, Madden kept criticism generic.... Under no circumstances would he ever publicly condemn a player's character. That didn't mean he wouldn't chew somebody out for making a mistake in practice, because he would. But even those outbursts would be tempered with a wink or a nudge.... Who was this guy? I began to wonder. What experiences could have forged such a humane perspective?"

Former 49ers coach Bill Walsh, who won three Super Bowls, summed up Madden's attributes this way when interviewed by NFL Films:

"His personality, his intensity, his persona, everything about John—his appearance—was ideally suited for the Raiders. These guys responded to him, when possibly they couldn't have responded to anyone else, no matter how smart or gifted they'd be."[11]

After the final whistle of Super Bowl XI, Oakland players lifted Madden onto their shoulders. He had a smile to last a lifetime.

The famous photo of the Raiders carrying Madden off the field after winning Super Bowl XI. COURTESY OF AP PHOTOS

∽

The Raiders were very tough again in 1977, finishing 11-3, but losing another heartbreaking AFC title game, this time to the Denver Broncos, 21–17. It was all starting to take a toll on Madden. Although he didn't talk much about it, the stress and ulcers were eating away at him. Raiders center Jim Otto said he saw Madden taking Pepto-Bismol antacid tablets on a regular basis. Then on August 12, 1978, another event took its toll on the big man.

Oakland was hosting a preseason game with the New England Patriots. In the second quarter, New England wide receiver Darryl Stingley went across the middle for a pass that Pats quarterback Steve Grogan overthrew. Here's how Madden's biographer Peter Richmond described what happened next:

"[Oakland defender] Jack Tatum was heading for Stingley. When Tatum saw that the pass had sailed high, Tatum turned his head to the left and led with his right shoulder pad, readying to collide with Stingley's chest. But Stingley ducked and his head slammed into Tatum's right shoulder pad. Stingley collapsed to the ground. His neck was broken."[12]

Stingley was paralyzed. He was strapped to a gurney and whisked off to Eden Hospital in Castro Valley. When Madden arrived at the hospital after the game, he became incensed that no one from the Patriots was there. Neither the Patriots' coach nor the team doctor nor any of the team trainers nor the team owner had stayed with Stingley. They all got on the team plane to head back to New England.

Madden picked up the phone, called the airport, and somehow got through to the cockpit of the charter plane that was getting ready to take off. When he reached someone from the team, he was irate. How dare they leave Stingley, paralyzed, alone. The plane stopped taxiing, turned around, and returned to the gate. The Patriots' business manager then deplaned and went to the hospital.

Then somehow Madden talked his way into the operating room, putting on scrubs to be with Stingley. Madden slept at the hospital that Saturday night, wanting to be there for Stingley when he woke up. For the next three months, both John and Virginia made daily trips to the hospital, which was more than an hour's drive from the Oakland practice facility. They brought clothes for Stingley's wife, Tina, and tried to make Stingley's life as good as possible.

"On that day he [Madden] revealed who he was," said Pat Toomay. "A man with a heart."[13]

That 1978 season was more stressful for Madden. The team went 9-7, marking the 10th straight year under Madden with a winning record. But he told Al Davis he'd had enough. Davis asked him to coach one more year, but Madden said no.

Virginia Madden thought it was important enough to take their two sons, Mike and Joe, out of school to attend the press conference. "I was crying, and he was crying," she said. "It wasn't what he wanted to do, but I think he knew he had to do it." Seeing the stress it caused, she told him, "John, we don't need football. We need you."[14]

At his retirement press conference, Madden tried to hold back tears and said, "I'm not resigning, quitting to do anything else. I'm retiring. I'll never coach another game of football. I gave it everything I had for 10 years, and I don't have any more."[15]

When John announced his retirement, Virginia thought it was important for her boys, Joe (left) and Mike (right), to be there, along with Raiders players showing their love. COURTESY OF JOE MADDEN

It surprised many, but not safety George Atkinson. "It was probably the stress," he said, "that and the fear of flying.... Plus, I think the Stingley thing had a real effect on him."[16]

So, John Madden was sitting at home with his bulldogs trying to figure out what was next. His oldest son, Mike, had some insight into that decision:

"He knew the pitfalls of retiring at the age of 42," Mike said. "He knew that he could do something else. He knew his potential. He knew he had two or three more careers in him, he just didn't know what they were. And the fact that one of them became television surprised him.

"He didn't respect TV [announcers]—[he thought] that they didn't know what they were talking about. He called them hair-dos, they're lazy, and blah, blah, blah. He didn't respect the profession. Then he did that first game with [Bob] Costas, and he said, 'This is okay; this might be a thing [for me].' So, he did it, he liked it and the rest is history."[17]

While Madden was establishing himself as one of the great coaches in the NFL, Pat Summerall was quickly rising in the ranks of CBS Sports. For Pat Summerall, less was always more. Even before he was switched from an NFL color man to play-by-play in 1974, he was demonstrating his minimalist virtues on two of the biggest sporting events in the world: the Masters Golf Tournament and the U.S. Open Tennis Championships. He was becoming the new face—and voice—of CBS Sports.

In 1968, Summerall was added to the CBS golf broadcast team, which didn't make producer-director Frank Chirkinian happy. Chirkinian, who practically invented golf on television, had no desire to put Summerall on the air.

"The first year he showed up, I was shocked they sent me this football player to be a golf announcer," said Chirkinian. "I really resented the idea someone would do such a thing. I thought the people in New York had lost their minds. I came to realize Mr. Summerall is completely devoid of ego and is probably the premier broadcaster in any sport because of that."

Chirkinian first put Summerall on the course at the 14th hole, which according to Chirkinian was "the black hole of Calcutta, where rookies go." Soon, however, Summerall was calling the tournament from the 18th tower with longtime partner Ken Venturi. Chirkinian impressed upon Summerall that it was a visual medium. "If I ever hear you say," Chirkinian told him, "that he made that putt, I'll fire you."[18]

Summerall's "less-is-more" delivery seemed to work for almost any sport. When Chirkinian discovered that Summerall was also a schoolboy tennis champion, he made him the lead voice of the U.S. Open beginning in 1973.

Summerall's style was brevity, sometimes with a little wit thrown in. *The New York Times'* TV Sports columnist Richard Sandomir wrote that Summerall's calls "are as trimmed down as a Hemingway sentence." He called Pat "the Marlboro man when the microphone is on, displaying his shorthand announcing—the anti-radio call." He also wrote that "Summerall lets his partners bake the verbal cake. He'll apply the icing."

A perfect example of that, Sandomir wrote, occurred when he and partner Tony Trabert were calling a 1992 U.S. Open match between Pete Sampras and Stefan Edberg.

> **Trabert:** "I'll say it once more. It's not a good strategy by Sampras, rather than go for that big second serve, get a good first serve in and come in and say, 'Come on and beat me.' Good job by that guy right there. He's been Houdini for two weeks."
>
> **Summerall:** "He's all business. And, well, a lot of talent."

The Washington Post's Chuck Culpepper wrote that "Summerall's voice was the voice you wanted to hear underlying the utmost sporting drama—good, true, modest and soothing." He said it was "the soundtrack of the American Sunday." He went on to add that "it came to convey . . . the feeling in the air, the season of the year and the bigness of the game."

Steve Tignor, of Tennis.com and *Tennis* magazine, wrote nostalgically of Summerall's calls from the U.S. Open. "When the Open came around, and you heard Summerall's bourbon-smoothed baritone beaming in from the concrete jungle of New York City," Tignor wrote, "you knew summer was over. Serious business, on and off the tennis court, was about to begin again.

Madden and Summerall Rise to New Heights

"Summerall's presence alone added to the importance of the Open. With him in the booth, tennis took its place, however briefly, as a major American sport." And Tignor loved the way Pat would say, "That's James Scott Connors," with a little extra snap in each of the words, anytime Connors was acting up trying to rev up the crowd.

"Summerall, who was the Voice of Fall in both tennis and football," Tignor concluded, "gave the Open a distinctive sound."[19]

Golf, tennis, football, basketball, hosting a morning radio show—there didn't seem to be anything Pat Summerall couldn't do behind a microphone. And soon he would be doing play-by-play for CBS at Super Bowl X.

Chapter Six
THE RISE AND FALL OF BROOKSHIER—AND SUMMERALL

Tom Brookshier entered the NFL with a bang. A Depression baby born in 1931, Brookshier was the Philadelphia Eagles' 10th-round draft choice in 1953 and seemed to have very little chance of making the team.

Vince McNally, the Eagles' general manager, reached Brookshier on campus at the University of Colorado where he was a defensive back on the football team even though he went to Colorado on a basketball scholarship.

"He offered me $5,500. I thought, 'Hot damn! Now I can get married,'" said Brookshier. Then he found out that he only could keep the $5,500 if he made the final roster.

At training camp, he looked around and counted 90 players trying out. "How many will they keep?" he asked a veteran. "Thirty-three," he was told.

"That afternoon I hit a first-round draft choice harder than I knew I could hit," he said. Head coach Jim Trimble screamed out, "B-r-o-o-k-s-h-i-e-r!!!" and ran over to the scene of the collision. Brookshier thought he was getting cut right there on the spot. But instead, Trimble said, "I like that."

"It's amazing what fear and desperation can do for you," Brookshier said, and continued to hit anything that got in his path.[1]

That season Brookshier not only made the team but was a starter and intercepted eight passes in the Eagles' 12-game schedule. By comparison, in the NFL's 2022 and '23 17-game seasons, only one player intercepted more than eight passes.

"Brookie," as everyone called him, grew up in Roswell, New Mexico, where his father had a filling station. In 1947, a conspiracy theory had a UFO landing site near Roswell after the Army reported it had found a "flying disk" nearby. That turned out to be just a weather balloon, but for years people would stop at the filling station where Tom would not only fill their car with gas but clean their windows and check under the hood.

"I had to greet people I didn't know," he said, "and a lot of people came through looking for Martians." He watched his father work 15-hour days, which made Tom realize that because of the Depression, "everything could be taken away."[2]

In high school, besides playing defensive back, Brookshier made all-state second team as a quarterback in his senior year, and football wasn't even his best sport. He wound up going to Colorado on a basketball scholarship, not football. He did, however, receive All-Big-Eight Conference honors as a defensive back with the Buffaloes.

After his rookie year with the Eagles, he served two years with the Air Force, and when he returned, the league had gotten tougher. In 1957, Jimmy Brown was a rookie running back with the Cleveland Browns and soon would be recognized as possibly the best running back the NFL had ever known, and certainly the hardest to tackle.

Ray Didinger, a Philadelphia-based, award-winning sportswriter, author, radio personality, and screenwriter, said that Brookshier was "the most physical cornerback and best open-field tackler in Eagles history."

"The rules of the day allowed defenders to rough up receivers," Didinger said, "and knock them off their routes, and no one did it better than Brookshier. Even the great Jim Brown said: 'I could run over most [defensive] backs, but not Brookshier. He came in low and hard.'"[3]

In 1958, Brookshier was named All-Pro, and the Eagles' fortunes began to change. Buck Shaw was hired as the coach that year after Vince Lombardi had previously accepted the job then turned it down, electing to remain offensive coordinator for the Giants. Shaw brought in Norm Van Brocklin as his quarterback and also made him offensive coordinator, and in 1960 the Eagles won the NFL championship, defeating Lombardi's Green Bay Packers, 17–13.

"The day after the NFL championship game," Didinger said, "Brookshier went into one of the department stores opposite City Hall to buy a set of 'Eagles Win NFL championship' glasses. The guy behind the counter said to Tom, 'Oh, hi. Nice game, Tom.' There was no big parade after the NFL championship game; it was just, 'Nice game, Tom.'"[4]

It looked like the Eagles might have been on their way to another title game in 1961 after Brookie had his right leg crushed while tackling Willie Galimore just off the Chicago Bears' sideline. Upon seeing it, Bears coach and owner George Halas said to Brookshier, who was writhing in pain, "Tough break, kid."

It was more than a tough break. It needed three surgeries for him to walk correctly again, and in effect ended his playing career. "Like an idiot," he said, "I tried to play again. I thought they were holding a spot for me." Instead, the Eagles retired his number 40, and later that season a rookie from Northwestern named Irv Cross took his place.

In 1975, Cross became a mainstay of CBS's pregame show, *The NFL Today*. Brookshier would often exchange banter with Cross and Brent Musburger about that day's game.

Brookshier had always been a Philadelphia favorite for his quick wit, and in 1962 the local CBS station, WCAU, hired Brookshier to do sports reports. By 1970 he had become the station's sports director, and sometime around 1965 he began doing work for the NFL Films show *This Week in the NFL*. He was invited to cohost the program with former Giants opponent Pat Summerall. It turned out that they got along just fine.

And by the early '70s, Brookshier was also moonlighting weekends for the CBS Network as an analyst on NFL games. Brookshier's success was partly due to his magnetic personality. He was almost immediately likeable. He was quick and clever and always seemed to be in a great mood. When he told a joke, he always made you feel like you were in on it.

In 1971, Frank Gifford moved from CBS to ABC, with the blessing of CBS Sports president Bill MacPhail, to be the play-by-play man for *Monday Night Football*. Gifford had been CBS's sideline reporter for Super Bowl IV, and he also emceed the trophy presentation.

By 1972, Brookshier was already drawing quite a bit of attention even though he was not yet paired with Summerall (who was still working with Ray Scott). For Super Bowl VI, between Dallas and Miami, Brookshier was chosen to work the sidelines and handle the postgame interviews. The first interviewee after the Cowboys' 20–7 victory was MVP Duane Thomas.

After his rookie season in 1970, Thomas told the Cowboys he wanted to renegotiate his contract. Dallas said they would only do it if Thomas agreed to an extension, which Thomas refused. At that point Thomas called Cowboys coach Tom Landry "a plastic man," general manager Tex Schramm "totally demented,'" and personnel head Gil Brandt "a liar." Then he stopped talking—period—for the rest of the season, until he agreed to talk to Brookshier.

The interview was far from a layup for Brookie because Thomas was being escorted by Jim Brown, who had been enshrined in the Pro Football Hall of Fame the previous year. Brown was also part of a Black athletes' summit, along with Kareem Abdul-Jabbar and Bill Russell, that met in Cleveland in 1971 in support of Muhammad Ali's stand against being inducted into the Army. To complicate matters, the interview was being conducted in the Cowboys' very tight dressing room, with reporters walking in and out of the picture throughout. Brookshier, for maybe his first time ever on TV, was nervous.

Brookshier: "Duane, hi, I'm Tom Brookshier, and behind you the great Jim Brown, a fellow who used to run over me for a living." After some quick hellos, Brookshier went into a long, winding statement in the form of a question: "Duane, you do things in quick speed, but you never hurry. You never hurry like Jim Brown. You never hurry into a hole, you take your time, make a spin. Are you that fast? Are you that quick?"

America and Cowboy fans had waited all season to hear Thomas speak, and when he finally did, it was just a one-word answer to Brookshier's question:

Thomas: "Evidently."

Jim Brown: "Are you nervous, Tom?"

Brookshier: "Yes, I'm nervous." (Brookshier then follows with another long, winding question about Thomas's playing weight. Was it 205 or 215?)

Thomas: "I weigh what I need to."

Brookshier: "They tell me in practice you run farther than anyone else with the ball. You must like the game of football."

Thomas: "I do. Yes, I do. That's why I play pro ball. That's why I'm a football player. That's why I can do it."[5]

At that point, Brown bailed Brookshier out and ended the interview, and he and Thomas proceeded to exit by walking in front of Brookshier's camera shot. Years later, Brookshier told ProFootballDaily.com: "I still have nightmares about that interview. I think of it and break into a cold sweat."

If you watched any of their *This Week in the NFL* shows from 1965 to 1974, you'd know that Summerall and Brookshier were a natural together. When CBS approved them working games together in '74, it was like watching two longtime friends at a bar talking football. The timing was perfect—the NFL was becoming a major television event.

"We were Frick and Frack," Brookshier said. "We had fun, and we fit. Pat can say anything in two or three words, where I'll need two or three paragraphs."

"The ironic part," Brookshier continued, "was that on the field we had been mortal enemies. Everywhere else we clicked. Pat never left you hanging when you were on the air. And I'd need him to pull me back off the ledge. I'd lapse into some stream-of-consciousness thing and wonder what my point was, and Patrick would decipher it all in a sentence. He was wonderful at filling in my blanks."

Summerall agreed. "With Brookie," he said, "it was more of a conversation. Like two guys in a saloon."[6]

As a broadcast team, they quickly became CBS's best. Brookie was clever and fast with the one-liners. Summerall was fun, too, but always reeled them back in. By the end of the 1975 season, it was clear that the two would be broadcasting Super Bowl X in Miami. The more they worked together, the more they wanted to celebrate.

At CBS, Brookie was loved by almost everyone. He was fun, he was glib, he was smart, he was irreverent, and he was always the life of the party. But sometimes he took it too far. If you happened to notice that he was too raucous or had one too many, you certainly didn't want to be the one to say something and end the fun. Which meant there were no guardrails out there for him.

"All of us drank, smoked, chased women, and stayed up all night," wrote Gary Cartwright in a 2007 issue of *Texas Monthly*. "But Summerall and Brookshier did it with an enthusiasm that people still talk about years later. 'I loved traveling with Brookie,' Summerall acknowledged. 'We'd meet up on Thursday and not get home until Tuesday. We had a good time on the air and off the air and stayed up late and enjoyed life.'"

Some of their weekend escapades became legendary. "Out of the booth, they were Butch Cassidy and The Sundance Kid, night riders who drank from every upholstered watering hole on the circuit," wrote *Philadelphia Inquirer* columnist Bill Lyon. "'They'd tell us we had a great time,' Summerall said, 'and we'd have to take their word for it.'"[7]

Their longtime producer, Bob Stenner, knew they were trouble once they got together at night. "They really liked each other," Stenner said. "They were drinkers, and I mean drinkers in the utmost sense of the word. And they didn't have a good governor on when it was time to stop. Brookie had a way of egging Pat on. Brookie had a way of pushing the right buttons with Pat. They were great friends and they never stopped being great friends, but they weren't necessarily great for each other when it came to alcohol."[8]

One weekend they were assigned a Saturday game in Washington and a late Sunday game the next day in Philadelphia. Their assistant Lance Barrow drove Summerall, Brookshier, producer Chuck Milton, and director Sandy Grossman in a large van from one stadium to the next. On the way they all decided to have a drinking contest, with Summerall and Brookshier on the Jack Daniel's team while Milton and Grossman were on the Scotch team. When they got to the outskirts of the Eagles' training site, with all of them completely soused and giggling,

Brookshier said, "I've got an idea. Why don't you guys tie me to the front of the van like we've been deer hunting?"

They did, but when the van pulled into the parking area, the Eagles players were not amused.

Said Chuck Milton about Brookshier: "He thinks he's a cowboy, a Western gunslinger. He wants to fight every guy in every bar every Saturday night."[9]

Another time they were drinking at the famous King Cole Bar in the St. Regis Hotel in Manhattan when Brookshier noticed that the piano player was wearing a toupee. Summerall couldn't stop him.

"He scampered around the bar, and dove over the top of the piano," Summerall wrote, "and snatched the toupee off the pianist's head. Then to my dismay he brought it back to me like a retriever with a stick." Bedlam hit the bar at that point, but when things settled down the manager bargained with Summerall to let them off the hook if they promised to never come back.

After working a West Coast game, they drank Jack Daniel's the whole flight home and landed in New York on Monday morning not wanting to end the party. In Manhattan they met the golf commentator Ben Wright and proceeded to get thrown out of another establishment. Unable to flag down a cab, Brookshier decided to lie down in the middle of Second Avenue.

Taxi drivers stayed clear, but a horse-drawn carriage did pull up. They decided to take it, Brookie riding shotgun with Summerall in the back. When Brookshier stood up to view the scenery, he fell out and landed on his head. None the worse for wear, they continued to the Plaza Hotel where they invited the driver to join them.

"What am I going to do with my horse?" the driver asked.

"Bring the horse," Summerall said. So they unhitched the horse and led him up the back steps of the Plaza until the horse balked at the sliding glass door.

When the horse reared up and whinnied, the hotel security came running to the rescue.

As Summerall explained in his autobiography, "We had [hotel] reservations. The horse didn't."[10]

Despite, or maybe because of, these weekend escapades, Summerall and Brookshier continued to get good reviews. At Super Bowl XII in New Orleans, where the Dallas Cowboys handled the Denver Broncos, 27–10, the pair had a very good game. *Sports Illustrated*'s William Leggett couldn't have been more complimentary.

"Thankfully, CBS did not also increase the number of announcers, staying with its 'first team' of Pat Summerall and Tom Brookshier, the best combination doing football on any network," Leggett wrote in the magazine's January 23, 1978, article "Insightful and Delightful."

"While Summerall and Brookshier have been called the Sunshine Boys, in broadcasting terms they are the Odd Couple. Standard CBS practice is to use a professional announcer for play-by-play and an ex-jock for filler. These two are ex-players who are also first-rate broadcasters. They share the airtime so evenly and smoothly that viewers get the impression they have been working together for a lifetime. Well, they have, almost, though they became a Sunday combination only 2½ years ago.

"Between them, Summerall and Brookshier have 28 years of broadcasting experience, and a lot of that time was spent doing things other than football. Brookshier served as the sports director of Philadelphia's WCAU for 12 years, and in recent years he has been handling some major prizefights. Summerall's background in sports and sportscasting is even more varied. He was a Florida tennis champion, and he had a tryout with the baseball Cardinals. He was considered such an able announcer by WCBS Radio in New York that he once worked as the station's 5:30–10 A.M. "Morning Man."

"During the NFL season CBS used 18 regular announcers and a few standbys. Being selected for the Super Bowl is the big enchilada for these broadcasters, and Summerall and Brookshier, well informed and low key, were the obvious choices. Their selection also reflects a slowly evolving trend: the networks are finally picking their best announcers, not necessarily their most famous ones, for big games. Summerall and Brookshier got the assignment though they were not the most familiar voices and though they were not the resident experts on the teams competing in the Super Bowl. 'As we go into the game,' Summerall said last week, 'the odd thing is that neither Tommy nor I saw Denver during the season.'

"Nevertheless, the pair handled the Broncos, and the game itself, with aplomb. They were intelligent and insightful and occasionally made a stab at being witty, as at the end of the first half following Cowboy Efren Herrera's third missed field-goal attempt."

Summerall: "It'll be a long halftime for him."
Brookshier: "Depending on which dressing room he goes in."

Unfortunately, their carousing also took them down two years later at Super Bowl XIV in Los Angeles, when Pittsburgh came from behind to defeat the Los Angeles Rams, 31–19.

Here is what producer Bob Stenner had to say about how they prepared for the game: "They were sitting by the pool ordering food and drinks all day long, and I had to drag them out of there to go see the two teams practice. They were enjoying themselves so much that they didn't put the effort in, in my opinion, to prepare for the Super Bowl as they should have. In my gut they weren't prepared. They got away with it because they were quick and clever, but they couldn't get away with that stuff today."[11]

Sports Illustrated wasn't so kind to them this time—especially Brookshier. The magazine hired freelance TV critic Stan Issacs. Here is a sample of his review from the January 28, 1980 article.

"As for Brookshier, he rambled on in his ever-chuckling, star-adoring way. Brookshier's almost unwavering pattern was this: stalwart makes a good play; Brookshier says how good play was; Brookshier says what a great man stalwart is. When Pittsburgh's Jack Lambert made an ordinary tackle, Brookshier said, 'He's quite an athlete . . .' Upon [Terry] Bradshaw's second long pass completion to John Stallworth, Brookshier reported that Bradshaw is a born-again Christian and that 'I love him.' For many viewers love is not enough."

Shortly after his disappointing performance calling, Brookshier admitted to a reporter, "I let all the parties get in the way of my concentration. A few hours before the game, I suddenly realized that I didn't have a single intelligent thing to say about either team."[12]

The negative reviews and the persistent stories of their carousing led to this public comment by CBS executive Ted Shaker: "Something has to be done."

Forty-four years later, Shaker added, "At Super Bowl XIV they were drunk the night before [the game] and you could tell on the broadcast. That's when John [Madden] presented himself as a real alternative. He had an everyman quality about him and could explain plays in a way that were informative and entertaining. You always wanted to hear more from John. As for Pat, he always seemed to be able to pull it together."[13]

When Van Gordon Sauter became the new president of CBS Sports in July 1980, something was done. Sauter ordered Summerall and Brookshier to be split apart for any further broadcasts. And in January '81, Sauter announced the hiring of former *Monday Night Football* producer Terry O'Neil as executive producer for all of CBS's NFL broadcasts and production.

Said Stenner afterward: "I'm glad they're being broken up. Somebody was going to get hurt. I mean it. All the drinking, the late nights before the games. Some Sunday you were going to turn on the television, and one of them wasn't going to be there."

"I still recall my days on the road with Brookie as one of the most enjoyable periods of my life," Summerall wrote in his autobiography. "We painted every town red, and we had so much fun doing our jobs that the fans could feel it too.... We were only focused on the next broadcast and how many drinks it would take to get us there and back. We didn't pay much attention to anyone or anything else—including our wives and our families.... It got to the point we never wanted to go home."[14]

Of the split, Brookshier told a Knight-Ridder columnist: "We were saddle buddies, almost like brothers. I guess it's something we're just going to have to learn to live with. It's going to be work now."

In his book *The Game Behind the Game*, O'Neil wrote about the events that led to Brookshier's downfall, and in doing so was extremely critical of producers and other CBS Sports executives.

"So, they deserted him [Brookshier]," O'Neil wrote. "His buddies. Guys with titles and supposedly the authority to take him in hand—for his personal welfare and for the good of their telecasts. They had never shown any strength and now they abandoned him. All except Summerall.

"You could make the argument that Brookshier wasn't solely to blame. CBS had been in town for a full week before the [Super Bowl] game. What kind of schedule was he on? Where was his leadership?"

After the split, Brookshier, like Summerall, asked to be switched to play-by-play. CBS agreed and chose former Eagles coach Dick Vermeil as his partner. Unlike Summerall, Vermeil was straitlaced and never visited any late-night bars.

In 1983, while working a college game with Charley Waters, Brookshier got into more hot water when reading a promo regarding a University of Louisville basketball game.

> **Brookshier:** "Denny Crum has a great team at Louisville, but they have a collective IQ of about 40, but they can play basketball."
> **Waters:** "Don't say things like that."
> **Brookshier:** "It's the truth."

CBS had to apologize to Louisville and to its viewers. The network spokesman, Doug Richardson, said that Brookshier's remarks were "intemperate, insensitive and off the cuff . . . and they don't reflect the views of CBS Sports." CBS also decided to suspend Tom for the final week of the season.

He later apologized to the Louisville team, telling United Press International that "my remarks were just dumb and flippant on my part, but I'm not going to be judged on one comment. After 20 years with CBS I deserve better than this."

In 1987, Brookie parted ways with CBS and became part owner of WIP All-Sports-Radio in Philadelphia. Although he had stopped working with Pat Summerall, they never stopped being friends. Unfortunately, Summerall's drinking got worse. Eleven years after CBS split them up, Brookshier was part of a major intervention for Summerall.

Summerall often said they were like brothers. For Pat, Brookshier's friendship went even further than brotherly love.

Chapter Seven
FOR JOHN MADDEN, 1980 "TASTED GREAT!"

For John Madden, 1980 turned out to be a very good year. Once Van Gordon Sauter, the new head of CBS Sports, identified Madden as his No. 1 analyst, everything changed for John. He went from being with a different play-by-play partner and a different crew each game he worked in 1979 to working exclusively with Gary Bender, who was one of the network's top announcers. In fact, Bender soon would be chosen as the lead announcer for the NBA on CBS.

Bender was a handsome 35-year-old announcer from the Midwest who was the voice of the Green Bay Packers when CBS hired him in 1975. He got to CBS in a very unusual way.

Agent Bob Rosen was in a New York delicatessen meeting with CBS Sports president Bob Wussler. When they got up to leave, Wussler said: "We just found out that we lost Jack Buck. He's leaving to go to NBC. We're looking for a younger guy. Do you have anybody? Rosen was stumped, but a guy at an adjacent table walked over and said, 'Gentleman, I couldn't help but overhear your conversation. I have somebody to recommend.'"

Wussler: "Well, who are you?"

He said he was Ron Lubell from the TVS Network. "I do the Big Ten game of the week and I recommend Gary Bender."

"And that's how I got to CBS," Bender said. "I went from the Green Bay radio booth to the CBS Green Bay booth working with Johnny Unitas. You send out these tapes and think you're going to get to the network on your own, only to have a guy in a delicatessen recommend you. You never know who's listening."[1]

When first paired with Madden, he was told by senior producer Chuck Milton, "We need you to coach a coach."

John was also now working with CBS's top NFL producer and director, Bob Stenner and Sandy Grossman. But adjusting to all of that still took some getting used to.

"I remember two incidents," Bender said when contacted for this book. "One was in the Silverdome where the [Detroit] Lions were playing. We'd open with a two-shot with John and I on camera, then I'd slide off camera to get ready for the kickoff. John would fill and I'd slide over, and then I'd take it.

"But this one time in the Silverdome we started out on headsets, but his headset didn't work. He couldn't hear himself. He couldn't hear me, and he really got upset. We got to a commercial, and I said, 'John what's the problem?' He said, 'I can't hear anything.' I reminded him that we had to fight through these technical problems."

Madden responded, "Yeah, yeah, yeah," Bender recalled.

Bender: "People were crawling around underneath John, trying to figure out what was wrong. We finally got to the point where he just shut down. He's not doing much of anything. So they took his headset away and gave him a stick mic. And he still wasn't giving us much. When we got to another commercial, we found out what was wrong."

John: "Gary, I know what the problem is. I can't talk with anything in my hand."

Talking with his hands open and his arms flailing reminded Bender of another time when John almost knocked Gary out.

"One time in Philadelphia," said Bender, "he knocked my glasses off and we had to send someone into the stands of Veterans Stadium to retrieve them. So I gave John my headset, and I took the stick mic and we continued on.

For John Madden, 1980 "Tasted Great!"

"Another time in Foxboro, Sandy Grossman was our director and Bob Stenner our producer. Sandy was talking too much to John [in his earpiece], and John was getting really irritated. At one point he said, 'I can't take this. I can't have people talking to me all the time [while I'm trying to concentrate on the game].'"

At the break, Bender told Stenner, "Bob, you better back off a little bit with talking to him. John's getting frustrated. We came back [on the air] and the talking continued, and John ripped off his headset and walked out of the press box. It got very quiet in the truck.

"I said to Sandy, 'You just chased the coach out of the press box.' He eventually came back in and put his headset on, and they didn't talk to him nearly as much after that."

John Madden may have been named the No. 1 analyst, but he still had a lot to learn—especially adjusting to the director talking to him during the game. He was making progress fitting his stories in, and he got very comfortable working with Gary. Here's what John said of the relationship on Fox's *All Madden* special:

"My second year I worked the whole season with Gary Bender, and we were [CBS's number] two or three or four [broadcast team] or whatever we were. But he was good, and he worked with me, and the good thing about Gary Bender is that he was real religious and didn't swear. So, when I was with him on the weekends I never swore. Because that's a nightmare you always have that you'll get all excited and BOOM you pop off with a swear word. Gary Bender was a good broadcaster and a good guy, and I thought that he really helped me there."

⌒๏⌒

Despite the theories that the Miller Lite commercials came John Madden's way because of the hilarious routine he performed at that January 1980 pre–Super Bowl luncheon, it more likely happened thanks to a recommendation from Raiders owner Al Davis.

When contacted for this book, both of John's sons, Joe and Mike Madden, recall Davis having something to do with it. The advertising campaign featured retired players who were a little bit wacky, like Dick Butkus, Bob Uecker, Bubba Smith, Billy Martin, and Madden. The

Virginia and John flanked by their sons, Joe (no. 77 for Brown) and Mike, who played for Harvard. COURTESY OF JOE MADDEN

campaign also included comedian Rodney Dangerfield, the mystery writer Mickey Spillane, and the sexy blond actress Lee Meredith.

"The Miller Lite commercial was really where my dad got his start," said Joe Madden. "Initially it wasn't intended for my dad but for Al Davis, and Al said [to the advertising agency], 'Why don't you think about [using] John [Madden] instead [of me]. John's retired now.'" Then it was suggested to John in a family meeting.

> **John Madden:** "Well, I don't even drink beer. Why the heck would I do something like this?"
>
> **Virginia Madden:** "Because you've got nothing else going on. Why not?"
>
> **Joe Madden:** "So she spurred him on to do it."
>
> **Mike Madden:** "Al [Davis] used to take credit for that [commercial]. Al wasn't a bullshitter, so it very well could have happened that way."
>
> **Joe Madden:** "Then a year later he's doing skits on *Saturday Night Live*."

Madden recalled being contacted by the McCann Erickson advertising agency to discuss doing the commercial. The agency guy told Madden, "More people will know you after you do this than have ever known you."[2]

"I said, 'No, no, you don't understand. I was the head coach for the Oakland Raiders for 10 years. . . . I played and coached in regular-season games, playoff games, championship games, Super Bowl games, Pro Bowl games—the biggest games in the world. How can more people know me?'"

"He said, 'Just believe me, they will.'

"And they did! It was a bridge to life from coaching. I went from John Madden, the coach, to John Madden, the Miller Lite guy who breaks through the wall. It was so big that I didn't believe them. And then after I got in the commercial, you just become part of the team. It was an amazing experience. It was big. A game changer for me and a game changer for [beer] drinkers. I mean light beer—this was 40 years ago. People didn't know about light beer."[3]

Light beer with fewer calories was a relatively new concept in 1980. It was first developed by a Swiss chemist in 1964, improved by a chemist from Rheingold Brewery, and eventually sold to a company that went bankrupt in 1972. In stepped the Miller Brewing Company of Milwaukee, which bought the process for light beer, rebranded it as Miller Lite, and launched it nationally in 1973.

And it was the McCann Erickson art director Bob Lenz who came up with the idea of using a macho retired athlete to promote the beer. In 1974, the New York Jets' 1969 Super Bowl hero, Matt Snell, was the first to say, "Lite beer from Miller is everything you always wanted from a beer . . . and less." He went on to explain that there were one-third fewer calories than a regular beer, but the copywriters eventually cut the line down to "less filling." As more rugged ex-player types were hired, they were divided into two camps chanting their favorite aspect of the beer: "Less filling!/Tastes great!"

In 1980, Madden joined the cast, exclaiming that he is no longer that crazy coach yelling at officials. Madden's first commercial appeared in the middle of that year. It starts off with him calmly talking to the crowd at a bar:

"Excuse me, I'm not the same crazy coach who used to storm around the sidelines yelling at the officials. I've learned to relax. And I drink Lite beer from Miller [holds bottle up]." Then he gradually gets more and more excited and louder, flailing his arms around until he finally says, "And let me tell you this . . ."

After the announcer's one line about Lite beer, viewers are shocked to see Madden bursting through a huge sign made of paper. He's waving his arms and says:

"As I was saying, I don't care what anybody else says . . ."

In his next commercial Madden wore a gray crew-neck sweater and sported a page-boy-length hairstyle. The first thing we see is John as he comes bursting through the wall of the bar. People scatter. John strolls over to the bar. The chyron reads: "John Madden, Famous Ex–Football Coach."

His opening line is, "Boy, could I go for an ice-cold Lite beer from Miller. And get this, it's less filling."

As John leans an elbow on the bar, the bartender taps him on the shoulder and says, "John, how many times have I told you? Use the door, huh?"

After the announcer says his line, John bursts through the door holding a Lite beer and says, "Like I was saying, Lite beer tastes great . . ."

Eventually they'd have a big group commercial with everyone divided into two teams, each proclaiming its own theme of either "Tastes great!" or "Less filling!" Madden loved being a part of it. CBS broadcast associate Richie Zyontz remembers Madden telling him about the trip they all made to the field where the commercial was shot.

"John said all those crazy players rode over together in a bus Miller Lite rented for them," said Zyontz. "All except Rodney [Dangerfield]. He arrived in a limo."[4]

Looking back after John died on December 28, 2021, *USA Today* wrote that Madden saved the campaign for Miller, that he more than legitimized it for the average Joe out there.

"The brand's first pitchmen were athletes like Bubba Smith, Joe Frazier, and Mickey Mantle. But those guys were supermen compared to the group of average Joes Miller was courting. . . . They needed a figure who oozed respectability while still being entirely relatable to normal Americans. Enter John Madden.... By 1980, his budding commentary career had him calling lower-level games to regional broadcasts. Miller Lite put him back on a national stage: He was exactly what the company was looking for; a credible and recognizable voice willing to make fun of himself in the kind of aw-shucks manner that raised both his profile and the product he was pitching. In the end, the saga played out the way most things do with Madden. He came in, took a product that already existed, and pushed it to new heights.

Madden didn't create light beer, but he legitimized it. He wasn't the first sports celebrity to make a beer ad, but he made the genre his own. And like the Raiders or sports video games or the commentary booth, he left an oversized imprint on the way Americans consume the product he was hawking. Madden wasn't a salesman, but he was always selling."[5]

After seeing Madden entertain a packed audience of advertisers, CBS affiliates, and media members at that pre-1980 Super Bowl luncheon, I also saw John in a new light. I pictured him as someone Johnny Carson would enjoy chatting with on The Tonight Show. So I set about contacting the talent coordinators for both The Tonight Show and The Tomorrow Show, starring Tom Snyder, which followed The Tonight Show. The Tomorrow Show got back to me first and loved the idea of John going on with Snyder. I accompanied John to the taping, which took place at 5:00 p.m. for broadcast that night.

I suggested he tell Snyder his right foot/left foot routine about NFL officials. While John was on, I sat quietly at one end of the green room with the next guest star, the actress Madelyn Kahn, at the other end. We did not speak. When John jumped up, arms waving, to imitate the officials marking the spot, two things happened: (1) Tom Snyder said, "You're driving my director crazy," and (2) Madeline Kahn asked me, "You know this crazy man?"

After the show I was about to walk John the few short blocks from NBC's studio back to CBS when he opened the door of a waiting limo and said, "You're coming to dinner with me." Dinner was at Tavern on the Green, where the entire Miller Lite team of celebrities was waiting for us, including Dangerfield, who had us laughing all night. It was a reunion dinner for the celebs, and I was a lucky fly on the wall thanks to the kindness of John Madden. As CBS associate director Joan Vitrano put it: "John treasured loyalty. If John liked you, he'd do anything for you."

After one of those 1980 games John Madden did in Tampa with Gary Bender, Madden decided he had already taken his last plane ride. He had gotten on a flight from Tampa with Bender, and when the plane doors closed, he had a panic attack.

"I was either going to get up, open the door and jump out," he later said, "or I was going to gut it out. Well, I gutted it out, and I said [to myself] if I land, and I'm still alive, I'll never get on another plane again. And I didn't."[6]

"I had a quick turnaround Thanksgiving Day game," Bender said, "and I had to be in Dallas. John was flying back to San Francisco. He's sweating profusely just thinking about the next flight. Finally, he said he wasn't taking another flight, no matter what."

"I'm not getting on," he told Bender. And he turned around, got on a train, and went back home. He said he could fly when he was with the Raiders because he could move around the plane, but he had always been claustrophobic. Then Bender recalled a very uncomfortable time with John in Anaheim.

"One day we went down on the field," Bender said, "and did a bunch of promos for the local stations. It was so hot that we sweated right through our dress shirts and had to go back to the hotel to change. We went on the press elevator in Anaheim. There were a bunch of people on it, and they shut the door and John lost it. He started banging his head against the wall, like a fugitive. They thought he was being funny, but I was desperately trying to get us off the elevator. And they all thought he was just being a character."[7]

The first time it really hit John that he hated to be in a tight place was on a plane ride back home in 1957 when he was playing for Cal Poly. On the return trip from playing at New Mexico State in Las Cruces,

New Mexico, the pilot told the passengers that he didn't think the wheels would come down for landing at the nearby Paso Robles airport.

"We circled Santa Margarita Lake for several minutes," said fellow teammate Johnny Nettleship in a 1985 account to *The Tampa Tribune*, "while crew members pumped coffee and other available liquid into the hydraulic system. The wheels came down, but there still was some concern as to whether the brakes would hold. Fire trucks and emergency vehicles were on the scene as we landed successfully."

The entire experience shook Madden up. Three years later, on October 29, 1960, after Madden had graduated Cal Poly and was coaching, a flight from Toledo Express Airport carrying the Cal Poly football team crashed on takeoff, killing 16 players, the team manager, a team booster, and four others including both pilots.

With zero visibility and a pilot whose license had been revoked by the Federal Aviation Administration, the flight should never have taken off, said Nettleship in his report on the 25th anniversary of the crash. To make it worse, the plane was an antiquated World War II C-46 aircraft, which exploded and split in two on takeoff.

The next day, Madden drove up to San Luis Obispo to spend time comforting friends of the family members of the team that he knew. Despite how easy it is for the news media to point to this incident as the reason Madden doesn't fly, he always said that he feared flying before the crash ever happened.

In his book *Hey, Wait a Minute (I Wrote a Book)*, he said: "I think the Cal Poly crash ... probably had a subconscious effect on my attitude toward planes. I thought about the crash for a long time.... I flew when I had to, but not when I didn't have to, not if I had a choice."

One time in the early '80s, producer Bob Stenner held a production meeting in his New York hotel suite which was on the 40th floor. Taking an elevator was never one of John Madden's favorite things—especially one 40 floors above the ground. Upon leaving the meeting, the doors on the elevator opened and closed several times once Madden was inside. When safely back down in the lobby, Madden told stage manager Rich Nelson, "Tell Bob Stenner, I'm not going to any more meetings on the 40th floor. Never!"

"From then on," Nelson said, "We tagged all of John's hotel reservations 'Big Bed/Low Floor.'"[8]

Once John started taking the train to the game sites that season, he was arriving a day or two earlier than everyone else, and he began going to team practices. What he learned from the coaches and the players helped him even more, and he also passed some tidbits along to his broadcast partner.

"He made those players more human," Bender said, "and he gave me insight to what was going on. [In return] I gave him room to work. You hear people say that we're in a 10-second world, but we're really not. You couldn't slow John down to 10 seconds. You had to give him time to do what he had to do. I'd be ready to pick up the pieces and be ready for the snap of the next play. He had a unique ability to support you. I remember one time he told me, 'Don't you worry about the [NFL] rules. I know the rules. I have your back.'

"He also had a heart of gold. When I was being considered at CBS as the lead guy for the NBA, he counseled me, encouraged me, and talked to me about how to get it. And when I got it, he was so excited, there were times he would just phone me from out of the blue and he wanted to know how we were doing."

Being able to work every game with an easygoing play-by-play man like Gary Bender and getting used to the top producer and director all season long helped Madden make the necessary adjustments he was missing his rookie year. Then, one day, Bender realized that John Madden was the future of the business.

"We were in Cincinnati and the thought occurred to me," Gary said: "He's got it. He has now got it. This guy is gonna be something special. It came down to the confidence, the timing, the interaction. I could just feel it. And I knew it was in his voice. We were a real team. If John Madden was a success, I think I had something to do with it."

After the season, Gary, his wife, and his two sons visited the Maddens at John's home in Pleasanton, California. John and Virginia took them out on their boat, named *Time Out*. They took them under the

For John Madden, 1980 "Tasted Great!"

Golden Gate Bridge. Virginia drove while John sat back drinking Tabs. The two families were becoming friends. Bender wanted to keep working with Madden, but that's not what the boss had in mind.

"I wasn't a big enough name to work with John," Bender said. "He became bigger than life. We met with (new CBS Sports president) Van Gordon Sauter [after the season], and John fought for me. He said, 'I want to work with Gary.' I thought that said a lot about John. I understood it [the decision] perfectly, but that doesn't mean you liked it.

"He was loyal: We'd go to games or practices and he'd bring his two boys, Mike and Joe, and I'd bring my two and they'd be playing touch football at Candlestick Park, and John would just sit back and laugh and enjoy the moment. You realize he's a real guy. He's a heck of a deal."[9]

After the 1980 season, things were changing at CBS Sports. Sauter was about to hire 31-year-old Terry O'Neil to bring CBS Sports production into the 20th century. And Sauter had his own choice to work alongside John Madden. His name was Vin Scully.

Chapter Eight

THE CONTEST

Would It Be Summerall or Scully?

Richie Zyontz, a sports fanatic, was an industrious young man who always worked summers for CBS in New York during his four years at Boston University. When he graduated in 1979, he was hoping to get a job at CBS Sports, but with nothing available, he took a job with security on the second floor of CBS's famous Black Rock building on 52nd Street and 6th Avenue in Manhattan. In 1980, he moved up to the stations group on the 24th floor.

Twenty-four was the floor where many CBS executives were located. Part of Zyontz's job was to sit at the front desk by the elevator and check everyone's badge and identification who entered. That year, one new executive whom Zyontz gradually got to know was Van Gordon Sauter. Van, who was 44, didn't look like any other executive at CBS. Here's how future CBS executive Terry O'Neil described him:

"He was a great bear of a man, perhaps 260 pounds, handsomely layered in sweaters and tweeds, even on the warmest days. His face, too, was covered by large glasses and a salt-and-pepper beard. He cut the figure of an academic favoring bow ties and a pipe."[1] *Sports Illustrated* also suggested that he had a remarkable resemblance to King Henry VIII.[2]

Sauter could have been the guy Johnny Cash was singing about in his rendition of the song "I've Been Everywhere, Man." Sauter began his career reporting on Vietnam for *The Detroit News* in the '60s, then talked his bosses into letting him go on a national road tour with the Motown stars and write about it. He almost quit his job to stay with Motown, but eventually found his way in 1970 to become program director of WBBM-AM radio in Chicago, and he was the man who hired Brent Musburger to do sports reports. In 1972, he became news director for WBBM radio at first and then WBBM-TV. From there he spent a joyous year as CBS News's Paris bureau chief before they pulled him back to be the television network's chief censor. It was a job that found him arguing with Norman Lear, creator of *All in the Family* and other shows, on a regular basis.

Sauter was then sent to New York to run the CBS Sports division, a job that had seen five different presidents in the previous six years. The previous head man was Frank Smith, who came from sales and didn't know much about sports on television. Sauter, admittedly, didn't know much about sports either.

"I didn't know a thing about sports," said Sauter, who was 88 when we sat down to lunch at Palmeri Ristorante, his favorite spot in Brentwood, California. "I used to read four papers a day but never read the sports pages." However, he did know good television, and one thing he was very good at was judging talent.

CBS Sports had a laid-back country-club reputation until Bob Wussler took over in 1974 and installed the live version of *The NFL Today*, which won 13 Emmy Awards its first season. However, after Wussler's departure in March 1978, the place slowly went back to old customs under Smith. Sauter was chosen to bring it back.

"I was a surprise choice for that job," he said. "I realized that place had bad morale and inadequate commitment to quality broadcasting. I had just got married and my wife [Kathleen Brown, whose brother is Jerry Brown, the four-term governor of California] said, 'Let's go to New York.' It wasn't a job. It was the game department. It was a fabulous place to work."[3]

Sauter was appointed president of CBS Sports on July 11, 1980. One thing it lacked was a journalistic approach, which was something Sauter definitely knew something about.

"One Sunday I was sitting 24 floors above the street in my office watching the Tour de France on our *CBS Sports Spectacular*," Van told

Sports Illustrated for its September 8, 1980, issue. "Now this was a great event to have on, but I was yelling at the TV because, one, we failed to capture the beauty of the French countryside; two, we failed to explain to the guy in Middletown, Ohio [Sauter's hometown], why this race captures the hearts and mind of Western Europe; three, we haven't told them what wonderful athletes these bicyclists are; and four, we haven't explained why their bikes are different from the Schwinn sitting in the garage. We failed to build a bridge between France and Middletown, which is something we will do next year."

The author with 88-year-old Van Gordon Sauter at Palmeri Ristorante in Brentwood.
COURTESY OF THE AUTHOR

To do that and bring CBS's production side up to the network standards set by Roone Arledge's group at ABC Sports, Sauter searched for the right leader and finally hired 31-year-old Terry O'Neil, who had risen quickly through the ranks at ABC Sports to become the producer of *Monday Night Football*, one of the most highly regarded positions in the business, and a position that the great Don Ohlmeyer had originated. After graduating Notre Dame in 1971, O'Neil quickly distinguished himself journalistically covering events for ABC in the 1972 Munich Olympics.

In 1974, the studious-looking O'Neil added a master's degree from the Columbia University Graduate School of Journalism, and in his spare time he wrote the popular book *Fighting Back*, about Pittsburgh Steelers star Rocky Bleier, who although wounded in Vietnam was able to make it all the way back to play pro football. O'Neil and Bleier were friends from their Notre Dame days together, and the book also became a successful TV movie by the same name in 1980.

But O'Neil's star flamed out when, as the producer of *Monday Night Football*, he had to battle hard-drinking Howard Cosell each week for editorial control. On November 23, 1970, Cosell missed the second half of the Eagles-Giants game when he threw up on boothmate Frank Gifford's shoes. Even though ABC executives detested Cosell's drinking and bullying tactics, his popularity was such that he prevailed against O'Neil and had him removed from the Monday Night assignment.

Rather than be demoted to another position at ABC Sports, O'Neil felt he would be better off resigning. When Sauter took over at CBS, he confided in executive Kevin O'Malley that he needed to find someone who could turn things around. O'Malley suggested O'Neil because CBS Sports publicist Beano Cook, who had previously spent 10 years working at ABC Sports, had regaled O'Malley with stories of how brilliant O'Neil was. They were also fellow Pittsburghers, where a coterie of brilliant sports journalists thrived: George Kiseda, Myron Cope, Roy McHugh, and Jim O'Brien. Sauter and O'Neil met for lunch late that summer of 1980, and in January 1981, O'Neil officially became executive producer in charge of production at CBS Sports.

One of the first things Sauter wanted to do was split up the No. 1 broadcast team of Pat Summerall and Tom Brookshier. The latter pair had called Super Bowls X, XII, and XIV for CBS Sports, with their call of Super Bowl XIV being widely panned. Sauter wanted to separate them because of many reports of their carousing and hard drinking together. Once Brookshier bragged with his classic chuckle on his Philadelphia radio show that they drank their Thanksgiving dinner. And Sauter already knew who his No. 1 analyst should be.

One late Friday night in the fall of 1980, as Sauter was leaving the 24th floor, he stopped to chat with young Richie Zyontz at the front desk.

"What football announcers do you like?" he asked him.

"I like John Madden," said Zyontz.

"I like him too," Sauter said. "He's real."[4]

The Contest

In 1980, Madden was working six games of a 16-game season for CBS in what was his second broadcasting season. His performance had improved, but he still wasn't the jovial, talkative John Madden we all got to love. Most of his games that season were with Gary Bender, and none of them had been broadcast back to New York. But Miller Lite started to run Madden's hugely popular commercial that had him bursting through the wall in his local bar. Perhaps that's when Sauter became captivated by Madden.

"I thought he had television magic," Sauter said when I asked him at our lunch meeting how he decided Madden should be the No. 1 analyst. "He was so real. He looked real, he sounded real, and he was a great raconteur. He could tell stories to a crowd at a bar—he could entertain all night. I'm not even tapping into the depth of what he had. I thought he would appeal to the audience. He was the guy you wanted to be sitting next to at the television set in your living room."[5]

When Sauter and O'Neil sat down to talk about it a month or so after O'Neil's arrival at CBS, O'Neil was shocked to learn that CBS didn't have a program similar to ABC Sports of hiring production assistants out of college in entry-level positions. This was the bedrock of ABC Sports. Its primary responsibility was the building and timely retrieval of graphics on live telecasts. They'd take orders through headsets from the producer and director. This is how they learned the craft—by listening and reacting and getting screamed at, so they'd be ready when promoted to associate producer or associate director.

"Without this position," explained one former network executive, "CBS Sports suffered a double whammy. Their graphics, executed by freelancers, were bad and inconsistent. The other half of the double whammy was that CBS Sports developed no production staff from within, so the vets [like Bob Stenner, Chuck Milton and Tony Verna] were unchallenged; their jobs never threatened by hungry, up-and-coming young prospects, thereby allowing those vets to grow old and lazy."

And to Sauter's credit, he understood why the "broadcast associate" positions (as CBS called them) were so important. He went directly to Jim McKenna, CFO, and told him to find the money for this initiative. That same day, McKenna walked into O'Neil's office and said the funds were available and that he and Van wanted O'Neil to start interviewing and hiring. By mid-July 1981, CBS Sports had hired nine broadcast associates. Among those nine were Mike Arnold, who at this writing has directed seven Super Bowls for CBS, and Richie Zyontz, who has produced six Super Bowls for Fox and is the man responsible for breaking in Tom Brady.

At that first lunch meeting with O'Neil, Sauter also offered up that he fell in love with Madden from his Miller Lite commercials.

"Have you seen any of his games?" O'Neil asked.

"No, no," said Sauter. "All I know is that he's the guy."

At that point, O'Neil had only seen Madden 30 seconds at a time, thanks to Miller Lite. Like most of America, the regional games John was doing only went back to the two teams' markets, and never to New York.

"Madden showed promise," O'Neil stated in his 1989 book *The Game Behind the Game*. He wrote: "At that point he was not the funny, outrageous guy who America would later revere. He was not doing the boom, bam, whap routine yet. But he had something that was honest, real. The quality was hard to define, which made it all the more appealing. The tapes of his games revealed an emotional love of football. Sauter and I would take it. Madden was on board."

But Sauter wanted the legendary Los Angeles Dodgers broadcaster Vin Scully for play-by-play. Scully, who was 53, had been calling football and golf for CBS since 1975. Sauter saw Scully as the best CBS had. O'Neil respected Scully's work as well but knew that Madden and Scully together would be a deadly mix.

"As a partner with Madden, I felt he [Scully] was 180 degrees the wrong choice," O'Neil said. "At his enshrinement into the Baseball Hall of Fame [in 1982], Scully painted a self-portrait: 'I like to talk, and I relish words . . . where you can put word pictures on the air.' It didn't fit with Madden, who had plenty to say and often used the full 30 seconds between plays to say it. The combination would be too much. The viewer would be wrung out by halftime, I told Sauter."[6] Besides, Scully worked alone in the Dodgers radio booth most of his 66-year career.

Sauter shared the same agent as Scully—the clever Los Angeles–based attorney Ed Hookstratten, who at times also represented Elvis

Presley and Johnny Carson. It's possible that "Hook" had already lobbied Sauter to pick Scully by the time Van sat down with O'Neil.

"Scully is an elegant broadcaster," Sauter would say. "But football isn't an elegant game," O'Neil would retort. "It's a question of styles. After six weeks, we'll all be saying they talk too much, and then we'll have to fight with both of them to cut back."

Of course O'Neil was right. History is the judge of that. After watching tapes of CBS games, O'Neil felt strongly that Summerall was the right choice, despite his history with Brookshier. Pat was always the perfect play-by-play announcer, known for being a minimalist with his words. Here's how former CBS executive Kevin O'Malley described his style: "Pat Summerall never used ten words to describe something if five words were possible."[7]

O'Neil came up with a solution that Sauter endorsed. Scully would work four consecutive Sundays with Madden in September (while Summerall was doing the U.S. Open for CBS). Then Pat would work four straight Sundays with John in October, with eight weeks remaining in the season. On Monday, October 26, a vote of top CBS Sports executives would be taken and a winner declared. One reason this was so important was that CBS would be broadcasting Super Bowl XVI at the conclusion of the 1981 season, in Detroit in January 1982.

Before the season even started, Summerall was feeling uneasy when told of his split with Brookshier and the contest to see who would work with Madden. Richie Zyontz was one who understood what Summerall was going through.

"Think about Pat coming off his great association with Brookshier," Zyontz said. "They were as close as can be. They were regarded as the best in the business; and that gets broken up and now Pat finds himself in a competition, to be the No. 1 guy. And now it's John Madden that's getting all the attention."[8]

For the first time in his career, Summerall hired an agent, Bob Rosen, who had several sports broadcasting clients. Rosen told Summerall to inform O'Neil that he intended to go to NBC if things didn't work out. This was a shock to hear coming from Pat who was in his 20th year at CBS and loved it.

O'Neil wanted to get a preview of what might be ahead and assigned John and Pat to work together on a preseason game in Dallas near the end of August. The week of the game, Pat gave an interview to *The Dallas Morning News* for its August 28, 1981, issue. The newspaper wanted to know what it would be like to work with someone other than Tom Brookshier.

The headline read: **"Summerall: 'The Heat's on Madden.'"**

Here's what followed:

For Pat Summerall the party's over. When he joins John Madden Saturday night for the first time to do the Cowboys-Oilers game, it will mark the first time in 6½ years he hasn't worked with color analyst and running buddy Tom Brookshier. And Summerall doesn't mind admitting that he doesn't look forward to the prospect. "It puts me in a tough position," he said. "Deep down, it's really true that I'd rather be with Brookshier. It's not like going to work when Brookie and I did the games. . . . When we arrived, we were laughing and when we left Sunday night we were still laughing. If it were Brookshier and me, we would have had the production meeting and then we would have been out having margaritas. Now I'm not sure what's going to happen."

Summerall said he received more public and media response from the breakup with Brookshier than any other incident in his 20-year broadcasting career. "I went into a restaurant in Flint, Michigan, last week" he said. "The owner was so irate he almost threw me out of the place. He said, 'Why'd you do that?' I told him I didn't do it," he said. He later added: "I'm not sure it was going to be as good as what we had."

Fifteen years later, in a guest editorial for *USA Today*, O'Neil described what happened the morning that *Dallas Morning News* article appeared:

At 8 a.m. that day, fully one hour before departing to visit the Cowboys, Madden was in the lobby of CBS's hotel. His newspaper was folded double and triple, very tightly, so that the only article facing him was Summerall's. He shifted frequently in his chair. One eyebrow was arched at an acute angle. His nostrils flared as, every minute or so, he exhaled deeply. His florid Irish face was raging. But he said absolutely nothing.

Summerall appeared and said good morning. Madden said nothing. The ride to the Cowboys' training complex left frost on the car windows. For the next 38 hours virtually the only words the two spoke to each other were on the air. But when the game ended, Summerall knew what he had hooked—an analyst for the ages who would reinvigorate him and propel his career to a new beginning.

O'Neil, who produced that game, thought that Summerall gave that public interview because Pat had to give some sort of nod to his old buddy Brookshier. "As far as being friends was concerned [for Pat and John], this was the lowest moment for them," O'Neil observed.

Although the chill quickly wore off, Summerall was looking at other possibilities besides NBC. The chance of being relieved of his No. 1 position didn't sit well with him. When he told O'Neil that he might go to NBC, O'Neil pleaded with him to wait until a decision was reached on October 26.

In the meantime, O'Neil and Sauter woke up to this news on the morning of October 8, 1981, in *The New York Times*: "Pat Summerall, the former Giant tight end and place-kicker who is now a CBS broadcaster, is thinking about running for the Senate next year as a Republican in Florida. He said that the race 'has been suggested to me and it interested me.'"

A UPI story dated the same day quoted Summerall as saying, "It has been mentioned to me and suggested to me. I really, frankly, never gave it any thought. The more I think about it—the more exciting it sounds."

Regardless of his threats, Summerall was a total professional working his four games with Madden, and Madden's performance began to shine through.

While doing research for this book, I reviewed a YouTube copy of the final game Scully and Madden worked together in Week 4 of the 1981 NFL season, Cleveland and Atlanta. My conclusion, like so many others', was that Scully could have done the game without an analyst. He had done so much homework and had so many bits of stories to tell us that there was hardly any room for Madden to talk. Narrating alone was his style.

But in contrast, the first pairing of Summerall and Madden reaped immediate rewards. The game between the visiting Dallas Cowboys and the St. Louis Cardinals was decided with 23 seconds to go when the Cardinals' Neil O'Donoghue kicked a 37-yard field goal. As John Madden's son Mike told me, "It was like peanut butter meeting jelly for the first time."[9]

> **Madden:** "See Neil O'Donoghue there? He's 6'6". See how they have to jump up to congratulate him?"
> **Summerall:** "He's about 6-9 right now."
> **Madden:** "6-9 going on 7-2. You have to get a stepladder to pat him on the head."

O'Neil recalled: "For his four games in October of '81 with Madden, Summerall reacted like the athlete-competitor he had been for a lifetime. ... You could actually hear a heartbeat in his play-by-play. Wisely though, he turned up the intensity without increasing the quantity. There was still enough space in Summerall-Madden despite John's growing verbosity. In fact, compared to Scully-Madden, it was easy listening."[10]

Imagine you're Madden. It's 1981 and all your life you either played or coached football. You love the game, and the game loved you back until bleeding ulcers forced you to stop coaching. Because you want to share that love, you have a microphone in your hand far from the field where you were so comfortable yelling at the officials. This is your third year trying to spin your stories for CBS, but it's not quite working with whoever they put next to you.

The Contest

Then one day suddenly it all flows beautifully, like a smooth cabernet after the bottle has been uncorked. The man next to you is the reason. His name is Pat Summerall, a man who, like yourself, played and loves the game. More important, he understands your love for the game. Each time the teams on the field exchange the football, your conversations begin to sound natural and inviting. You begin to relax. The two of you laugh. You finish each other's sentences. By the end of the game, the two of you realize you have struck gold.

After just that first game they worked together in Week 5, senior producer Chuck Milton told O'Neil and CBS talent executive Janis Delson, "They can be one of the all-time [broadcast] teams."[11]

For the October 26 meeting, Sauter invited the following executives: Kevin O'Malley (college sports), Chuck Milton (senior producer), Ted Shaker (*The NFL Today* producer), Jim Harrington (programming), Carl Lindemann (programming), and O'Neil to the CBS executive dining room on the 36th floor for lunch.

Harrington was the only one of that group that seemed completely misplaced. He was the perfect example of the Peter Principle, rising to his level of incompetence, eventually becoming head of programming at CBS Sports.

He had zero background in sports. His CBS background was personnel and program standards.

"Then [former CBS president] Frank Smith drafted him to keep an eye on us to make sure our camera shots didn't give away any free advertising from signage," said one former CBS executive. "One day at the U.S. Open, he actually called the LaGuardia Tower and asked the controllers to reroute all planes on their takeoffs and landings away from the tennis courts because Pat Summerall couldn't hear the cues in his headset. Harrington couldn't decide whether to cross the street on the red or the green, let alone make broadcasting decisions."

According to O'Neil, they were served chicken and asparagus on elegant CBS china. Once the plates were cleared away, they began to discuss the subject at hand. Van Sauter began making his case for Vin Scully. "He's a great broadcaster, an elegant broadcaster," Van repeated. Then the remaining group went around the table and voted one by one. Before O'Neil concluded the voting, Chuck Milton and O'Malley made impassioned speeches for Summerall.

Here's how O'Malley recalled it: "We came loaded for bear. I said [to Van], 'You shouldn't do this. Talk to your sales department. They will tell you that having Summerall is worth 5 to 10 percent more in revenues over NBC—because our talent is so much better regarded. Our talent is personified by Pat Summerall. And if you tell your sales department that you are demoting Pat Summerall, they will all hyperventilate.'"[12]

The vote was unanimous for Summerall, except for Sauter. O'Neil, who had the last vote, started to say how he agreed with the rest of table when, according to O'Neil, "Van slammed his fist on the table and said, 'Okay, I've heard enough. If you people want him, you can have him. But mark my words, you'll have to manage him.... I'm not going to be responsible for his alcoholic binges.'"[13]

When presented with this version of events, Sauter said (by email) that he didn't recall slamming his fist on the table. "If I pounded my fist, it was not in anger. I went into that job not knowing anything about sports. That group at CBS, which had gone through some hard times, was very bright and flexible and had the right to create a better business than they had been allowed to create. There was real talent there."

"It wasn't my decision," Sauter continued. "It was just another day of making decisions at a company.... I wanted it to be the best broadcast we could get. In all my years of making decisions, I never ran into a decision that was more unacceptable to my employees than that. They just knocked me out of the box. And part of being a manager is respecting the opinions of your colleagues, but also capitulating when you are at the face of an open rebellion. That's how it went."[14]

It is to Sauter's credit that he allowed the majority to rule. He could have vetoed their decision and replaced it with his own choice. But now somebody had to tell Scully he lost. Scully was in New York that afternoon to call the Yankees-Dodgers World Series game the next day on radio. O'Neil volunteered to give him the bad news.

He called Scully in his hotel room and asked if he could walk over to give him the decision. Scully wanted an immediate answer. "Just tell me," Scully said. O'Neil tried to spin the bad news into what he told Scully was "good news," that he and his partner Hank Stram would be calling the NFC championship game instead.

O'Neil knew he'd made a mistake by not telling him straight. In his book, O'Neil wrote that Scully was "spitting mad," but he later revised that to say, "Vin's tone in the phone call was not angry, rude or 'spitting mad,'" he later told friends. "He was too gentlemanly for that."[15]

Scully did in fact call the NFC championship game, which saw Joe Montana hit Dwight Clark with the game-winning pass with just 51 seconds remaining. For that game the Cowboys were favored after they crushed the Tampa Bay Buccaneers, 38–0, the week before. The winner would represent the NFC in Super Bowl XVI at the Pontiac (Michigan) Silverdome. O'Neil produced that game, and Scully's call, of what has become known as "The Catch," was perfect.

Scully: "For the upstart 49ers, they're six yards from Pontiac. . . . Montana, looking, looking, throwing in the end zone. Clark caught it! Dwight Clark! It's a madhouse at Candlestick with 51 seconds left." Final score, 49ers 28, Cowboys 27.

Several months later, Scully turned down a 10-year, $7 million deal to stay at CBS and went to NBC. Years later he told a reporter, "I got on a plane and I thought, 'You know, it doesn't get much better than that.'"[16] "And I told my family, 'That's a great game on which to call it a football career.'"[17]

Although Sauter admired his technical brilliance, it turned out that O'Neil was a little too rough around the edges for Sauter, especially in delivering direction to underlings. In reviewing the Scully "good news" call, here's how Van summed up O'Neil's leadership skills:

"Terry O'Neil was the worst at human relations [Scully]. The problem was he always made good decisions. He always had [good] ideas. And if you would embrace the idea, and send him off to execute it, you always knew there would be bloodshed."[18]

"I'm not sure I've always handled people as well as I could," O'Neil admitted to *Sports Illustrated* in 1984. "I've failed at times when I might have done the job in a more diplomatic way."[19]

Dick Stockton was one of the top play-by-play broadcasters CBS had when O'Neil arrived, and Stockton remained near the top of his profession for decades to come. He understood how important it was for Sauter to hire O'Neil.

"Terry knew more about the games, the Olympics, and television than anyone at CBS," Stockton said when interviewed for this book. "This guy was a brilliant, knowledgeable sports guy. He knew stories better than you could know them even after you had researched them. He knew football, and he knew more, and he knew television better than anyone knew television. He just couldn't handle people."[20]

Madden once said to O'Neil, "You remind me of Al Davis." To O'Neil, any comparison to Madden's ruthless former boss was the ultimate compliment coming from Madden.

While both feared and respected by all those who worked for him, O'Neil easily made enemies. One was Bob Stenner, who O'Neil thought was a mediocre producer.

Stenner: "He [O'Neil] took two Super Bowls away from me [to produce them himself], and I think that was pretty shitty."[21]

"He was reviled and hated by just about everyone on the NFL broadcast team," said one former CBS executive. "At the 1984 Super Bowl, a cameraman said that at halftime O'Neil screamed at all the cameramen something like, 'If you don't give me better shots [pictures], I'm going to go over there and pull your fingernails out.'"

He's been called a bully, rude, and a tyrant, but he was brought in to bring CBS Sports' production from the '60s into the '80s. "Like Sinatra," wrote *Sports Illustrated* of O'Neil's management style in its January 30, 1984, issue, "he did it his way." O'Neil also had the unusual habit of calling nearly everyone "Dude."

Regardless, here are some of the things O'Neil instituted in his five years at CBS Sports that definitely contributed to Madden's success:

The Contest

- He introduced new replay angles and camera framing that allowed Madden to display his expertise. If two receivers were running a combination route, O'Neil had cameramen frame the receivers together and track them downfield so we could see a combo-play design. This kind of production was brand new in 1981.
- He introduced the Telestrator, renamed it the CBS Chalkboard, and designed it to allow Madden to diagram plays the average fan could understand. It became a major breakthrough in broadcasting the NFL, allowing viewers to see all 22 players in a single frame.
- He got more cameras approved for games and placed cameras on the 20-yard lines like the other two networks had done, instead of just the 50-yard line.
- He had a "playbook" for his cameramen on isolated replays and rehearsed them before games on the team formations that were most likely to provide the best replays. He installed a fresh, new low-angle replay for Super Bowl XVI that became a standard thereafter in the business.
- He also received the okay to hire a slew of broadcast associates in 1981, many of whom are today's great producers and directors.
- Prior to O'Neil's arrival, CBS's production and talent traveled Saturday for a Sunday game, arriving Saturday afternoon, speaking to the teams' PR men (no players or coaches), then had a quick production meeting and they were off to Saturday night follies. When hired, O'Neil informed Sauter that they needed to travel Friday, stay at the visiting-team hotel, wake up Saturday morning for a 12-hour day, then arrive at 8 a.m. at the home-team facility, screen videotape, watch home-team practice, speak individually to home-team players and coaches, then back to their hotel, where the visiting team would be arriving for more meetings with players and coaches. That was followed by a production meeting in the producer's suite with room-service dinner. There was no time to go out for dinner. Van understood and got it approved in less than 24 hours.

- And O'Neil, along with Madden, was instrumental in getting the entire crew to arrive at game sites early to study the coaches' game film, with Madden leading the sessions. Madden even kept the room at 60 degrees to make sure everyone stayed awake.
- O'Neil, along with Madden and John Robinson, helped create the All-Madden Team—a team of bruising, hard-nosed players that Madden selected, and adored, which the public absolutely loved. At each season's end, awards would be presented to the All-Madden Team.
- And in Super Bowl XVIII in Tampa in 1984, O'Neil even used Tampa's Jesuit High football team for an on-field CBS dress rehearsal of Raiders' and Redskins' plays.

"We used to have directors blow into town the morning of a playoff game," O'Neil told *Sports Illustrated*, referring to the years before his arrival. "We've convinced people it won't be done that way here anymore."

Regardless, Van Gordon Sauter will always be the one most responsible for choosing John Madden, and Terry O'Neil will always get the credit for pairing him with Pat Summerall. Together they formed the greatest broadcast team of all time.

Terry O'Neil's departure several years later from CBS was as much a victory for Brent Musburger as it was a loss for all those young production people and technicians O'Neil had trained, not to mention how much Summerall and Madden would miss him.

Like others at CBS Sports, O'Neil lost a bitter battle with Musburger, whom O'Neil had tagged as an "anchor monster." The problem began before O'Neil even arrived at CBS during *The NFL Today* producer Mike Pearl's regime.

Pearl had initiated a segment in the pregame show where the network would go from one live site to another and quickly get any new information from the game announcers before kickoff. They'd report things like injury and weather updates, or any change in starters at key positions. The fans, especially the gamblers, tuned in for this information.

The problem was that Musburger had the ability to key into each site and listen to the announcers' rehearsals before they went live on the air. If there was a key injury, Brent knew it before the on-site guys would tell the live audience, and Brent would often lead into their news by saying something like, "Tell us about that injury to Roger Staubach."

This would infuriate the guys announcing the games, especially Summerall and Brookshier before O'Neil joined CBS. "You know, Brookshier would like to kill the son of a bitch," Summerall said, referring to Musburger. "He literally wants to kill him."[22]

Pearl once had to separate the game crew from the pregame crew at a playoff dinner to keep Musburger safe. And CBS executive Janis Delson mentioned in *You Are Looking Live!* that Brookshier traveled from El Paso to Dallas with a gun looking for Musburger, who was working in Dallas for the Cotton Bowl game.

Pearl referred to Musburger's eavesdropping on their rehearsals as "stealing the headlines." Brent's best example of this was when he stole Jimmy the Greek's big scoop about Notre Dame about to fire its football coach and replace him with high-school coach Gerry Faust, before the Greek could deliver the news during his live segment. This led to their famous one-punch brawl at Peartrees restaurant in Manhattan.

According to O'Neil, to get more firsthand information, Musburger insisted that his *NFL Today* partner, Irv Cross, should be allowed to join the private meetings John Madden and Summerall had with the coaches and star players on Saturdays. Madden and O'Neil had talked the NFL into allowing them access after they promised that no news from the interviews would be dispensed before the games. Cross would then relay any news back to Brent, who would then try to scoop Pat and John before they could deliver it on the air, and in so doing default on CBS's promise to the NFL.

After Madden and Summerall protested vehemently about the intrusion, O'Neil was able to force Cross out of the meetings, which infuriated Musburger. In addition, O'Neil managed to block the airwaves between the game site and the studio during rehearsal time only, preventing Brent from listening in and stealing the on-site guys' news. This really made Musburger crazy.

Then there were the in-game studio updates with highlights of games happening live. Musburger voiced them, and they gave him maximum exposure. Madden and Summerall complained bitterly about the constant interruptions. O'Neil didn't like them either and went to Peter Lund (who by 1985 had replaced Van Sauter as the CBS Sports president). Lund wasn't interested in deciding who was right or wrong. He just wanted it to stop.

In his book *The Game Behind the Game*, O'Neil wrote that after he forced Cross out of the coaches' meetings, Musburger "attacked me savagely to Peter Lund, saying I was disruptive and bent on sabotaging his show." Soon after, O'Neil wrote that Lund called him into his office and said, "All I can tell you is that when you have one of the 800-pound gorillas [Brent] mad at you, you've got a problem."

Terry O'Neil pictured here as he looked in 1989, when, after working as an executive at ABC and CBS, he began working for Dick Ebersol at NBC Sports. COURTESY OF NBC SPORTS

The Contest

There was no doubt that Musburger was the 800-pound gorilla at CBS Sports in the mid-'80s. He had just signed a five-year, $10 million contract that would run through 1989. That was probably 8 to 10 times more than anybody else was earning in those years, including Madden and Summerall. Musburger was not only hosting and controlling *The NFL Today*, he was also CBS's lead broadcaster for the NBA, NCAA football, and the Belmont Stakes, which led to O'Neil's "anchor monster" assessment. In the next few years, Musburger would add the Masters and the U.S. Open tennis to that list.

At Madden's suggestion, O'Neil asked Musburger to lunch to try and make peace. Of the get-together, O'Neil wrote, "Before we finished our soup, he [Brent] had (1) threatened to use his influence with Gene Jankowski [chairman of the Broadcast Group] to get me fired, and (2) declared that our exclusion of Irv Cross from the Saturday meetings was potentially a racial issue which might bring an NAACP protest."[23]

From that point on, Musburger tried to undermine everything O'Neil did. Eventually he was successful, mainly because Lund didn't have the stomach to settle the political battles. Musburger thrived on them. During the first week in June 1986, *The New York Post*'s columnist Phil Mushnick wrote:

"The hills are alive with the sound of a shakeup coming at CBS Sports that could slay some high-profile executive producer types."

On the morning of June 23, 1986, Lund walked into O'Neil's office and simply said, "T. O., the rumors are true." O'Neil was out. Musburger had temporarily won, only to be fired himself a few years later by Ted Shaker and Neal Pilson.

As for O'Neil, he once again landed on his feet. His book *The Game Behind the Game*, describing his careers at ABC and CBS, was published in early 1989 and became a guide for those who would be working for him a few months later when he was named executive producer at NBC Sports by Dick Ebersol.

CHAPTER NINE

WHAT MADE THEM GREAT

When two people are as great a broadcast team as Pat Summerall and John Madden were for nearly all of their 21 years together, viewers become so comfortable listening to them that it's sometimes difficult to point to a single reason why they are considered the best of all time. With the help of the dozens of people interviewed for this book from both CBS and Fox, several explanations become obvious:

Pat's Unselfishness

When Terry O'Neil put them together in 1981, Summerall was already considered the best play-by-play broadcaster there was, regardless of the shenanigans with Brookshier. Pat's strength was taking the broadcast in the right direction, and when Brookshier got out on a limb, pulling him back in. Before that, Summerall had spent nearly seven years as an analyst himself, mostly with his mentor, Ray Scott, who let the pictures do the talking and said as little as possible.

O'Neil knew that Summerall's minimalist style of calling a game would fit perfectly with Madden's desire to be America's NFL nutty professor. No matter how far Madden would stray telling his stories, Summerall would have the perfect capper to move things back to neutral.

In an August 26, 1996, column for *USA Today*, nearly 15 years exactly after their first official pairing, O'Neil wrote about the cold atmosphere that existed between the two before that preseason game. The cold atmosphere was the result of an interview Summerall gave to *The Dallas Morning News*, saying, "It wouldn't be the same [without Brookshier]."

O'Neil described Pat and John as "two strangers who had reached an accommodation, for the sake of the broadcast," but they both knew what they had. In that 1996 column, O'Neil also marveled about Madden. "Madden is largely unchanged from that first game," he wrote. "Virtually everything he does can be broken into categories: vivid word pictures that capture the players exquisitely—their mannerisms, their slang, their essence—and a stunning ability to coach both teams simultaneously better than they are being coached on the field."

But in those roles, O'Neil noted that Summerall was capable of participating more. "The dimensions of '90s football are too many for even Madden to shoulder alone. Too often, he is leading every dance with Summerall and the production truck following in close choreography. Pat is capable of so much more, and often his perspective is needed."

Time after time while interviewing Summerall's and Madden's coworkers, other broadcasters and executives, and even the media, the general theme projected as the key to their success was Pat's unselfishness. Here are some of those opinions:

Dick Stockton, who was with both CBS and Fox as one of their top play-by-play men, said: "I don't know whether Pat and John ever had a dinner together alone. That comment speaks to how separate they were away from the booth. They were different people.

"Even John knew when to lay out. But Pat was so concise and authoritative. He could say, 'First down Packers,' instead of [screaming it]. And it would just penetrate. And he would be conversational. He never lost his cool, and he always was in command. So he gave himself up. He was the guy that played in the NFL and was a hero in the National Football League. John never played a down. Pat Summerall was just as majestic as a broadcaster. And even as a player he was that way—kicking that great 50-yard field goal [in the snow] against the Browns. He was just magnificent. So those two were a match made in heaven, because John would not have been as great if he had a garrulous, yelling egomaniac next to him."[1]

Richie Zyontz, who was a broadcast associate at CBS working closely with Summerall and Madden and has become one of Fox Sports' top producers, said: "John needed the space to be John. He didn't speak in complete sentences. If you read a transcript of one of John's broadcasts, you might think, 'Did this guy go to school?' It was just a bunch of random words and sounds, but when you put it on TV it was brilliant. And in order for John to be brilliant, he needed a partner who gave him the space to be brilliant. And that was Pat.

"And not for one moment of time did Pat ever reveal any sort of jealousy or bitterness. Pat was just a great teammate. And he was kind to everybody. He wasn't just kind to John; he was kind to the kids on the crew like myself.

"As one of those kids back in the early '80s, it felt like you were walking with giants. In today's world it doesn't feel the same, but those guys were titans."[2]

And as for Madden in those early days, Zyontz said, "I felt like I was at the birth of a star. I saw it develop. I saw him become what he became."

When Richie Zyontz started working with Madden fresh out of college, he described himself as an "honest New York street kid who loved sports." He took Madden for cannolis, kosher deli, and "the whole New York culture thing." They became fast friends. COURTESY OF RICHIE ZYONTZ

Ed Goren, who was a senior producer with CBS before he was a top executive running Fox Sports, said when interviewed for this book: "John changed the culture of football coverage at CBS. Back then the pregame meeting consisted of the producer and director, the play-by-play man, and the analyst meeting the team's PR director at the bar to go through the three-deep [player positions] and go through pronunciations. That was the meeting.

"When John came in, he brought the coaching mentality to the broadcast meetings and the broadcast itself. They were the best two-man broadcasting team ever. And you could say it goes beyond sports. They're up there with some of the great two-man teams in the history of entertainment—like [Dean] Martin and [Jerry] Lewis.

"The real star of CBS's Saturday all-day tape sessions was Pat Summerall. At that time, there wasn't one play-by-play guy at CBS who watched any tape. Pat had every right after an hour of watching tape to say, 'All right, guys, I'll see you later.' But he didn't. He understood the value that John brought. Pat was the perfect partner. He didn't say much, but he always had the perfect tagline to something goofy that Madden had just said."[3]

Richard Sandomir, who was *The New York Times'* TV Sports columnist for 25 years, all through Summerall and Madden's partnership, and had a front-row seat to the change they brought about, wrote by email:

"They were opposites—maybe more than any partnership in NFL TV history—whose disparate styles meshed perfectly. Pat was terse; if other play-by-play announcers needed 100 words to express something, Pat could do it in 10 words.

"And in that concision rested the secret of his teamwork with John. He was a great straight man, like Bud Abbott to John's Lou Costello. Pat could utter one word, like 'Yes?' or 'Really?' which would let John ramble on. And John was a rambler. When he found his footing on CBS, John was exciting, Rabelaisian, amusing, and, more than anything, informative—much as he was as a coach. When he parsed plays with the Telestrator, he became America's football professor. Pat was deeply informed about football, but he gave John all the room he needed to deal with X's and O's, as well as distractions like turkey drumsticks, and turduckens."[4]

Many years later for *Sports Illustrated*'s September 30, 2002, article "Split Personalities," Madden said: "He [Summerall] saved my bacon all the time. He had this way of taking my babbling and making sense out of it."

Dick Stockton and John had become good friends with both living in Manhattan. They'd often watch the *Monday Night Football* game together at Madden's apartment in The Dakota, the famous building on Central Park West, along with Stockton's wife at that time, Lesley Visser. One day Stockton asked Madden what he wanted from his partner.

"John said, 'I want the play-by-play guy to call the play concisely, accurately, and then shut up. Don't lead me anywhere. Don't lead me. Because you might want to talk about the quarterback and I've been watching the linebacker, so just get out. Let me get in quickly.' This is why their impact [of Pat and John] worked so well together. It wasn't Pat leading John. It was John coming in and taking them where he wanted to go and Pat coming back with the perfect exclamation point.

"John was the best of all time in a blowout. Nobody was better. I think [director] Sandy [Grossman] was the key to that success. When they arrived at a game, they were on headsets throughout the entire practice time. And the cameramen were looking for unusual shots or unusual people that he [John] could use in the game. If some guy had his hat off and was lying in the sun in a chair, Sandy would say, 'Get that.' After a while they didn't have to tell them what to get. They'd know what to get. Once during a time-out, the cameraman showed the guy with the Gatorade tray, putting his finger in each one of those cups. And John would say, 'Look at this. This guy's got his finger in every one of those cups.' And he'd draw circles around this stuff, and the game was like 31 to nothing at the time. Stuff like that—that's what made the broadcast."[5]

Jim Nantz, CBS's all-around broadcaster since 1985, said: "Pat was a rarity. He made the transition from former player to analyst to play-by-play. You don't see that happen very often, when someone who played the game winds up calling the game. There's usually only a one-way ticket to the booth.

"It was all meant to be for those two [Pat and John] to be paired together. That's the gold standard of two broadcasters working together."[6]

How Madden Changed the Culture of NFL Broadcasts

John Madden's reluctance to try broadcasting stemmed from his lack of respect for what he had heard on the air. When Terry O'Neil began revamping CBS Sports' coverage after he was hired in January 1981, he finally got around to having lunch with Madden that May. O'Neil talked about that lunch during an interview with Neil Amdur of *The New York Times* before Super Bowl XVIII, in Tampa, three years later.

"I remember the first time Madden and I sat down and talked," O'Neil said. "John was complaining and moaning about the work ethic that was commensurate with some of the people at the time, and that he couldn't analyze something during a game if he didn't have the pictures."

Madden also complained to O'Neil about how the production people always called it a "show." "Our people are always calling it the show this, and the show that," Madden said. "Hell, it isn't a show. *Kukla, Fran and Ollie* is a show. *Laverne and Shirley* is a show! This is a game!"[7]

By the time O'Neil was changing things at CBS, Madden was already taking the train, and many weeks he was arriving at game sites a day or two ahead of the crew. So John started visiting the teams' practices on his own and discussing the upcoming game with the coaches. O'Neil did him one better.

In the spring of 1981, O'Neil went to the NFL's vice president of broadcasting, Val Pinchbeck, and asked him for permission to do something the networks had never done. Here's their exchange:

O'Neil: "I want access to the coaches and players. We won't quote anybody, but we need that information."
Pinchbeck: "You want what?"

O'Neil convinced Pinchbeck to give them that access. Then he mentioned it to Madden. "When I brought this to Madden," O'Neil said, "he just lit up. John said, 'My biggest bitch about television is that nobody knows anything about football, starting with the producer and director all the way down to the crew [based on his first two years there], and that nobody cares about football.'"[8]

O'Neil put a plan in place that included trips to the visiting- and home-team practices on Fridays and then all-day film sessions on Saturdays, with Madden running the projector and teaching the producer, director, associate directors, and cameramen what formations to expect. If they knew what was coming, he reasoned, they could react to it that much faster, resulting in better replays. The sessions would almost always go into Saturday nights, with O'Neil ordering a food delivery for everyone.

When they would all watch film together, Madden would start by focusing on the center and then the guards and so forth. John always worked inside out. It became an art form for the crew. That's how he would teach them to watch the game.

"We would sit in production meetings [Saturdays]," said Joan Vitrano, "and he'd get the coaches' real film, and he'd play it on a projector just like he was running a meeting with his players. He'd teach the crew and the cameramen a lot about football and how to cover it. John was coaching his own team again."[9]

For Super Bowl XVIII in Tampa in January 1984, O'Neil made it even easier for his crew to recognize the formations the Washington Redskins and Oakland Raiders would use. Here's how O'Neil explained the crew's Friday schedule to Amdur, *The New York Times*' TV Sports columnist: "Friday morning—Between 8:30 A.M. and 11 A.M., Madden will diagram 'potentially troublesome' formations and plays so that cameramen and crew will be better able to follow the flow. Between 11 A.M. and 1 P.M., players from the Tampa Jesuit High football team will run some of the formations and plays of both teams for the cameras."[10]

Imagine hiring a football team to rehearse your cameramen! It wasn't the first time O'Neil did this. Before Super Bowl XVI in Pontiac, Michigan, O'Neil hired the Wayne State University football team to run formations used by the two Super Bowl teams for the benefit of his cameramen and crew. O'Neil was one who didn't care how much of CBS's money he had to spend if he could improve a broadcast. Before an extremely windy playoff game between the New York Giants and the Chicago Bears, O'Neil had broadcast associate Mike Frank track down three anemometers and had them shipped overnight to the stadium in order to track the speed and direction of the wind.

George "Hulk" Rothweiler is one of the all-time great sports cameramen. He's been nominated for 11 Emmy Awards, winning twice. He was just 21 years old and was part of the CBS game crew in 1981 when O'Neil and Madden came on board. He was a keen observer of what was happening.

"When Terry came in, he forced us to really understand the game of football," Rothweiler said when interviewed for this book. "He made everybody smarter, from the tape guys to the graphic guys to the camera guys. In the early years with Brookie and Pat [and Stenner and Grossman], we didn't have meetings with the coaches. When John and Terry came on, we started having meetings and watching film with John. John kept the room cold to make sure we didn't fall asleep in the meeting. Somebody said, 'John, it's fucking cold in here.' He laughed and said, 'That's what I used to do with my players in Oakland.'"

Rothweiler was quick to recall how things used to be before O'Neil's arrival:

"We never had this kind of communication," he said. "We never had this information before Terry came to the table. At Christmas time, John would give a speech at the party. We were just a bunch of jocks living the dream. We didn't realize the history we were a part of with Pat and John."

Rothweiler then gave an amazing example of how the communication between Madden, the director, and the cameramen paid off during a San Francisco 49ers game:

"I was always a close-up guy. I shot [Mike] Singletary's eyes—everybody loved those shots. Now with the high-speed camera you had more frames per second than with a standard replay machine.... I said to John, when you're talking to [director] Sandy [Grossman], we're missing a lot of live shots because Sandy's only talking to you. I told him what a high-speed camera can do to enhance some things that he would like. I said, 'John, tell me what you're looking for.' The last thing he said to me was that Joe Montana sees the whole field. That his eyes get real big.

What Made Them Great

... Now they're coming at me, and I have Montana on a full-face shot. Most guys would widen out from there. Montana rolled out and then his eyes lit up real wide. I stayed with his eyes. When that replay came in, John loved it. He even talked about it after the game when we did a postgame on the bus. We relived that shot, and I said to him, 'I wouldn't have known that had you not told me about his eyes.'"[11]

When you looked around the room those Saturday nights, what you came to realize was that Madden once again had put together his own championship team. And he was coaching them every weekend during a football season.

> When Tom Brady was approved as a minority owner of the Las Vegas Raiders, the NFL threw in the stipulation that he is no longer permitted to sit in on Fox's pregame meetings with coaches and players. It's as if nobody else from Fox in those meetings would tell Brady what new information was ascertained.
>
> It has come to be known as "the Tom Brady rule." It's as if the NFL wanted the flair of having Brady as an owner but also wanted to keep its skirts clean by punishing him as a broadcaster. And indeed they have at Fox's expense. Fox has paid Brady $375 million for 10 years to be its No. 1 analyst. Fox even assigned its top producer, Richie Zyontz, who once was Madden's broadcast associate at CBS. If Brady can't have direct access to this information, he will be missing a key piece to his preparation. After five years, one of the other sports reporters suggested that Brady will be distant from the freshness to the game he once commanded.

Matt Millen was an All-American defensive tackle and a linebacker at Penn State who was drafted in 1980 by the Raiders after Madden had retired. Once the two stalwarts met, they always remained close. After Madden's death, Millen talked about how John never really stopped coaching.

"John was a teacher first," Millen told his Fox broadcasting colleagues. "When John retired and he said, 'I'm never going to coach again,' that was wrong. John never stopped being a head coach. He was a head coach with his television crew, and he was a head coach with me every time I was around him.

"John was my mentor. We always had a lot of fun. I loved the guy. I took a lot from John. Like, just the way you see the game. One of the first things John told me in this business is that there's always gonna be a guy who makes the play. He said, 'Try and find the guy who doesn't make the tackle but makes the play.' I've always stuck with that. I know he'll always be with me."[12]

In 1987, after O'Neil had departed from CBS, Ted Shaker was the executive producer for the division. That April, Shaker was at Augusta National supervising coverage of the Masters when he got an unusual phone call.

"Madden called and reached me at Butler Cabin," said Shaker, which is where CBS broadcasters sometimes interviewed finishing players. "I was surprised because I didn't expect to hear from John for several months. He wanted us to do a retreat for different groups of production people. I reminded him that we had our annual seminar in August, but he was not having any of that."

Madden asked: "How can anyone give us a picture of a nickel defense if they don't know what a nickel defense is and the purpose of it?"

Then Madden gave Shaker an example of what he meant that stayed with him the rest of his life:

"You're climbing a mountain," Madden said. "You get halfway up and once you stop trying to go higher, you start sliding down. I don't want us to slide down."[13]

The CBS Chalkboard

The other incredibly important aspect to the success of Summerall and Madden that first year was the appearance late in the season of the CBS Chalkboard. Invented by Dr. Leonard Reiffel, the University of Chicago physicist, it was a Telestrator that began as a tool for illustrating weather broadcasts on WBBM-TV in Chicago.

During their May lunch, Madden asked O'Neil, "Why can't we show the game the way coaches watch it on film—with all 22 men?"

"One autumn morning a little package landed on my desk," said O'Neil. "I swear it was from heaven, but the return address said Chicago, a company called Interand. They'd developed an electronic stylus, connected to a special monitor, that allowed commentators to draw freehand over television pictures. They wanted to know if I was interested. *Was I interested?*"[14]

He immediately picked up the phone and called Madden. They both believed *The Philadelphia Inquirer* was right when it called the CBS Chalkboard "the most significant improvement in football coverage since the development of instant replay."

Madden loved the Chalkboard: "In coaching you tape 22 players. Everything is in relationship to the other guy," he said. "Everything reacts to what the other players are doing. When I first came into TV, I realized you never get to see the whole game of football. All you see is parts of it. You see a little part here and a little part there. I wanted to do something where you can show all 22. The problem is when you do that, the players become too small, so you need something to point them out. That's what the Chalkboard does."[15]

This was the process: When a play ended, if O'Neil wanted Madden to draw, he would simultaneously issue a command to Madden and director Sandy Grossman: "Chalkboard." That alerted John to pick up the stylus, Sandy to tell the technical director to insert the Chalkboard video effect, and the videotape operator to cue them one second before they snap the ball.

In Super Bowl XVI, for instance, two Cincinnati linebackers were drawn forward by a Joe Montana play fake, creating space for a completion behind them. So O'Neil said to John, "Circle the two inside linebackers." John would draw and then narrate. When he finished drawing, they would erase his drawing and roll the replay.

At first they used the Chalkboard only over a wide view of all 22 players. Later they realized it was sometimes more effective over a different framing, depending on the play. For example, the Redskins had a play called "Counter Trey" in which guard Russ Grimm and offensive tackle

Joe Jacoby led running back John Riggins through a hole. Since wide receivers were not involved, there was no need for framing all 22 players. This "Counter Trey" became one of Madden's best-known Chalkboards: "Here comes big Grimm," he'd say. "Bam. Here comes big Jacoby. Bam. And right behind them, here comes big Riggins. Bam, bam."

Before the Chalkboard showed up, they would need something like a laser pointer to guide the home viewer's eye through a screen with all 22 players. Chalkboard technology solved it. After O'Neil's exit from CBS, producer Bob Stenner was reluctant to make the live call for the Chalkboard. Instead, Madden would make the decision and press a switch in the booth that muted his mic but allowed the truck alone to hear him. He would alert Grossman to insert the Chalkboard video effect, and Madden would do the rest.

The first time they tried using the Chalkboard over live TV was during the New York Giants–San Francisco 49ers divisional playoff game on January 3, 1982. O'Neil and Madden hoped to use it twice during the game, and never until after a commercial, to allow Madden the time to rehearse what he was showing during the break. But as O'Neil wrote, once the game started, instinct took over, and they used the CBS Chalkboard eight different times that first game, and only twice with Madden getting a commercial break beforehand.

The perfect example of how instructive it was happened when Joe Montana hit Dwight Clark with a pass in the first half for a 39-yard gain. It was a typical 49er play, drawn up by Coach Bill Walsh, because no defender was within 10 yards of Clark when he caught it. Without the Chalkboard, the usual close-ups and isolated replays of Clark could not show why he was so wide open. But with Madden running the Chalkboard, the viewer could see how another receiver had taken the defensive safety with him, leaving Clark all alone in that area of the field.

The Chalkboard was such a huge hit with both viewers and TV sports writers that three nights before Super Bowl XVI in Detroit, CBS Sports held a dinner for selected members of the news media to allow Madden to demonstrate how he worked his magic with it. Madden was even more dazzling that night than he usually was on the air. Nobody at CBS bothered to count the number of times it was used in the Super Bowl itself, but it was highly complimented when the reviews came in.

> *Two nights before the Super Bowl, I met* Saturday Night Live *writer Jim Downey for dinner. Downey was there because Dick Ebersol, who was the producer of* SNL *that year, had called me saying he wanted Madden to host* Saturday Night Live *the week after the Super Bowl. A month earlier I met Ebersol at a 50th birthday party I threw for Beano Cook at Runyon's. When I told Ebersol about Madden needing extra time to get to New York because he only took the train, Dick said, "No problem. I'll send Jim Downey to travel with him along with a camera crew." Six nights after the game, Madden made history, and I was one of the lucky ones to be in the audience for the* SNL *show.*

Before they could even get to New York, however, the snowstorm that hit Detroit the weekend of the game was still lingering in the Northeast, and when the train reached the Buffalo area, it came to a stop. "We were told it might be a few hours before we could move again," said Downey, "but John had an idea. He called a friend who picked us up and took us to a local sports bar near the Buffalo train station. When we got there it was practically empty. But once word got out that John was there, it filled up pretty fast. We did manage to get to New York in plenty of time for John to rehearse his skits, which he was great in."[16] Later that year, Downey became the head writer for *Late Night with David Letterman*.

The 49ers won Super Bowl XVI, 26–21, after leading 20–0 at halftime. From CBS's standpoint, it was a complete success, earning the highest rating (49.1) of any Super Bowl at that point. And the reviews of the TV sports writers were just as glorious, for not only Summerall and Madden but for O'Neil and director Sandy Grossman too.

O'Neil and Madden thought Dr. Reiffel's Telestrator contraption was a gift from heaven. And it allowed Madden to teach America what the game looks like with all 22 players on the field.

Because Super Bowl XVI was so successful for CBS and its new No. 1 broadcast team, the network gave Pat and John an extra minute at its conclusion to express their feelings.

Summerall: "I can't tell you what a joy it's been to be with you all year."

Madden: "And thank you for putting up with all the goofy things I do."

Summerall: "Well, I hope the rest of the year continues to be as good for you, and may no trains pass you by."

When John Madden won his first Emmy in May 1982 for Outstanding Sports Personality (Event Analyst), among his acknowledgments in his acceptance speech was this: "Terry O'Neil came over and made something happen. I don't know what he knows about television, but he knows an awful lot about football."[17]

Humanity

Hal Trencher was the head of sports sales at CBS for the early years that Summerall and Madden were together. He had a different perspective on why the combination worked so well.

"The truth is, these guys were user friendly," Trencher said. "They valued and understood this was a commercial medium. They both embraced and initiated a sense of humanity. They were approachable, they were touchable. They were real.

"They weren't just doing a broadcast and then it was 'leave me alone, I'm going home.' There was a humanity to them. And that, in itself, was incredibly important in having them embraced in the marketplace. The clients not only thought they were good guys, but Pat and John really cared about them. They got acceptance before people asked, 'Who's the matchup?' Viewers said, 'Hey, I've got appointment TV with John and Pat because they come into my house every Sunday. They're my guys!' That's what breeds success, and they sure as shit had it!"[18]

One of the pieces of business that Summerall always took care of during the broadcasts was reading the promos for the upcoming network shows. In his early years working weekends for CBS, he taught middle school English in Lake City, so he particularly enjoyed reading the promo in 1984 for a new murder mystery series starring Angela Lansbury, *Murder, She Wrote*. And while reading it, Pat would always give an accentuated pause (reflecting the comma) after the word "Murder."

"Pat started the pause thing on his own," said broadcast associate Mike Frank. "So I started typing up the cue cards, and I would put in my own little gap. I'd write: 'Murder, comma, space, space, and then She Wrote.' Some weeks Pat would screw with us by using a big pause . . . some weeks a little pause. One week I didn't even include 'She Wrote' on the card. The next week he brings it up in the meeting, teasing us. This went on for years.

"In the January '87 playoff game where the Giants beat the Redskins, 17–0, Pat's reading the cue card and says it straight without a pause, 'Murder She Wrote,' then he adds, 'followed by Gone . . . long pause . . . with the Wind.' John drops the mic he's laughing so hard, and Pat was giggling."[19]

The series lasted 12 years, and Pat and John were already at Fox Sports when it ended. But the joy of doing those promos for the two of them was never forgotten.

Love, Respect, and Loyalty

> **Bob Stenner:** "They had different agendas. They had total respect for each other and knew the combination was going to work. They recognized they were different people. But when it came to Sunday and game preparations, I never heard a cross word between them. I never heard either of them talking behind the other's back. They were very happy with each other. They knew what they had. They just weren't asshole buddies. I don't know that they ever had a dinner together, just the two of them."[20]
>
> **Director Sandy Grossman:** "John knew that Pat always had his back."

Former broadcast associate **Mike Arnold** recalled Madden's generosity and loyalty: "When he hosted *Saturday Night Live*, he asked me if

I wanted two tickets to see the live broadcast. I said, 'Yeah, but don't you have somebody more important to give the tickets to?' And John said, 'No, I want you to have them. I want YOU to come.' That's the way he was."[21]

Sometime in the mid- to late '80s (no one recalls the exact year), CBS Sports was hosting its annual NFL seminar for broadcasters and production people in late July. The large meeting, with about 120 in attendance, was on the 19th floor of CBS's famous Black Rock headquarters building at 52nd Street and Sixth Avenue in Manhattan.

The previous May, John Madden had won either his third, or fourth, or maybe his fifth Sports Emmy Award. For the first time, John did not make the trip to New York for the ceremony, staying with his family in California.

One of the CBS Sports execs (maybe Ted Shaker) said, "Instead of wrapping it in a package and mailing it back to John in Pleasanton, let's give it to him at our NFL seminar in July." And that's exactly what happened. With everyone in attendance, Shaker started off the meeting saying a few nice words about the No. 1 broadcast team and then proceeded to call John up to receive his Emmy.

One of those in attendance that day was operations colleague Janis Delson.

> **Janis Delson:** "John was sitting in the back [like he always did in grade school]. He walked halfway to the front where Ted met him and handed him the statuette."
>
> **Ted Shaker:** "When I handed it to him, almost the entire room stood up and applauded. John was so loved by everyone in that room. It was heartwarming."
>
> **Delson:** "But then John did something that surprised us. He said, 'This doesn't belong to me. This should go to my partner.' And then he walked over and handed it to Pat."[22]

Among the many honors Summerall has had, including being named Sportscaster of the Year in 1977 by the National Sportscasters and Sportswriters Association and being inducted into its Hall of Fame, he also was the recipient of the prestigious Pete Rozelle Radio-Television Award from the Pro Football Hall of Fame in 1994, and he was inducted in 2010 into the Sports Broadcasting Hall of Fame. But in all his years as a broadcaster, Pat Summerall had never received an Emmy Award. That day, in the late '80s, on the 19th floor of Black Rock, John Madden corrected that mistake.

(In 1994, possibly realizing that Summerall may have had just a little something to do with all the Emmys Madden was winning, the National Academy of Television Arts & Sciences honored Pat with a Lifetime Achievement Award.)

In 1998, both Summerall and Madden were part of a small contingent from Fox Sports speaking at a charity dinner to raise $1 million to prevent birth defects. The event was at the Beverly Wilshire Hotel's ballroom—the same ballroom where Madden had his coming-out party 18 years earlier.

Both Pat and John were headlined on the program as speakers, and each indeed spoke at length—but mainly about their loyalty and friendship with each other. Summerall went first.

"This will be our 18th year together," he began. "I recall the first game we did together at Tampa, which was a very hard stadium to work from. We were high up, and it was hot, and he was sweating like I never saw anybody sweating in my life. I thought, 'This is the wrong business for this guy.' I soon realized he was sweating because of the height, and after a quarter, I thought, 'This guy is going to be pretty good.' I didn't know he was going to be THIS good!

"Over the years, I've learned when to duck [from his swinging arms]. I've learned to interpret the hieroglyphs he calls the Telestrator.... We've become very good friends. I think at the beginning, we were acquaintances, and out of the respect we developed for each other we've become closer—and in recent years, we've developed a friendship that we don't have to say too much about. It's just there, and I hope it always will be."[23]

And then Pat introduced John, saying, "He's the best there is. He's the best there ever was, and he's the best there ever will be."

Madden began by telling a story about broadcasting their first Super Bowl together in January 1982 in Detroit.

"I knew things were going to work out with Pat," said Madden. "The first Super Bowl we do, we were in Detroit. What you do [at the opening of a game broadcast], you have a stand up, and you have a hand mic and telex. You know you have the hand mic [fakes holding one] and you talk, talk, talk. Then you have to put down your hand mic and you go put on your headset to do the game. So I'm there, and Pat would do the hand mic and telex and he'd ask the last question and then they'd do a one-shot of me, and then Pat would go and put his headset on so he could announce the Super Bowl.

"I finish what I'm saying and I'm sitting there, and Pat doesn't have his headset on. So I'm looking, but you can't talk because you've got live mics. I can't say, 'Hey Pat, what's wrong with you?' So, I'm sittin' there and I'm looking at him and he's looking at me and it's the Super Bowl. There's no air. Finally, he starts pointing down below me. You know, I was saying that fat guys sweat, well, I was sitting on his headset. True story [he raises his hand up]. [The in-house camera takes a shot of Summerall standing in the wings, laughing.] So I realize I'm sitting on his headset, so I pull it out and hand it to him. He just takes it and puts it on and makes a few adjustments and says [in baritone], 'The San Francisco 49ers and Cincinnati Bengals,' etc., and they kick off. . . . [Madden is laughing.] So anyway, that's a friend, and that's a pro."[24]

The Things Madden Would Say

Once Madden knew he was the guy, the No. 1 analyst, and had a partner who made him feel like he always had a safety net to catch him, he became the John Madden we all grew to love. He felt free enough to say whatever came to mind, some of them classic Maddenisms. Here are a few examples:

When six Blue Angel jets flew low over the stadium: "Holy moly, they were close," Madden gasped. "I haven't been that close to a plane in 18 years."

When Dallas Cowboys lineman Larry Allen made an impressive block: "Watch what Larry Allen does to Atlanta's Cornelius Bennett. He knocks him clear out of the picture."

Having fun with the Telestrator, drawing around Dallas lineman Nate Newton's bald head: "You can see the heat escaping from his head. You can have a barbecue on that. Now you're talking. When you've got steam coming out of your head, now you're talking football."

Having fun with Troy Aikman's facial growth: "If that's all you've got after four days [of trying], I'd quit. If the going gets tough just quit."

On blimps: "Blimps—they always get to go to games. If I could come back in another life, I'd like to be either a blimp or a seagull."

"Nobody taught Madden how to be a broadcaster," said one former CBS executive. "Some people have taken partial credit, but John figured it out on his own. He brought with him phrasing from his coaching career." Former All-Pro Raiders linebacker Phil Villapiano once told Terry O'Neil, "I hear him [Madden] on Sundays, and this is the same shit I used to hear for years in team meetings."[25]

Camaraderie

In an attempt to increase the camaraderie between the talent, the producers, and the crew, O'Neil initiated a four-team touch football series during the '84 playoffs. The touch games were played on a local field in Fullerton, California, prior to the Giants-Rams wild-card game. The four captains were Madden, O'Neil, Summerall, and director Sandy Grossman.

Broadcast associates were assigned to arrange for a playing field and whatever else was possible to make it fun. In '85, broadcast associate Mike Frank rented a park from the city of Chicago, hired a referee, arranged for color-coded uniforms, and even got the Chicago Bears' Honey Bear cheerleaders to cheer at the game.

"My team won the first tournament," O'Neil later recalled. "Cameramen and tape operators on my team trash-talked John for a year

Terry O'Neil celebrating his touch-football victory over Madden's team in the Chicago snow. COURTESY OF JOAN VITRANO PAPEN

about it. Pissed John off. For much of the '85 season, he talked about a rematch. He was very competitive in the rematch. For John, he looked and sounded like he was playing the Vikings in Super Bowl XI."

Cameraman George "Hulk" Rothweiler recalled just how competitive Madden was for that rematch:

"I was on John's team against Terry, and Terry shows up in this one-piece jumpsuit. We thought, 'What a hot dog.' They knew me as 'Hulk' because I worked in the weight room. 'Hulk' stuck."

Madden: "Hulk, on this kickoff you come down and you kick Terry's ass."
Hulk: "John, really?"
Madden: "Yeah, you get him. I want you to nail him."

What Made Them Great

Madden bundled up with producer Chuck Milton on the left and broadcast associate Mike Arnold between them. COURTESY OF JOAN VITRANO PAPEN

"The kickoff comes, and Terry comes up to me and I nail him, flat on his ass. He's lying in the snow, his glasses are twisted, he looks up at me and says, 'You mother fucker.'

"The next morning, Terry pulls up with Pat and Sandy. He says, 'Hulk, my man, I want to apologize for what I said to you yesterday.' It made me feel like he didn't take it personally. He could have been pissed off all day, but he took the hit, the next morning apologized, and off we went. I never lost respect for that man because of that.

"Because they [John and Terry] were now closer with the crew, we did more things than in previous championship games. We got together more, we had barbecues, it was fun. Everybody was invested."[26]

Madden's team wound up winning the '85 game, which gave John a chance to return some of the trash talk he had taken from O'Neil's team the past 12 months. In the semifinals, Summerall, who was 55, pulled a hamstring and gimped his way to the booth that Sunday.

Chapter Ten

THE TRAIN, THE BUS, THE GAME, THE ALL-MADDEN TEAM, AND THE MATCHMAKER

In 2019, Syracuse University's well-known sports communications school, S. I. Newhouse, presented agent Sandy Montag with its annual Marty Glickman[1] Award for leadership in sports media. The funny thing was that Montag, who idolized Marv Albert and wanted to be a broadcaster himself, couldn't get into the Newhouse program when he was at Syracuse. If he had, he might never have taken the incredibly successful path that he has since graduating in 1985.

As an undergrad, Montag started his sports management path by doing stats for ESPN and CBS Sports. "I told my dad, 'This is unbelievable. I get to sit on the front row next to two great announcers. All I have to do is give them points and rebounds, and they pay me 50 dollars!'"

When Montag found out he could get two jobs per weekend if he was willing to travel, he took a part-time job as a reservationist with People's Express, a low-budget airline at the time, just so he could get free travel. When he graduated, CBS needed someone both knowledgeable and reliable to travel with John Madden on the train. Montag fit the bill. It turned out that CBS and Madden's agency, International Management Group (IMG), were both paying Montag's salary. In the off-season, he worked in the IMG offices and began learning how to be an agent.

"Anything that came in for John," said Montag, "they threw my way. In the '80s there was no degree available in representation. My degree was from Mark McCormack and Barry Frank, which I earned by sitting on their couch and listening to them negotiate deals."[2]

Madden's traveling by train, due to his claustrophobia, became well known. It was the type of story *Sports Illustrated* liked. In the fall of 1980, they assigned Ray Kennedy to travel with Madden and report. Here's what Madden told him:

"There aren't too many big fat redheaded guys around like me. But you meet some great people on trains, and I enjoy talking football with them because it gives me a chance to find out what people want to hear from an announcer. I know one phrase they won't hear from me—'skill positions.' What are the poor slobs who block? Unskilled? I've always wanted to slow down and, like Steinbeck says in *Travels with Charley*, 'get to see and know our land.' And now I'm doing it. There isn't a train I wouldn't take. No matter where it's going. I don't know what state we're in, what time it is, or even what day it is. Give me a train any day."

Traveling with Madden by train was "peaceful," Montag said, mainly because there was no internet in the '80s and no cell phones to interrupt. But it took 72 hours to go coast to coast, and Amtrak often missed Madden's Chicago connection to the West Coast, forcing them to wait an entire day until the next one.

Once CBS scheduled Madden to do a billiards event midweek somewhere in the Midwest, but there was no train that could get him there in time. Madden meeting "Minnesota Fats" seemed like a natural. Instead, producer Terry O'Neil arranged to rent Dolly Parton's tour bus, and Madden never wanted to look back. John told Montag, "We've got to get ourselves one of these."

Shortly afterward, Madden did an interview for PBS that was broadcast as part of *The MacNeil/Lehrer Report*. The president of Greyhound Bus Lines saw it and called IMG wanting to make a deal. Montag worked out the details.

"They gave us the bus free," said Montag, "plus revolving drivers, and John got to keep the bus. All he had to do in return was make a few speeches at Greyhound depots whenever he'd arrive at a city for a game. He'd shake some hands, make a little speech, and that was it. I even went to Columbus, Ohio, to supervise the customization of the first Madden

The Train, the Bus, the Game, the All-Madden Team, and the Matchmaker

Sandy Montag (center) circa 1984, when Montag was an assistant for Pat and John. Sandy later became the agent for them both. COURTESY OF SANDY MONTAG

Cruiser for John. It had a bedroom, a workspace, a TV, and a three-quarter-inch tape machine so he could watch game film on the road.

"It changed his life. He could leave whenever he wanted to, and it no longer took 72 hours to go across the country. It just took 50. And he could go directly from New York to Dallas without having to get off the train in Meridian, Mississippi, and then driving 10 hours. At the game sites, I used to have to rent vans for the crew to meet John at the team practices. Now everyone traveled there in the bus."[3]

Madden always kept the temperature in the bus at 59 degrees. And he had these rules: Don't wait for anyone, finish any bottle of water you start, drink right out of the bottle, and never take I-80 in or out of New York.

A decade after Ray Kennedy's *Sports Illustrated* article on Madden's travels by train, the magazine sent Peter King to go cross-country with John on the Madden Cruiser.

"John Madden, 54, has a job most of us would love to have," King began. "He sleeps as late as he wants, and he wears whatever clothes he wants, almost every day of his life. He has to be somewhere with a tie on for only three hours a week. To do this job he criss-crosses the United States six months a year in the greatest bus you've ever seen.

"'What I've learned traveling around is this,' Madden told King. 'People are nice. You go to a big city, and you hear the world is going to hell, but it's not true. Small parts of it are. The whole isn't. You get out there and it makes you feel better about America. The thing works. . . .

"'If the claustrophobia thing didn't happen, I wouldn't know what this country is, or what these people are like. I would have been like everybody else: run, run, run. Airport, airport, airport. Hotel, hotel, hotel. City, city, city. I wouldn't have found time to see things like I see them now.

"'Sometimes I just like to break up the trip, and Omaha's kind of halfway. So, I stayed in Omaha one night, and we went to see the minor league baseball team play. Anyway, they have a raffle for a case of pork and beans. It's the seventh inning, and everybody's excited. They pick the winner, and the guy's sitting right behind home plate. His name is Elmer something, and he's jumping up and down. To him, it was like a trip to Hawaii or a new car or something. It was just a case of pork and beans. That was great.'"[4]

That first bus in 1987 was the first of five Madden Cruisers and is now at the Pro Football Hall of Fame in Canton, Ohio. After the Greyhound deal, other offers started coming in. One of them was for a football video game from a Harvard grad named Trip Hawkins, who later created Electronic Arts and EA Sports. He tried to get Joe Montana to put his name on it first, but Montana was already committed.

"He came on the train in '85 to pitch the game," said Montag. "John gave him the Raiders playbook, but it seemed like nothing really happened. They said they could do a 7-on-7 game. John strongly objected,"

Madden: "What happened to the other four?"

Hawkins: "Well, they're linemen."

The Train, the Bus, the Game, the All-Madden Team, and the Matchmaker

Madden: "You're talking to an offensive lineman. I'm not putting my name on any game unless it's 11-on-11."

"There were production problems," said Montag. "We never thought it would happen." Neither did the software guys working on it at EA. Privately they called it "Trip's Folly."

But by 1990, technology was such that EA was able to make it into a video game, and it took off. There have been over 130 million copies sold worldwide. In exchange for his name and strategy, Madden received a licensing deal to pay him a residual for every game that was sold. When the stock (symbol EA) went public, EA offered John 10,000 shares at the initial public offering (IPO) price of $6 a share.

"John thought he had done enough and didn't want to invest any money," said Montag. "We really didn't understand what an IPO was. ... The stock went to something like $200 [a share], and [passing on the IPO] cost us a few million. He still made more money through the video game than on anything else. Now the game is part of John's legacy. People know him three ways: as a coach, a broadcaster, or the video game guy."[5]

Madden NFL, the game, has become so influential that according to *The Athletic*, the New York Jets are now using Madden player ratings to determine trades. On December 19, 2024, *The Athletic* reported that the Jets nixed a trade for Denver wide receiver Jerry Jeudy because owner Woody Johnson's 18-year-old son, Brick, said Jeudy's Madden rating wasn't high enough. *The Athletic* wrote that Brick's influence is so prevalent in the locker room that former Jets general manager Joe Douglas said at the beginning of the 2024 season, "I take orders from a teenager."

In the '90s, Madden and Michael Jordan were the two biggest names in sports advertising. Jordan had Nike and Gatorade, and Madden had Ace Hardware, Tinactin, Outback Steakhouse, and Miller Lite. "We only got involved if it fit his brand," said Montag. "For Ace [whose slogan then was 'Ace is the place with the Helpful Hardware Man'], John would look for the 'helpful' guy. John wasn't handy. Virginia was, but John couldn't hang a picture. He was with Ace for a decade. It was true to his character. It was an important deal—it made him the everyman."

John's Favorite Food Stops

To understand John's food preferences, you need to know how much Madden loved to eat all kinds of food. "John is a lineman," Matt Millen began on the *All Madden* documentary. "You can tell by the shirts he wears what he had for breakfast, lunch, and dinner."

When John Madden's boyhood pal John Robinson would ride the bus, Robinson always wanted to stop at great restaurants with tablecloths and three-star ratings. Not so much Madden, who preferred diners and dives.

Lesley Visser wrote about one of John's favorite food stops, somewhere in West Texas, in a column for SportsBroadcastJournal.com.

"It was the kind of education you got on the Madden Cruiser, completely unexpected," Visser wrote. "I-20 hooked up to I-10 in a desolate stretch of West Texas near Kent, and we traveled quietly until we hit Van Horn, the site of John's favorite restaurant.

"Many people have heard about Chuy's in Van Horn. More than 120 miles from El Paso, in a dusty town of 1,800 people, the cantina founded in 1959 is now a must-see destination because it's the official Madden Hall of Fame. There's a John Madden room with a John Madden table and a huge John Madden chair. It was just what I had imagined—dark green plastic tablecloths, family recipe enchiladas, and people who really do say 'Howdy.'"

Visser had the opportunity to ride cross-country with John's crew and gave readers a firsthand feel for what it was like:

"The Madden Cruiser was set up for his comfort," she wrote. "Plasma TVs, bowls of M&M's, computers, a shower, and a bedroom in the back. My memory was that the temperature was always set at about 15 degrees, but no one was allowed to complain, even when my teeth were chattering. John once said that he didn't think anyone should run for President if he or she hadn't traveled the country on the ground. 'How the hell can you know America,' he said, 'if you've only seen the big cities? And you can't drive, you have to ride—so you can see it.'"[6]

Stopping for the Stubbs sandwich was a must for the Madden Cruiser as it was leaving Dallas. CBS's Janis Delson got to experience that once, recalling:

"There was some greasy food stand somewhere in Texas that they used to stop at if they were making a cross-country trip. They made these disgusting sandwiches—greasy cheap meat, processed cheese, onions, peppers, half a shaker of salt. The thing had about 5,000 calories. But John wanted it. We sent one to the nutrition department at the Mayo Clinic."[7]

The Stubbs was introduced to John by former Cowboys quarterback Troy Aikman, who over the years became close with Madden. Their friendship began during pregame production meetings when John would talk with the coaches and key players.

"I brought Pat and John their first Stubbs sandwich for a production meeting one year," Aikman emailed. "John loved it! He would get them every time he came to Dallas, and PR director of the Cowboys at the time, Rich Dalrymple, would pack several in an Igloo cooler and take them to him even when we were playing on the road, if John and Pat were covering our game. John made the Stubbs the official sandwich of the All-Madden Team, and he began serving them at his place in Carmel [California]."[8]

The Stubbs is named for former Dallas Cowboys lineman Danny Stubbs, who started a trend of Cowboy players eating it at the Coppell Deli outside of Dallas. In 2012, *The Dallas Observer* reviewed the sandwich, with the headline "The Stubbs Breakfast Sandwich Might Kill You, but What a Way to Go." It described the contents this way: "Wrapped in parchment paper, it felt like a book. I grabbed a seat and unwrapped my gift. The Stubbs special is a behemoth: an inch-thick layer of straight scrambled eggs, a sausage patty bigger than a hockey puck, too many bacon strips to count, and a slice of cheese slipped in to round it out, all book-ended by white toast, which I'm going to assume they toasted in bacon fat (why not?). It's super savory, greasy, and exactly what you want if you know what you're getting yourself into. The sandwich is so packed with meat that it's hard to even get your jaw around it."[9]

Madden's favorite stop was Chicago. CBS's Delson said Madden had his own favorite Mexican restaurant there:

"He spent many weeks between games at the Ritz-Carlton in Chicago if he was doing two games in the Midwest and didn't want to make a trip to either New York or the West Coast. Everyone else on the crew went home. A couple of times, Montag and I stayed in Chicago for a couple of days during these weeklong stays. He had a favorite Mexican joint that he visited that was two blocks from the Ritz. He said the food was terrific because the cops always ate there. That was news to me because I never heard of any police force that moonlighted as restaurant reviewers, and I wouldn't take the word of a cop when it came to culinary ratings.

"This place was quite below the standards we were used to. But he insisted it was fine, and he insisted on the joint every time he was in the Windy City. Odd, because he wanted the finest hotels, but the down and dirty restaurants were one of life's pleasures for him. He had a similar place in New York on Columbus Avenue, along with its Chinese cousin that was just as elegant. The noodles and dumplings were so oily you could see your reflection if you looked in the bowl. And he always over-ordered and we took the leftovers to the homeless people that would hang out on the benches near 72nd Street.

"He did have a few better places scattered across the country . . . ones that had tablecloths, stemmed glasses, and votives on the tables. They included Sambuca on West 72nd Street [across from The Dakota], Morton's in DC, The Palm in LA and in Denver, a couple of nicer Mexican cantinas in Dallas. When meals were on the weekends [company business time], he always let Stenner or me get the checks [we had the expense accounts], but if something was personal, like in New York on a Tuesday evening just gathering people to hang with him, he would always grab the check. He was most generous in that way.

"Decorum was important in restaurants for John. Tables had to be large and not too close together. If there was a place that had a semi-private room or area, that won him over. Needless to say, portions had to be plentiful. And drinking glasses had to have a large rim because he claimed if he drank from a smaller glass it would bump up against his nose."[10]

The Train, the Bus, the Game, the All-Madden Team, and the Matchmaker

Mike Arnold was one of the broadcast associates Terry O'Neil hired in 1982, after he was turned down the previous year by ABC Sports. "I was crushed when ABC didn't hire me," said Arnold. "I always thought it was because I didn't go to an Ivy League school." He graduated from Arizona State. Living just two blocks from Madden on Manhattan's West Side, Arnold spent a lot of time with him.

"John loved to go to [the restaurant] Sambuca and diagram plays on the paper tablecloth. He also loved the deli Fine and Shapiro a block away. He knew all the waitresses by name, and when he walked in, Mary would say, 'Hey John, want the usual?' And she'd bring it out."

"We did a Redskins playoff game, probably in '83," Arnold recalled, "and when we got to the hotel, they hand John a note from Ethel Kennedy [the widow of former attorney general and presidential candidate Robert F. Kennedy]. The note read: 'Dear John, we are big fans of yours. We'd love to have dinner sometime this weekend. Please get in touch. Signed, Ethel Kennedy.'"

> **Arnold:** "Wow, John! Are you going to have dinner with Ethel Kennedy?"
> **Madden:** "Nahhh. I'd rather have dinner with you guys."

"That's the way he was," Arnold concluded, "but I don't know how he turned her down."[11]

CBS associate director Joan Vitrano lived in Manhattan not far from John. "I lived in New York when he had his place at The Dakota," she said. "One night with Richie Zyontz we went on a pizza and egg cream tour. He heard about the egg cream [New York was famous for], and we went to the Upper East Side, and we finally found a small little candy store that had egg creams. But that wasn't good enough for John. Then he wanted to find a stoop so he could drink his New York egg cream like a real New Yorker on a stoop. He wanted the FULL experience."[12]

The Turducken

Madden made Thanksgiving special for the CBS crew. Celebrating Thanksgiving became a wonderful tradition, with families joining in.

"It evolved that we all had it together," said Vitrano. "It was really important that we had our families with us. There were speeches; there were thank-yous. Even the referees came."[13]

"In 1997, Fox was doing the Thanksgiving Day game in Dallas," Delson recalled. "Two days prior, there was an article in *The Wall Street Journal* about this place in Louisiana that made a Thanksgiving dish that was called turducken.

"It had a top layer that was the turkey, the middle layer was the duck, and the bottom layer was the chicken. The dish was heavily spiced, heavily salted, and heavily oiled. It was a long way from a spa meal of white meat turkey cooked in lemon juice.

"Well, sure enough, on game day a turducken showed up in the announce booth. John went gaga over it. It was the perfect Madden dish. The place where we got it from was called the Gourmet Butcher Block located in Gretna, Louisiana. They still call themselves the home of the All-Madden turducken. I believe it sells for $200 . . . not including the Rolaids.

"And so, yearly, a turducken made a trip to wherever they were doing the game. John loved most foods that were spicy and rich and filling. Turducken has now caught on and is available all over the country at just about every food outlet. But back, almost 30 years ago, it was a novelty."[14]

The All-Madden Team

Broadcast associate Mike Arnold (now CBS's top director) was there when the idea for an All-Madden Team was created.

Madden's boyhood pal John Robinson was coaching the Los Angeles Rams in '84. He would meet Madden whenever possible. One day Robinson was sitting around with Madden, Terry O'Neil, and John's agent, Sandy Montag, before a late-season game. They started talking about Madden's favorite players—one of them was Rams offensive lineman Bill Bain.

Madden: "He has a bad body. Stuff hanging out everywhere."

Robinson (to O'Neil and Montag): "You should get a list of these guys that John likes and put them together in an All-Madden Team."

(Everybody laughed, but a few days later O'Neil called Madden.)
O'Neil: "We need your picks for the All-Madden Team."
Madden: "What?"
O'Neil: "Yeah. You're going to announce the team on *CBS Sports Saturday* in a few weeks."
Madden: "What do the players get for being on the team?"
O'Neil: "Let's give them a statuette, like the Oscars."
Madden: "What will it look like?"
O'Neil: "Why don't you design it?"

Madden told O'Neil that it should be a player in a cold-weather cape. He said the player should not appear to be black or white but should be a blend, somebody like Anthony Muñoz of the Chargers. Madden and Arnold went through a few designs with a sculptor until they arrived at a player in a cape who looked like Muñoz.[15]

Mike Arnold: "There was a producer assigned to put together the All-Madden Team the first year. When he saw the photo array for the players chosen, Madden called O'Neil and said, 'I hate it, I hate the show.' The producer put Jack Youngblood in an all-white uniform making a play on AstroTurf. O'Neil called and asked me to find out what he's upset about. I called John."
Madden: "I see Youngblood in a clean white uniform. I want guys who are bloody and covered with dirt and blood on the uniform and sweat. This guy doesn't look tough."

"So basically I re-edited it," said Arnold, "and replaced the Youngblood photo with another photo of him. And John said, 'That's what I'm looking for!'"

The following year Madden made the turducken the official Thanksgiving meal for the All-Madden Team. "In 1997, we made and sold 250 Turduckens," said its creator, Glenn Mistich. "But when John made it the official turkey for the All-Madden Team, we went from 250 sold to 6,000 the following year."[16]

If you made the All-Madden Team, you got a statue in the first few years and later this plaque in commemoration. COURTESY OF MIKE ARNOLD

"Just to show how loyal John was," Arnold said, "when he went to Fox and I was still with CBS, Madden made sure I was involved in the All-Madden Team when it was at Fox and that I got paid a salary.

"I had an idea for the show that everybody who was on the All-Madden Team was going to have a dance when they found out they were on it. The end of it was going to be MC Hammer [himself] trying to teach Jerry Rice a touchdown dance. We were shooting the stand-ups with Pat and John before we had edited in the dance part. I knew how it was ending, so I asked Pat and John to play off it and react like it's funny, but I couldn't get them to laugh. So finally I said, '3, 2, 1, go,' and I made a lewd gesture and that got them to laugh. They never let me forget it."[17]

MADDEN THE MATCHMAKER

After working for security at CBS his first year out of college, Richie Zyontz was one of the broadcast associates hired at CBS Sports under Terry O'Neil in 1981.

"I don't remember Terry O'Neil fondly," Zyontz said. "John [Madden] definitely respected Terry, but Terry had that way of managing up. CBS in the early '70s was kind of like a country club, Bob Stenner would tell me. And then O'Neil came in and gave it that ABC swagger. He bullied people.

The Train, the Bus, the Game, the All-Madden Team, and the Matchmaker

"I did some games with John that first year ['81]. In 1982, I became his broadcast associate. He took a shine to me because I was just a New York kid, a street kid, who was honest and had no airs, and loved sports. We became fast friends."

They traveled the train in '82, which was before the bus. If Madden had a game in Dallas, they would take the train from New York to Meridian, Mississippi, and then drive 10 hours to Dallas. Amtrak didn't go any farther south then. Despite the 22-year age difference, they enjoyed being together.

"So, I was the BA-slash-friend, and he got the place at The Dakota, and I'd spend time with him on the West Side [of Manhattan]. I lived near The Dakota, so we'd go for a cannoli, we'd go to the Kosher deli on West 72nd Street—the whole culture thing. I'd teach him New York and he just loved to laugh, and with John the big thing was you had to bring something to the table. He took to me, and I was in awe of him. We just became really good friends and stayed that way until the day he died. I was more like a friend and a confidante, and he trusted my judgment."[18]

Now, the last person in the world that you'd think would play the role of Cupid was John Madden. But that's what happened a few years later. Janis Delson was a witness to how it began.

"I would say that Richie was probably the closest thing to a best friend for John," said Delson. "John took to hanging with a lot of the younger guys. There was something special about the Zyontz/Madden relationship.

"One day, back in the end of 1985, Madden was sitting in his office, Red Bear Productions, out in Pleasanton, California. It was during the week. He was talking on the phone to Richie Zyontz, who was in the CBS Sports office at Black Rock in New York. It was a typical midweek, 'check in and talk about the state of the world' call that Richie and John had frequently, both during the football season and in the off months. John had set up an office and small sound and production studio in Pleasanton to do some recordings and other production work. Lo and behold, while John was on the phone with Richie, one afternoon, in walks a lovely young lady named June Cervantes who was working on a real-estate property with one of John's buddies. John takes a look at June and says to her, 'You look a lot like the guy on the other end of this phone.' I guess there was a little back-and-forth, and eventually John hands the phone to June and they begin talking."

A few months later on another visit to the realtor friend, John mentioned to June that Richie was coming to town for a preseason game they were broadcasting, and she should meet Richie then. She did, and after the game Madden peppered her with questions about how it went.

Madden: "Hey, June, so how did it go with Richie?"

June: "It was terrible. He kept running to the pay phone to check the Mets score."

Madden: "What a schmuck, but give it a second try."

June: "I'll have to think about it."

Madden: "I'll talk to him."[19]

They hung up and June actually called Zyontz to relay that John said to give it a second try. And she did several days later.

"This was truly a different side of John," said Zyontz. "He was Madden the Matchmaker! He'd never get into the Matchmakers Hall of Fame."

But Richie and June kept dating, and she'd meet him at game sites all over the country. Fast-forward a couple of years: After trying New York, they relocated to the East Bay, a mile away from John and Virginia in Danville, California.

"John was the only one I knew in Danville," said Zyontz. "I spent a lot of time hanging out with John and Virginia, so when it came time to plan our wedding, John said, 'Why don't you just have it here?' So we had the wedding at John's house. John was my best man. There were about 30 people at the wedding. My family flew out there. At the time my dad was dying from cancer, and John was particularly kind to him. The wedding took place in his backyard, and John was attentive. It was a different side of Madden. A tender side.

"Janis Delson flew out, and so did some of my buddies. It was just such a wonderful thing the way they opened their home to us. He had a game room where I was playing pinball with John Madden on my wedding day."[20]

Madden hosted Richie Zyontz's wedding at his home in Pleasanton. Below, Virginia helps John with his tie.
COURTESY OF JUNE AND RICHIE ZYONTZ

The Zyontz wedding party. COURTESY OF JUNE AND RICHIE ZYONTZ

CHAPTER ELEVEN

DISASTER

How CBS Lost the NFL Contract

YOU COULDN'T REALLY BLAME NEAL PILSON FOR GETTING GREEDY. He had been at CBS Sports since 1976, and for most of that time all he heard was how wise, wonderful, and dominant ABC Sports had been. To the news media, Roone Arledge was a god. And the theme of ABC's *Wide World of Sports*, "The thrill of victory and the agony of defeat," was always on Pilson's mind.

In 1988, Pilson was president of CBS Sports, and he was in a position to do something about it. Larry Tisch, who made his money with the Loews Hotels chain, was the new owner of CBS, and Pilson had his ear. For once, ABC Sports was in a downward spiral, with Arledge now only running ABC News. NBC didn't appear to be competition, either, for the big sports properties that were about to hit the auction block. Pilson was licking his lips.

The first of those properties was Major League Baseball. Pilson wanted it. He thought its playoffs and World Series could help prop up CBS's sagging entertainment shows. Losing baseball was a crushing loss for NBC, which had it for years. Making money wasn't Pilson's top priority. But was losing $400 million on the package worth any promotion they would get out of it? At least that's what NBC and ABC suggested when CBS paid $1.1 billion for six years, or as *Time* magazine put it, "Is any baseball game worth $1 million an inning?"[1]

Sports Illustrated described Pilson as a "steady, abstemious, bespectacled 50-year-old with a Yale Law degree and a pharmacist's name." He bitterly resented the accusations his competitors made.

"There's a campaign of disinformation," Pilson said. "I just don't believe we were that far apart. Larry Tisch is not a plunger; he's a sound investor."

Pilson compared the MLB package to milk in a grocery store. "You don't judge baseball just by whether you're losing money or making money on it," he said. "In a supermarket, they put the milk in the back so the customer will have to go past everything in the store to buy milk, and in an airport newsstand, they put the newspapers at the back for the same reason. Now you don't ask a man whether he's losing money on milk or newspapers, because making money isn't the point of these products. On CBS, baseball is our milk and newspapers. There is so much exposure because of it. There is leverage on the affiliates because of it, and our stockholders and Wall Street are all happy because we have it."[2]

Not happy enough, apparently. Less than a year later the Associated Press reported that CBS was trying to claw back $100 million of its baseball deal. The headline of *The Los Angeles Times* on December 4, 1990, read: "CBS Wants Some of Its Money Back after Taking a Bath on Baseball Deal."

The next move for CBS would be a decision about its NBA package. CBS owned it cheap before Larry Bird and Magic Johnson restored the NBA to popularity beginning in 1979. Now Michael Jordan was becoming a huge star. Surely CBS would want to hitch its star to Jordan.

Not so much. By '89, Dick Ebersol was running NBC Sports, and he hired former ABC and CBS producer Terry O'Neil, who suggested that NBC could outbid CBS for the NBA because Tisch no longer trusted Pilson. NBC was able to get the four-year deal for $600 million. Pilson's reason for not bidding more: the NBA playoffs were in late May and June, after the sweeps ratings were already in. (Ratings are measured in February, May, and November and are called "sweeps" by the networks, who can then charge advertisers prices based on those results until the next ratings period.)

Disaster

"The NBC deal for the NBA closed November 9, 1989, for 40 percent less than the baseball deal," said a former NBC executive interviewed for this book who wished to be anonymous. "So CBS had 11 months of misery with baseball in the marketplace, leading to their choke on the NBA. CBS had Michael Jordan on its air beginning in 1984, but did the network know where Jordan and the Bulls were headed? Jordan debuted on NBC in the 1990–91 season. From 1991 through 1998, he won six NBA titles, was Finals MVP all six times, and was easily the most watchable athlete on television. So, not only did Pilson and his team not know the TV business, but they also didn't know anything about sports either."

Pilson continued his spending spree with a seven-year, $1 billion purchase of the NCAA basketball tournament, $543 million in total for the 1992 and '94 Winter Olympics in Albertville and Lillehammer, and a little over $1 billion for the 1990–93 NFC contract renewal (including the '92 Super Bowl).

Bidding that high for a Winter Olympics in European time zones made no sense. By the time CBS broadcast the events at night, ESPN's *SportsCenter* would have announced all the key winners. It wasn't like doing the 1980 games from Lake Placid in New York in the Eastern Standard time zone.

NBC Sports president Arthur Watson said of CBS's spending spree, "They've got to be out of their minds."[3] Pilson disagreed: "We're in as dominant a position as a sports network as anyone has ever been," he said. "There has never been a period when there were so many properties for sale that all had to be negotiated in such a brief time [December 1988 to March 1990]. We won a few and we lost a few, but we got everything we really wanted."

In response to Pilson's last comment, *Sports Illustrated* editorialized: "At enormous risk, he might have added. The future of CBS may be at stake in this decision."[4]

SI was right. The future of CBS was at stake, and it was about to turn ugly when the NFL began negotiating its next four-year contract for CBS's NFC package. Pilson, who by now looked like a mad bidder on

The Price Is Right, had lost the confidence of the man writing the checks, Larry Tisch.

After losing as much as $100 million in the first year of the baseball deal, Tisch didn't want to hear any more milk comparisons. He wasn't willing to lose a dime on anything they bought from that point forward.[5] Which was bad news for Pilson and CBS, and great news for Rupert Murdoch and Fox.

Murdoch was trying to build a network with Fox, which was established in 1986. It had 85 percent of its affiliates located on the hard-to-find UHF stations—from channel 14 to 83. In December 1992 when Fox submitted its bid to the NFL, it was a network of only 139 affiliates, 120 of which were on the UHF bandwidth. That compared to at least 200 affiliates each that the three major networks had.[6]

If Murdoch could capture the NFC contract (with teams in major cities like New York, Philadelphia, Chicago, Dallas, Los Angeles, San Francisco, and Detroit), it would mean that CBS affiliates would flock to Fox. The growth of Murdoch's Fox network had stalled, and he was shrewd enough to know that capturing the NFL contract would give it a huge boost. While Tisch was saying, "No way am I going to lose money on the NFL," Murdoch certainly was willing to. He looked at it as an investment in the network he was building, not a yearly dollar-and-cents proposition. In other words, the contract was worth way more to Murdoch than to anyone else.

And now new team owners, like Jerry Jones in Dallas, were taking charge of the negotiations, which meant Pilson's old relationships with owners like Cleveland's Art Modell, had little impact. CBS had paid $265 million for the final year of its current NFC deal, but because of a poor economic advertising market in 1991 and '92, all the networks lost money that year, and Tisch said he wouldn't pay more than $250 million a year going forward. All Tisch wanted to know was how CBS was going to make money on the deal. Pilson was in a bind.

In the early 1990s, shortly after Jerry Jones paid $140 million to purchase the Dallas Cowboys in 1989, the networks asked the NFL for a several-year reduction in their contracts. Jones was not about to let that happen.

"I couldn't afford that," Jones said when contacted for this book. "I was all in when I bought the Cowboys, and we had negative cash flow that first year. I couldn't afford a reduced price. I got together with five or six other owners, and we killed that deal. That's when Commissioner [Paul] Tagliabue asked me to be on the television committee."[7]

Murdoch's top sports executive, David Hill, promised the NFL 12 cameras for big games (versus the 1993 standard of seven that CBS and NBC used) and a much greater emphasis on the sounds of the NFL. Jones and the other new owners were impressed. "I was just mesmerized by their thinking," Jones said, according to The Ringer, a sports website created by former ESPN talent Bill Simmons.

"When Mr. Murdoch called," Jones recalled, "he said, 'If we [Fox] come to you with a substantially higher offer, would you consider it? We don't want to be a stalking horse again.' I said I had burned all my boats when I bought the Cowboys, and I had no way to get home, that of course we'd consider his offer."

Fox's initial bid was $300 million per year. CBS never imagined that Fox might go even higher. That's why Pilson thought a CBS bid of $295 million per year would win it, thinking that with such a small difference in bids, the NFL would stay loyal to CBS, which had broadcast the NFL for 38 years.

"Neal told the story late in the season, that [NFL commissioner Paul] Tagliabue came to the studio for his annual visit," a fellow CBS executive related. "He'd bring his wife and shake everybody's hand. Neal pulled him aside and asked, 'What's the number so I can go to Larry [Tisch] and get this done?' Tagliabue said he never gave Neal a definitive number. Neal said he was told 295. That was when CBS's number was 250. So Neal thinks that 295 gets it, but he didn't realize that with the new sheriff in town, no specific number was going to be a done deal with Jerry Jones."

Final bids were due that night. CBS president Howard Stringer was hosting a Christmas party at his Manhattan townhouse. Pilson thought $295 million per year would win it, but how could they convince Tisch? Former CBS president Peter Lund was now the network's executive vice president, with Pilson reporting to him. Here's how Lund remembered that night:

"At the end of the day, Larry wasn't willing to match Fox's offer," Lund began. "The pro forma looked like we'd lose money at least the beginning years of a new contract if we paid much more.

"Even when [NFL executive] Neil Austrian said Fox is now bidding, we couldn't get authority [from Tisch] to get a higher number [to make a bid]. The baseball deal had been a disaster for CBS. Larry was not a believer in pro forma projections from anybody [because] Larry had been burned by the sports deals. I was with Commissioner Paul Tagliabue at the St. Regis [Hotel], and he said, 'We're going to hear from Fox today or tonight.' We had the right of first refusal, so I wasn't panicked.

"They asked where I was going to be that night. I told him at a Christmas party at [CBS president] Howard Stringer's townhouse. No cell phones in those days, and they asked for the phone number of the townhouse. Everybody's there. That night, somebody says, 'There's a phone call for you.' So I go into the kitchen—I'll never forget it—the phone was hanging on the wall in the breakfast nook. I get on with [NFL executive] Neil Austrian."

Austrian: "Are you sitting down?"

Lund: "No, but I can lean against the wall."

Austrian: "That's a good idea because we got the number from Fox. Fox is offering $405 million a year for four years [$1.6 billion]."

Lund: "You're kidding?"

Austrian: "No."

Lund: "You're kidding."

Austrian: "We couldn't believe it either."

Lund: "Well, they're going to lose a fortune on that."

Austrian: "That's what we think, too."

"We all gather in Howard Stringer's bedroom, and I had the pleasure of telling everybody their number. Everybody's horrified except Larry. Larry says, 'The heck with them.' Howard especially is crushed because he's running the Broadcast Group. We all said, Larry, we can't do this; we need to keep the NFL. Larry basically said, 'Not gonna happen.'

"That was it. We could have offered 406 and kept it, but Larry wanted no part of it. We left and regrouped in the morning. We walked over to [NFL headquarters at] 410 Park Avenue to meet with Tagliabue and Austrian and handed them our letter. We said we'd like to bid on [NBC's] AFC package. And they said, 'It's too late. That deal has closed.'"[8]

Here's how people close to the negotiation reacted:

Pilson: "Nobody really had the balls or the instinct to say to Larry, 'We really should match that offer.' Which we had the right to do."

Steve Bornstein, ESPN president: "When the league took that package from CBS and Tisch and sent it to Rupert at Fox, it changed the dynamic for the next 30 years. In the past, the broadcaster had to always maintain a profit on all the content that you were buying from the NFL, the NBA, or Major League Baseball. Now you could rationalize that that's how you build a network."

Jay Rosenstein, who was the programming chief at CBS Sports in 1993, saw the big picture: "The kicker to the whole story is that four years later, when CBS had new management—Tisch was gone—we paid $500 million a year for the weaker [AFC] package. Four years later."[9]

"The real failure was," said a former CBS executive, "instead of telling Tisch what it would cost him to buy it, Pilson and Rosenstein and Lund should have had the foresight to say, 'Here's what it will cost you NOT to have the property. Here's what it will cost you if Rupert Murdoch can build a network on this acquisition.' The affiliates that had been loyal to CBS all those years never had an agreement longer than three years, and when those agreements ran out, they immediately jumped over to Fox. Especially in the NFC markets."

After the NFL accepted Fox's offer, Fox asked Jerry Jones and Pat Summerall to go on *Nightline*, ABC's nightly news program, to debate the deal. "Pat took the position that Fox didn't have any talent or production people," said Jones, "and he asked: 'How are they going to broadcast the games?' I knew that Murdoch didn't even have enough stations to cover the country, but he had invested so much in getting the NFL contract that he was certain to build his network fast enough to assure everyone. It was ironic that Pat and John were the first building blocks he chose."[10]

꩜

John Madden's and Pat Summerall's contracts were also coming to an end in 1993, which made them valuable commodities going forward. At the time, John was making $2 million a year. Sandy Montag, who was one of the IMG agents along with Barry Frank, negotiated Madden's deal with Murdoch.

"John was fascinated with Murdoch," said Montag. "He was impressed with what he had built in Australia and the UK, and yet hardly anyone knew him here."[11]

Madden may have been impressed with Murdoch's successes, but apparently he was unaware of a few of Murdoch's huge failures, including the onetime social-media darling MySpace. He bought MySpace in 2005 for $580 million and sold it a few years later for just $35 million.[12]

> **Lesley Visser:** "One night a bunch of us are watching *Monday Night Football* at John's place at The Dakota. In the middle of the game, he gets a call and in a flash he's out the door. I'm pretty sure he went to meet with Murdoch."[13]
>
> **Montag:** "John liked Murdoch right away. He saw him as a regular guy. He was blown away by his charm and his brain. One time we were at a barbecue at Rupert's, and Rupert is grilling hot dogs and accidentally drops one on the ground, but quickly picks it up and puts it back on the grill. John loved that. 'You're just like a regular schmuck like all of us,' John said. They had a great relationship."

At first Bob Iger, the CEO of Disney, which owned ABC, thought he had landed Madden for *Monday Night Football* by offering $2.5 million per year. But Barry Frank said he never gave him a final approval because he hadn't run it past John. Then Madden met with Murdoch, and everything changed. The next day Murdoch called IMG and told Frank, "Give me a number for what it will take to get John, and I'll call you back in five minutes with a yes or a no."

Disaster

Montag and Frank reached John on the phone, and they threw some numbers around as to what to ask for. According to Montag, "John suggested $6 million a year. Frank wanted $10 million a year. I thought that was a little greedy and suggested seven and a half. That's the number we gave them, plus an hour on Fox for the All-Madden Team, making it worth eight.

"We laid that out, and Rupert said, 'Okay, be back to you shortly.' He didn't call back, but he had his CFO for News Corp. call back, and all the guy said was, 'All right, what's the address for the contract?'"

Doing the deal for Summerall was a lot less complicated. Pat was never interested in taking part in the negotiations. He didn't enjoy the business end like John did.

"Pat was one of those guys," Montag said, "who would say, 'How much did we get from Fox?' I could say any number and he'd say okay, and that was it. Pat never said, 'I think we should ask for more.' Whatever I told him, he'd say, 'All right, Airball.'"

When Madden joined Fox in 1994, it seemed like their photographers and sound crew followed him everywhere. John obviously enjoyed the attention. COURTESY OF FOX SPORTS

"I'm only 5-6, and playing basketball in high school I was only good at free throws. A few years earlier, we all went to a barbecue at [*USA Today* TV sportswriter] Rudy Martzke's house. I take a shot in his backyard and missed everything. From then on, all Pat ever called me was 'Airball.' For a decade."

A few months later, Montag saw Murdoch at an event and thanked him for being so generous on Madden's deal by quadrupling his salary. "Young man," said Murdoch, "we've already made the contract back [for what we've sold against it]."[14]

Both CBS golf producer/director Frank Chirkinian and Summerall wanted Pat to keep broadcasting CBS's golf events through the spring and summer, until he needed to report to Fox for his NFL duties. Fox had no problem with it, but CBS officials citing Summerall's status as "the signature voice of CBS Sports" backed off.

Rupert Murdoch (center) enjoying the view from the booth along with John Madden and Pat Summerall after Murdoch outmaneuvered and outbid CBS for the NFL contract. When that happened Madden was fielding calls from every network, prompting one colleague to say, Madden became more valuable than a "van Gogh at a Christie's auction." COURTESY OF FOX SPORTS

"That's one of those philosophical things that was developed in some 36th-floor office," said Chirkinian. "A bunch of guys were sitting around, saying, 'Gee, we're really mad about losing football. How do we get even with the world? Let's kill Summerall.' One of our great strengths at CBS has been our continuity. It's like an old sports jacket—you put it on and you feel comfortable with it. To lose Pat, it's like losing one of the sleeves off this jacket."

"I wish they'd change their mind," Summerall said at the time. "I don't agree with the decision. I'll continue the friendships, whether I work here or not. I do feel I'm being penalized for being 'the signature voice.'"[15]

The news of CBS losing the contract was a shock to all of CBS's NFL staffers. Here's what some recalled when it happened:

Bob Stenner, the producer of CBS's NFL "A" game, had been at the network since the '60s and had never experienced a year that CBS wasn't broadcasting professional football.

"We had finished a Thursday game," Stenner recalled, "and we were on our way to Detroit. When we got to the lobby of our hotel in Detroit, that's when we found out from some of the technicians that we had lost the NFC contract. We also had thought that, oh, okay, now we will get the AFC contract. Then we found out that NBC had already made a deal prior to that. It just hadn't been announced yet. Then we realized we had nothing."

Many people in the CBS crew were consoling each other, not knowing where they would be working the following year. But Stenner was shocked by Madden's reaction.

"John was like [giddy], 'Oh this is all great,' kind of thing," Stenner said, "and I kind of got pissed off. I was thinking, 'Yeah, it's gonna be great for you, but a lot of people here, including myself, aren't going to have jobs.'"

Stenner, who spent many years in Los Angeles, may have tried to reinvigorate his brief acting career. In 1981, he appeared as a California Highway Patrol motorcycle cop in the Hal Needham film *The Cannonball Run*, which starred Burt Reynolds and Farrah Fawcett. He also was briefly in the 1985 film *Fever Pitch* starring Ryan O'Neal. Fortunately for Bob, Fox needed his services too.

"They [Fox] knew everyone would be watching how they televised the games," Stenner said. "You start with the best people, and that started with John. Barry Frank was his agent at the time, and he was in Europe, but he called me."

Frank: "Who's your agent?"
Stenner: "I don't have one."

"I didn't need one," Stenner said. "Pilson always told me, 'This is as much as we can give you for what you do,' and he wasn't being condescending. He was saying, 'Why would you give 10 percent to an agent? I'm telling you as a friend, this is where we're maxed out.'"

"So Barry said, 'I want to represent you.' Now somewhere along the line in those meetings Barry must've said, 'Well, John's going to want Bob Stenner.' I'm sure Rupert [Murdoch] didn't know who I was, but they probably said, 'Whoever this guy is, we're not going to let him get in the way of the deal for John.' So John and I were the first two that were hired. Then I believe it was Pat and [director] Sandy [Grossman], and I think [Terry] Bradshaw came after that."[16]

Dick Stockton stayed at CBS through the '94 Winter Olympic Games in Lillehammer, Norway. Then he got a phone call from Fox.

"Fox came to me and asked if I and Matt Millen wanted to be the No. 2 team," Stockton recalled.

At one point on CBS, Stockton had been a key contributor and the No. 1 play-by-play announcer for the NBA, which CBS lost to NBC in 1990.

"You know Pilson lost the NBA, too." Stockton said. "He went into that meeting—because I know this—with [former NBA commissioner] David Stern. He made his proposal, and David told him, 'Don't leave the room with that offer.' Pilson thought he was smarter, and [NBC's] Dick Ebersol was outside the door ready to grab it. Fox wanted it too, but that was a bigger gamble for the NBA because of Fox's weak station lineup.

"But getting John and Pat MADE IT [for Fox]! It didn't matter who else they had. It was John and Pat. And people said, 'Oh, I'm watching them.'

"CBS was outbid. They had somebody that was hungrier. I spent 27 years with Fox. That was the best company I ever worked for. They're unbelievable. They don't bother you. They support you. They're phenomenal."[17]

Richie Zyontz was a broadcast associate traveling with John Madden when he heard the news.

"It was the winter of '93–'94 right after CBS lost the contract," Zyontz recalled. "We were on John's bus traveling the country for his All-Madden Team. John was fielding calls from all the networks for his services. I'm literally sitting there at a truck stop in Wyoming as he's talking to his agent and reps from Fox, ABC, and NBC. For the worker bees like myself, we thought our career was over. For John, it was the best of times. I remember him saying, 'You need to have two [interested parties], but it's great to have three.'"[18]

CBS senior producer Ed Goren had heard rumors that Fox was going after NBC's NFL package, but he didn't believe it.

"Why wouldn't they go after the best [CBS's]?" he said. "I had that in my head and told my agent Bob Rosen to get me a meeting with someone at Fox. But for weeks nothing happened. 'You got to get me to somebody at Fox,' I told him, before it's official. Then Rudy Martzke [at *USA Today*] was about to write who was going to run Fox Sports, and my name was never mentioned.

"So, it came out of nowhere that I got a call from George Krieger, a Fox executive, who asked me to fly out to LA to meet with the head of Fox Sports, David Hill. I think the NFL was concerned that Fox didn't have anyone to oversee football. I think the NFL's vice president of broadcasting, Val Pinchbeck, did it—I gave them a comfort zone."[19]

> **Mike Arnold:** "I was traveling with Jim Nantz, and when we got the news, I was absolutely devastated. I was worried for my job, but shortly afterwards Rick Gentile [the executive producer at the time] said he wanted me to stay."[20]
>
> **Mike Frank:** "Everyone except John was worried. For John it was the greatest free-agency opening in sports TV history.... Director Sandy Grossman was ahead of the curve on this. We had a lot of Cowboy games in '93, and every time he saw Jerry Jones, he asked him about the contract. Sandy was the last of the four [John, Pat, Stenner, and Sandy] to sign his deal with Fox."[21]
>
> **Janis Delson:** "The entire week leading up to the tragic Friday [December 17, 1993], John Madden was on my phone a lot asking about the NFL rights negotiations. He kept asking what I was

hearing. Seriously. J. M. [Madden] insisted that Larry Tisch was just posturing. Everyone kept talking about loyalty and that the NFL would never abandon us. I told John that he was the only one who could get through to Tisch, that Tisch wouldn't listen to anyone else. On Friday, December 17, the decision came down that Fox had outbid us and that the NFC package was lost. That was about two or three in the afternoon. There was serious talk about bidding on the AFC package. But that was a dead issue very quickly.

"John announced [to colleagues], at the conclusion of the NFC championship game in Dallas, that he had accepted the Fox deal. He did it right in the announce booth where Rudy Martzke of *USA Today* could hear it. John wanted it to make the Monday papers. And so did Fox. They needed credibility in year one, and no one could deliver that better than Madden. As you know, he did have offers from the other two participants, so he had become a Van Gogh on the Christie's auction block."

"Ed Goren was hired several weeks later," Delson continued. "Ed called me a lot while I was in Lillehammer for the Olympics about how to do talent auditions [I did a lot of them at CBS]. I shared my information with him. At some point during my stay in ice-cold Norway, Ed said that when I came back, I should let him know what it would take for me to come to work for them. A week or so after Norway, Ed asked me if I would do the advance networking for their game assignments for all the stations.

"I did do it. It took me a few days, and no one knew about it. I don't remember when Ed actually asked me what I wanted to leave CBS. I was going to be Fox's main contact with the league. Val Pinchbeck was in charge of media for the NFL, and Val and I were longtime colleagues and had a great working relationship. I met David Hill at the Emmys, and we 'agreed' on terms. I started at Fox the very beginning of June."[22]

In his book *Lucky Bastard*, Joe Buck, now part of ESPN's No. 1 NFL broadcast team with Troy Aikman, summed up exactly how important the signing of Madden and Summerall was to Fox:

"Then they hired CBS's top NFL broadcast team of Pat Summerall and John Madden. That was brilliant, not just because they were the best, but because everybody knew they were the best. That shut up a lot of critics. It brought Fox Sports instant credibility. Fans could stop worrying that Bart Simpson would broadcast the Super Bowl. It was as if people said you couldn't put together a rock band, and then you brought in Mick Jagger and Keith Richards."

The '90s were a financially tumultuous time for sports television, and in the end, Pat Summerall and John Madden were two of its benefactors.

Madden in Albertville ... Huh?

"Neal got this idea that John should be part of our Albertville Winter Olympics coverage in France," said Janis Delson. "What was he going to do there? Then I had to explain the logistics to Neal of getting John there. San Fran to New York by bus. And then a boat? I told him that the Northern Atlantic in the middle of winter is quite wicked. The luxury boats don't make the crossings. What were you going to do, put him on a cargo ship? Oh boy! This idea went on for quite some time, but obviously and thankfully it died.

"The thought of Madden in Albertville is hysterical. All he had to do is get a look at those hotel rooms [three feet by four feet], and he would have been horrified. . . . And those miniature food portions!"[23]

Chapter Twelve

THE INTERVENTION

Pat's widow, Cheri Burns Summerall, recalled that they first met at the Colonial golf tournament in Fort Worth, Texas, in 1978. Brookshier and Summerall were in the fourth year of their partnership, and drinking their way through each weekend was part of it.

"When I first came on the scene," she said, "production meetings on Saturday nights finished fast so we could all go out and party. I didn't realize it at the time, but the people in charge [of the broadcasts] those weekends weren't doing them any favors." Asked if they were enabling their drinking by not saying anything to curtail it, she said, "They absolutely were."

Their imbibing almost forced Summerall and Brookshier to miss the kickoff of the NFC championship game on January 6, 1980, in Tampa, where the Buccaneers were hosting the Los Angeles Rams. "The morning of the game," Cheri Summerall said, "there was a brunch, and they let Pat and Brookie attend it." Driving them to the brunch was CBS Sports senior public-relations executive Bill Brendle, who was known to have a few cocktails himself. In fact, it was Brendle who, when presented with his tab, told the bartender at Rose Restaurant next to the CBS headquarters, "Date this for tomorrow, because I used up today last night." In CBS circles, cheating on your expense account was the norm, and that line became so famous it might as well have been on Brendle's tombstone.

They all had one too many Bloody Marys that morning when it came time to find Brendle's car in the parking lot and drive to the stadium. For 15 minutes, Brendle, Summerall, and Brookshier walked in circles looking for it, until someone finally asked Brendle, "What kind of car was it?" Without missing a beat, Brendle replied, "It's a Hertz."

"We all laughed when we heard the story," said Cheri, "but it was actually a sad account of how things were then. And Pat told me they barely made the game in time."[1]

"Alcohol was the lifeblood of the old CBS Sports," Terry O'Neil wrote of his time at CBS in his 1989 book, *The Game Behind the Game*.

And Pat and Brookie rarely missed an opportunity to partake.

When Bill MacPhail took over as the head of CBS Sports in 1956, he may not yet have become a heavy drinker. But 18 years later, his addiction to alcohol caused his departure. It seemed that anyone who was one of MacPhail's drinking buddies enjoyed their time at CBS. One of those buddies was Pat Summerall.

MacPhail hired Summerall in 1962 to be an analyst on New York Giants games. He and MacPhail would often go out for drinks at nearby spots like Mike Manuche's, Rose Restaurant, Toots Shor's, or even down the block on West 52nd Street at 21.

This was the atmosphere that prevailed when Summerall started his career. As one CBS assistant blatantly put it, everyone drank. But Summerall's habit didn't start when he came to CBS. It began when he played for the University of Arkansas. After Pat was drafted in the fourth round by the Detroit Lions, he bragged that his $500 bonus would at least pay off his bar tab.

And when he joined the Lions, he worked diligently to become part of hard-drinking quarterback Bobby Layne's inner circle. When he became WCBS Radio 88's entertaining morning man, he became a popular new face around Manhattan trying to get better guests for his show.

Summerall learned to hold his liquor. Often there was no telling how many drinks he'd had. His speech was never slurred. You could almost never tell unless he had been out all night with his pal Tom Brookshier. Some of their drinking escapades were covered in chapter 6, but the one that is most bizarre happened at six in the morning when, after carousing all night, they unhitched a horse from a hansom cab and tried to walk

The Intervention

him up the steps and into the Plaza Hotel. "We had a reservation," Summerall said. "The horse didn't."[2]

Tolerance changed for a time in 1981 when O'Neil came to CBS to shape up the network's NFL production. Sauter, the CBS Sports president, had heard the stories of Pat and Brookie's drinking, and no matter how popular they were on TV, Sauter wanted to split them up before someone got hurt. When O'Neil insisted that Summerall, rather than Vin Scully, was best suited to be Madden's on-air partner, Sauter warned O'Neil to keep a tight leash on Summerall.

In so doing, O'Neil laid down the law that there would not be a drop of alcohol consumed on the day of a game, at least not until after the broadcast had been completed. When O'Neil took over, Rich Nelson was associate director and stage manager, in charge of who and what got into the broadcast booth. O'Neil pulled him aside and said: "If I find out that there is liquor in the booth from this day forward, I'm going to fire you."[3]

Summerall was a professional and abided by O'Neil's rule and kept himself clean on game days during the five years O'Neil stayed at CBS.

However, once Terry left, Summerall and others slowly returned to their old habits. Broadcast associate Richie Zyontz revealed that Pat usually had a red to-go Solo cup nearby in the broadcast booth, which he presumed was half full of vodka and maybe a little Sprite. The cup, Zyontz said, was never seen on camera.[4]

Mike Frank, a broadcast associate working with Pat and John, was concerned about Pat's drinking. In 1989, he arranged a meeting for producer Bob Stenner and director Sandy Grossman to listen to Mike's uncle, a doctor who was an addiction specialist, and an interventionist his uncle brought with him.

Stenner: "I remember we met with Mike's uncle, and I do remember that everything they described should be done. But I don't remember if I called [executive producer Ted] Shaker or anyone at that point."

Stenner was Summerall's longtime producer, going back to the Tom Brookshier days of the 1970s when Summerall and Brookshier were known for their various drinking escapades on weekends before their Sunday broadcasts.

"Friday nights back in the Brookshier days were their nights," Stenner said.

"They would go out and get in trouble, and then they would talk about it with pride. So I knew about those things, but by the time Sunday rolled around it was never a factor."[5]

Shaker didn't recall hearing anything about the 1989 meeting: "This is something I'm sure I'd remember because I recall Pat's 1990 incident so vividly. But I don't remember getting a call from Bob Stenner or anyone at that time."[6]

Confronting addiction of someone close was difficult. Summerall's drinking was a widely known secret and nobody did anything about it. At least not until 1992 when it started affecting others.

In 1990, the excess behavior started to unravel. Summerall was hospitalized with a bleeding ulcer, which according to *The New York Times* was "aggravated by a toxic combination of painkillers and alcohol."

Mike Arnold recalled: "Once we were shooting the All-Madden Team on [John's] bus around 10 in the morning. They were sitting at the table, Pat on one side, John on the other, and Pat was drinking a can of Diet Coke. I said, 'We have to get rid of the Diet Coke because the can is right in the middle of the shot.' I reached for it, and Pat goes, 'Whoa, whoa, whoa, whoa. Where are you going with that?'

"I said, 'I'm going to throw it out,' and Pat said, 'Give it to me and let me put it right here.' So Pat put it on the seat next to him, out of the shot. We did that shot and a few more, and we broke for lunch, and I said, 'Boy, Pat was very protective of that Diet Coke.' And somebody said, 'Well, you know what was in there. It wasn't Coke; it was vodka.' I never saw Pat acting or looking or sounding drunk. He could hold his liquor like nobody you ever saw."[7]

A few years before, in 1986, Ted Shaker was named executive producer at CBS Sports by president Peter Lund. Previously there had been four separate executive producers, which resulted in confusion regarding who was in charge. Shaker said he didn't issue any alcohol ultimatums, but he also didn't change O'Neil's game-day rule.

The Intervention

"Pat Summerall was an amazing human being on so many levels," Shaker said when contacted for this book. "He was a special guy in so many ways, and in so many ways a flawed man."

"I guess the problems started after a [Washington] Redskins game [in 1990]," Shaker recalled. "Pat ended up on the bathroom floor of the plane that was returning him home to Florida after the game."[8]

Stenner, the producer, also recognized a big difference in Summerall before that 1990 game in Washington. "We were doing an on-camera [lead-in], and it took Pat three or four takes to get it. He didn't look like himself. I went into the truck and told Sandy [Grossman], 'I've never seen him like this.'"[9]

Ted Shaker: "I got a call the next morning that he was in a Florida hospital, and I flew down to Tampa to see how he was, see what he needed. I went directly to the hospital, and he was in bed in one of those hospital gowns, open in the back. He was not good. I was afraid that this guy was gonna die. I think he realized that it could have been fatal if he didn't get it together."[10]

When Summerall was released from the hospital, he was determined to stay sober, and did so for seven long months. And then he pronounced himself ready to resume "social" drinking. But this time it wasn't nearly as much fun.

"From his days as a football player to his career in sportscasting, he loved being the last guy at the bar, telling the best stories, having the grandest time. Now, at the age of 62, he had to hide the drinking and deny the problem," wrote Richard Sandomir in his *New York Times* TV Sports column. But it was hard for Pat to contain his social drinking. Especially when he was the lead voice for the CBS Sports PGA Tour. Shaker saw the tour as a big problem.

"The attitude at the time," said Shaker, "was that anything goes there. They'd spend weeks away from home going from one tournament to the next. Then [40 years ago] it was okay to do all that stuff. [CBS golf producer/director Frank] Chirkinian also recognized how dangerous this all became."[11]

But not much was done to curtail it. At one point CBS president Neal Pilson tried.

"Summerall had a drinking problem, and the president of CBS Sports told me to get him to stop drinking," senior producer Chuck Milton said. "I didn't know how I was gonna do that. My mother and father were both alcoholics, and I knew they wouldn't stop drinking until they wanted to."[12]

Pilson even tried personally, inviting Summerall to dinner along with Pat's friend and longtime CBS executive, Janis Delson. The meeting place was Gallaghers Steakhouse, the famous sports restaurant near CBS on West 52nd Street. Here's how Delson remembered the meeting:

"Pat ordered his usual vodka tonic, no fruit. He always said, 'No fruit.' I think Neal and I each ordered a glass of wine. At one point during the dinner, Pat said he wanted to help make CBS Sports the best in the business. He said to Neal, 'What can I do to help?' Neal paused for a moment and then motioned toward Pat's drink and said, 'You can have less of that.'"[13]

Delson was clear that Pilson was only trying to help and convince Pat to cut back. However, many experts have said that it's nearly impossible to get an alcoholic to stop by just asking him.

Another time, Summerall and a longtime CBS friend, who wished to remain anonymous, went to Campagnola, an Italian restaurant on East 61st Street around the corner from the Regency Hotel where Pat was staying. When they sat down, they noticed that Summerall's old friend Mickey Mantle was eating at a nearby table. Mantle motioned for them to come sit with him. When they arrived, the friend noticed that Mantle had already gone through two bottles of wine and had just ordered a third. "Before the night was over," the friend said, "they had gone through 10 bottles of wine." Many years later, after Summerall had had a successful recovery at the Betty Ford Center for his addiction, he sponsored Mantle's admission there.

According to Delson, Summerall even went as far as hiding a bottle of vodka on John Madden's bus. "There was a bottle of Absolut [vodka] on the bus, in the growler, as John used to call it [bathroom]. There was a vanity under the sink, and in it was a bottle. John used to say, 'There's never been any alcohol on the bus,' but we all knew that there was. Pat would go in there with a can of Sprite."[14]

The Intervention

Summerall stayed sober until a few months into 1991, and then he slowly returned to old habits. He was drinking more than ever, and friends were more concerned. It got to the point that even Brookshier felt Summerall needed to stop drinking. So, with the help of Peter Lund, Pat's boss at CBS, and others, Brookie organized "The Intervention."

Lund described how they convinced Summerall to go to the Betty Ford Center in Rancho Mirage, California, two weeks after his Masters broadcast on April 12, 1992:

"Here's how it got started. Deane and Judy Beman [the commissioner of the PGA Tour and his wife] lived next door to Pat and Kathy Summerall [Pat's first wife] at Marsh Landing in Ponte Vedra, Florida. And Jay Summerall, Pat's son, worked for the tour. After Pat threw up on the plane and it became apparent that this was at a crisis stage, it became clear that Pat needed some help. So Deane talked with Jay.

"Deane: 'I feel I need to do something to help him, because we can't just let Pat continue to go down this road.'

"Jay: 'That would be great, but you'll lose a friend. He'll resent it and never talk to you again.'

"Deane: 'I'd rather lose a friend than have him die on me and not do anything about it.'

"And then Deane called [the late longtime Tampa Bay Buccaneers owner] Hugh Culverhouse," Lund continued. "So, it was Deane and Hugh Culverhouse that put this intervention together. That's how it started, and once they contacted an interventionist, the rest of us came on board.

"Pat and I knew each other from the '70s. We had become fairly good friends. I was running a CBS radio station in San Diego from '72 to '75, and Pat would come in to do affiliate relations. For reasons I can't remember, we played tennis and golf together and got to know each other. I think they were CBS Radio affiliate conferences. So, before I came to sports, Pat and I had a relationship.

"Pat was always a very emotional guy. I was in Dallas for a conference, and Pat and I wound up having lunch that Saturday at some sports bar in Dallas, and because of something that came up, we both got emotional and both of us started tearing up. Pat would cry at a gas station opening.

So we're tearing up at a sports bar with all the college games going on, and people are looking at us like, who are those two guys over there?

"It [The Intervention] was held at a Stouffer's Inn in Camden, New Jersey, in April 1992. And the hook was that Brookshier had a huge client that was a fan, and it would be a great favor to him [Brookie] if Pat could stop in when he came to do a voice-over for nearby NFL Films. Tommy said, 'I'll send a car for you. All you have to do is stop by for a fast hello.'

"We all get the word that we're going to have this intervention, and we all fly in the night before. The next morning we met with the interventionist. In my memory, the people who were there were Deane Beman, Frank Chirkinian, Hugh Culverhouse, Kathy Summerall, Tommy Brookshier, and a couple of friends from Tampa. Pat said in his book that Pete Rozelle was there, but I don't recall him being there. I knew Pete well, and I would have remembered if Pete was there, and he wasn't there.

"In the morning we all meet, and the interventionist tells us how it's going to go. He says, 'I need you guys to write a letter to Pat. Go back to your rooms and write the letter, and I need you to reference how you got to know Pat and how you see alcohol affecting his life.' As an aside, I had a lot of alcohol in my family, so I was very emotional about this. Then we meet again and read the letters out loud to the interventionist, and he makes a few changes and orchestrates how it should go. Now we're waiting for Pat, and the interventionist says, 'Here's the order we're going to read the letters.'

"When Pat comes in the door and sees this whole crowd, he's going to know this isn't where he wants to be, so the interventionist assigns the two biggest guys, Brookshier and Culverhouse, to be waiting at the door so he can't get out. Pat comes in and says, 'I know what this is about.' But the interventionist says, 'Would you please come in and sit down for a minute? You don't have to stay if you don't want to, but all these people are friends of yours and they've all flown in and they've all written a letter to you, and we'd like you to just listen to the letters. And if you want to leave after that, you're welcome to leave, but please listen to the letters.' Pat reluctantly agrees. He sits down and then the letter reading begins.

The Intervention

"My role, besides reading my letter, was as 'the hammer.' Everybody reads the letters, and after, the interventionist says, 'Pat, as you can see, all these people love you and want you to get well. And we have a plane ready and a reservation at the Betty Ford Clinic in Palm Springs for you. Tommy is going to ride over to the plane with you to go to Betty Ford.' And as expected, Pat said, 'Okay, but I can't do it right now. I've got this Chicago Bears voice-over to do in an hour, and I've got some other things to do, and I've got to do the Hilton Head tournament, but after that we can talk about it.'

"I had a tough role for somebody who really liked Pat Summerall. So I said, 'Pat, here's the deal. If you don't go to Betty Ford, you're not working at CBS anymore.' This was a real hammer for Pat because he just loved working there. He loved being with everybody, the whole crowd. This was an extension of his playing career, the camaraderie, traveling together, having dinner together, and lots of drinks together. And he was stunned by it.

"And I said, 'We'll get somebody else to do that, but if you don't go, you're not working at CBS anymore.' We talked a little more, and I assured Pat and Kathy that if he did this, he would always have a job at CBS. When Pat said okay, kind of reluctantly, then two guys grabbed him and rushed him downstairs to the limo and got in the limo with him. Then we all went to this regional New Jersey airport to say good-bye. The plane is cleaned out, Brookshier is going to ride on the plane with Pat to hold his hand, and they're all ready to go, but then the plane has a mechanical problem and an hour delay. Panic breaks out. How are we going to keep this guy calm? We barely got him to the airport. So the interventionist assigns us each to sit and talk to him for 15 minutes until the plane is ready. We hung in there, and he got on the plane and went to Betty Ford."

"The amazing thing about it," Lund concluded, "is that 30-day programs have a low percentage of success. But Pat got it in 33 days and stayed sober. He took those letters and carried them around with him and read them all the time. It really worked for him."

Of all the letters they read to Pat the one that affected him the most was from his daughter, Susan, who couldn't be there. But Tom Brookshier emotionally read the letter for her. Among the words she wrote that moved her father tremendously was: "I'd always been proud we'd had the same last name, but now I can't say that."[15]

(Susan Summerall's married name is Susan Wiles, and recently she was named Donald Trump's chief of staff at the White House. A longtime Republican, she first worked for Ronald Reagan and Florida governor Ron DeSantis before Trump.)

The Intervention took place shortly before Summerall left CBS for Fox in 1994. When he left Betty Ford, he went back home to Florida to rest for more than two months until he felt capable of working again. He returned for the Buick Open in Westchester, New York, on June 26, 1992, where he met with a few members of the media. That's when he divulged what his daughter wrote in her letter.

Neal Pilson, who was then the head of CBS Sports, made the following statement: "We've worked with Pat for a period of time as he's struggled with his problem with alcoholism. We've provided various levels of support. We were very pleased when he agreed to a course of treatment at the Betty Ford Center, and we assured him that he could return to his work provided he successfully completed treatment. We were in close touch with the professionals at Betty Ford and continue to stay in touch."[16]

That sounded very nice, but there wasn't much evidence that Pilson or CBS had ever tried to slow Summerall's drinking, other than Pilson once asking senior producer Chuck Milton to get him to stop. Summerall's longtime NFL producer Bob Stenner had witnessed it for decades, going back to Pat's years with Tom Brookshier, but he may have felt it wasn't his job to say something.

Peter Lund felt that wasn't part of a producer's job. "It seems to me their job was to produce games at a high level," he said. "Their job is not to babysit Pat Summerall. If Pat performed in those games like we know he did every Sunday, then I'm not sure that it was Stenner and [director Sandy] Grossman's responsibility to have to deal with Pat's personal life."

Lund continued: "If you would see Pat drinking too much other than on Sundays and if you blow the whistle on Pat, you know that he's going to turn on you. Then you'd have a shitstorm on your hands. You can look at it both ways: maybe it would have been best if somebody tried to do something about it sooner, but I don't see how it would have been Stenner and Grossman's job. What could they do? A talk with Pat would have accomplished nothing. I don't know a single alcoholic who would respond to that. I don't know; it's a bit of a stretch."[17]

His time at Betty Ford helped him reflect more clearly. He wrote letters to friends and coworkers telling them how much he appreciated them. And in his autobiography, he wrote: "As the years and the parties passed, I became more erratic in my judgment and less patient as I drank more frequently and recovered more slowly. In addition, I had lowered my standards along the way—professionally, personally, and physically. To my shame, I had become a practiced liar and a seasoned cover-up

Cheri Summerall surrounded by her two favorite men: John (on the left) and her husband, Pat. COURTESY OF CHERI SUMMERALL

man. I was spending more and more time on the road just to be around the party scene, always to the detriment of my family. I had walked away from my marriage and alienated my three kids. They didn't deserve that treatment."

Summerall's accomplishment was all the more remarkable because he managed to remain sober the rest of his life. In August 1992, he returned to CBS and the NFL with John Madden. Fox executive producer Ed Goren, who knew Summerall going back decades when they were both at CBS, was incredibly proud.

"Pat's greatest achievement was staying sober all those years," said Goren. "Of all the things that he accomplished, that was the greatest of all. All the experts say you have to change your lifestyle. That you can't go to the same places and be with the same people as before. Well, wait a minute. Pat Summerall had to be on the road every week. He was with his crew every week, and they drank, and he managed to survive through that and not get dragged back in. You can't change your whole lifestyle if you're on the road every week. It was a tremendous achievement."[18]

In 2008, Summerall met with a writer from the NFLThread.com to discuss his career. He was no longer in denial about his past.

"I was drinking myself to death," he said. "Everyone saw it but me."

Chapter Thirteen
IT WAS THE PERFECT MARRIAGE— UNTIL IT WASN'T

When John Madden and Pat Summerall first signed with Fox in 1994, they were all Fox had. Even Madden joked that it should be called "Fox Sport" rather than "Fox Sports," "because the only sport we had at Fox was football, NFL football," and they didn't even have any idea then how to put the games on the air.

Summerall's and Madden's jumping on board ended the hilarious rumors of Bart Simpson broadcasting the games and gave Rupert Murdoch and his fledgling network instant credibility. In short order, Fox hired CBS senior producer Ed Goren, and he helped Fox raid the CBS pantry. They quickly signed enough announcers, supervisors, and production people to get the product on the air. Those signings included the lead NFL producer and director team, Bob Stenner and Sandy Grossman.

Even after 13 years together at CBS, Summerall and Madden continued to excel. Madden had already won eight Emmy Awards on his way to winning a total of 16. And Summerall was recognized as one of the all-time great all-around broadcasters, also excelling at golf (the Masters) and tennis (the U.S. Open).

David Hill was the man Rupert Murdoch chose to run Fox Sports. Hill grew up in Sydney, Australia, and at age 17 began as a copy boy for *The Sydney Daily Telegraph*. He progressed quickly to reporter and at 19 moved to television, working for Australia's Nine Network. Eventually he became vice president of sports at Nine, and in 1988, at the age of

42, Hill accepted Murdoch's offer to move to Great Britain to help get England's first satellite TV station, Sky Television, off the ground. He followed that by launching Eurosport, a multilingual sports channel throughout all of Europe. After British Sky Broadcasting merged with Sky Television, he was asked to run the BSkyB sports channel, and in 1991, he started Sky Sports.

So, with all that experience, in 1994, when Murdoch bid for and won the NFL broadcast rights that CBS formerly had, David Hill was the first one Murdoch called to get things started in the United States.

"When the announcement was made that Fox had the NFL, my father-in-law, who lived in Omaha, Nebraska, called me in a panic," Hill said when contacted for this book. "The reason for the panic was that he didn't have Fox on his cable system and therefore couldn't watch the NFL. 'Don't worry, Wilbur,' I said, 'It'll be there by the start of the season.' And it was. Fox distribution jumped from around 65 percent [of the country] to 98 percent within six months, from the announcement to the start of the 1994 season. And that was in the day of mom-and-pop cable companies! The UHF stations were rapidly replaced by the high-powered VHF stations. And the Fox O&O [owned and operated] group [of stations] grew by leaps and bounds."[1]

One of the first things Hill did as president of Fox Sports was something he did on Europe's televised soccer matches with Sky Sports—he added a score box that stayed on the screen that recorded not only the score of the game but the time remaining as well. His "Fox Box," as they called it for NFL games, wound up being a big hit, but not without its early detractors. Today, it is ubiquitous.

"I didn't know football, but I knew how to produce television," he recalled. "And television is simply a human being speaking to another human being. The score box in the corner was something I dreamed up in England, but when I introduced it here, I got five death threats: (1) 'You're a foreigner,' (2) 'You're screwing with football,' (3) 'We know where you live,' (4) 'We're gonna kill you,' and (5) 'Welcome to America!'"

In addition to the "Fox Box," Hill helped invent the yellow first-down line for televised football. Those two things alone have made the game much easier to watch.

"I didn't grow up watching American football," Hill said, "and [those things] made it easier for me to understand what was going on. Simple as that!"[2]

Hill was elected to the Sports Broadcasting Hall of Fame in 2014.

During the 1999 season, Fox executives and others spotted some slippage in Summerall's performance. He just wasn't as sharp as he'd always seemed to be. The Fox executives weren't the only ones to notice it. John Madden noticed it, too. Summerall was approaching his 70th birthday, and maybe it was time for a tune-up.

But according to *The Los Angeles Times* media critic Larry Stewart in his January 25, 2002, column, Summerall had a good excuse for his mistakes. Here's some of what Stewart wrote about the situation:

"He was taking pain medication for a bum knee, and the medication was affecting his play-by-play. The knee was replaced in March 2000, and the 2000 football season was a better one for Summerall."

At the conclusion of the 1999 season, Hill and executive producer Ed Goren approached Summerall with a three-year plan that would conclude with him doing Super Bowl XXXVI with Madden in 2002 and then retiring.

"The bottom line is that we tried to provide him with a soft landing," Goren said when contacted for this book. "This isn't the way you want to end a Hall of Fame career. Some broadcasters late in their careers know they've lost a step or two or more. The industry has a history, unfortunately, of great, great broadcasters who just aren't ready to leave. And I understand it. Why would you? It's one of the greatest jobs ever. It's unfortunate that it ended this way."[3]

Before Goren and Hill approached Summerall, Hill had seen some obvious missteps, and he said that he consulted with Madden every step of the way. Did Madden help push Summerall out the door?

"John was very upset, and there was only one way out of this," Hill said. "He [Madden] came to us and said, 'Something has to be done.'" Then paraphrasing, Hill added: "'You know Pat's been terrific, but it's now time.'"[4]

(It should be noted that Summerall was six years older than Madden.)

"It's one of the worst things in the world when you can sense the viewer saying, 'It's time this guy stopped,'" Hill continued. "It got to the point the mistakes were making an appearance in the commentary. I've been working with talent [broadcasters] all my career, and you become friends, and at some point you have to make the ultimate call because you're running the business, and it's tough. Unfortunately, when you become friends with someone, the emotion can cloud your judgment, which is why I tried to make it as easy as possible with Pat."

Hill was asked how involved John Madden was with the decision. "I didn't make any decisions without talking to John," Hill said. "John was totally brought in, and every conversation I had with Pat, I would repeat it to John. So he [John] knew exactly what was happening."[5]

It's very likely Madden noticed the same mistakes and simply wanted to know if the executives knew something he didn't know. It certainly didn't mean he was being selfish or that he loved Pat any less.

Richard Sandomir was *The New York Times*' sports television critic for 25 years, from 1991 through 2016. He covered Madden and Summerall on their move from CBS to Fox and all through their Fox years together. In an email, he summed up their final years together when contacted for this book.

"I think Pat knew, as Ed Goren and David Hill knew," Sandomir emailed, "that there was much more top-tier mileage left in Madden than there was in Summerall. . . . And the difference for what they offered on games was obvious, in Madden still being Madden when he left."

"John knew that Pat didn't have the skills to stay as a No. 1 announcer," Sandomir continued. "And John clearly wanted to ensure that he continued to work with a No. 1 announcer, even if he had to do it with other networks. And Fox knew they had a younger crew [Joe Buck and Troy Aikman] ready to replace both of them."

Having Summerall retire after the 2002 Super Bowl would signify 50 years in professional football for Pat, and 40 years in broadcasting. So Hill and Goren traveled to Pat's home near Dallas to propose their three-year plan.

"We even wanted to make his final season into a grand tour for Pat to celebrate his career," Goren said. As far as the slippage was a concern,

Goren said: "There's not much more to say. [Howard] Cosell and Dick Enberg left [broadcasting] bitter. There's a whole list of Hall of Famers who left the industry bitter [because they stayed too long]."[6]

In July 2000, a press conference was called in which Fox would introduce Summerall, who would then officially announce that he would retire after the 2002 Super Bowl in Los Angeles. The room was packed at the Park Hyatt Hotel in Century City, with dozens of other media members listening in from around the country. Pat Summerall retiring from football after 50 years was a big deal. Fox even leaked the announcement to the media the night before the conference.

However, knowing Summerall for so many years, one of the Fox Sports publicity guys was concerned. "Are you sure he's going to say he's retiring?" he asked Ed Goren twice. "Are you sure?"

"So we had a press conference," Hill said. "The world was there. I said a few words, and then Pat said, '**I'm not retiring.**' When I look back, it's very funny. What it came down to was Pat saying, 'I'm not retiring.' Listen, shit happens. It's not the end of the world. I'm never shocked by anything. What I was surprised by was how John handled his surprise. John was legitimately shocked. John said, 'It was like Mom and apple pie. Pat and John.'"[7]

Fox got whipsawed by the press. The *Sports Business Journal* headlined its July 25, 2000, story: "**That's Not All from Pat; Summerall Not Retiring.**" The *Business Journal* then listed the headlines and lead sentences from many news sources from around the country, including:

> *New York Newsday*: "Summerall refused to go quietly into the night."
>
> *The Boston Herald*: "Summerall said 'Not so fast!'"
>
> *The Dallas Morning News*: "It was all a misunderstanding."
>
> *USA Today*: "Summerall: 'I'm not retiring from broadcasting.'"

On January 28, 2000, *The Seattle Times*' great sports columnist Steve Kelley wrote an impassioned piece about Summerall. Here's an excerpt:

The geniuses who run Fox have decided Pat Summerall is too old. Summerall is 71, which is about 450 in Fox years. At the Rupert Murdoch Network, anybody older than Ally McBeal is viewed with suspicion. . . . Summerall has been a witness to almost every important game the league has seen, and he brings that sense of history with him every Sunday. There is a difference between being old and being experienced. A difference too subtle for Fox. But Summerall is being treated like the last mastodon, the same way CBS once treated Ray Scott and NBC treated Curt Gowdy. Both were shoved aside before their time. . . .

Pat Summerall has spent the last half century with the NFL. He belongs with the league, with Madden on every important Sunday in the season. If only the geniuses at Fox, those same guys who think Tom Arnold speaks for the true American sports fan, understood.

What Summerall said at the news conference was that he felt he was in relatively good health and that he wanted to continue to work with Madden for years to come. Taken by surprise, Hill and Goren did a quick reversal and indicated that it was Summerall's decision to make, and that he and Madden would continue to work together.

Summerall's widow, Cheri Burns Summerall, held no ill will toward Hill and Goren when contacted for this book. "Pat had a hard time with retirement, stepping aside, because he loved it," she said. "There was never a bitter bone in his body. I would hear him making little mistakes too. It's easy to sit back and point fingers at David Hill or Ed Goren, but that's not what Pat would say or do. David Hill and Ed Goren—they were always good to Pat. They were good people. They were good friends. They were grateful for what Pat and John brought to Fox [credibility]. A lot of that [mistakes] I truly believe was the brain disease."

After Summerall's death, it was discovered that he suffered from a rare brain disease known as PSP (progressive supranuclear palsy). According to national institutes, PSP is a rare neurological disorder that affects the brain and can cause problems with movement, balance, vision, and speech.

It Was the Perfect Marriage—Until It Wasn't

"I know they [Hill and Goren] were trying to do the right thing at the end with the exit," Cheri Summerall said. "Unfortunately, it didn't go that way. And that was Pat's choosing. But looking back, it was a gift from the doctor who helped me understand the things I was puzzled by."[8]

Two years later, in the actual week before that 2002 Super Bowl, after consulting with his agents and his friends Stenner and Grossman, Summerall called his own press conference and announced that he was stepping down from the "A" team, but he wanted to continue working.

"Goren and Hill are fond of Summerall," Larry Stewart wrote in his January 25, 2002, column in The Los Angeles Times. "And they respect him. They wanted his exit, or whatever you want to call it, to be classy and amiable. And they wanted an open line of communication. According to Goren, one thing they tried to convey to Summerall was that it might be in everyone's best interest for him to make a decision about his future before Super Bowl week. 'It was his decision,' Goren said."

"Summerall said the same, only he added, 'However, I'm not saying they are not glad I decided to do this.' Summerall didn't say so, but maybe he was feeling unappreciated."

The flip side of the coin was written by *The New York Post*'s media critic Phil Mushnick, who had a reputation of never seeing a sports broadcaster he ever liked. Mushnick rarely had a kind word for any of them, and once he ripped you, he almost never let up.

Under the headline, NO SYMPATHY FOR SUMMERALL; FRAUDULENT PAT WAS BAD GUY IN SPLIT WITH FOX, Mushnick wrote about Summerall on February 3, 2002:

I HATE writing this. I don't like kicking 71-year-old men who are perceived to be down. And out. But enough is enough. Fox actually wanted Summerall to exit gracefully a contract ago, but he didn't see the light.... The fallout is the same that Fox had previously tried to avoid: Fox did dirt to sweet, venerable Pat Summerall. And that's bunk. In truth, Fox was far better to Summerall than Summerall was to Fox. And the bashing it has taken since Summerall's announcement represents the latest in no good deed going unpunished.

What it came down to was that Summerall wasn't exactly forced out, but he felt pressured to make some kind of decision before the Super Bowl. So, he met Fox in the middle. According to Larry Stewart, Summerall apprised Madden of his decision three days earlier. After Summerall announced his decision, it meant that that Sunday's Super Bowl would be the last time the two would work together. Madden spoke from his heart when he talked with reporters during a conference call that Wednesday.

"When the announcement came out, it was like a kick in the stomach," he said. "That's when it hit me. You think about the 21 years you've been with someone and you're not gonna be with them anymore. It's been 21 more-than-great years. I'm not the smoothest or the easiest guy to get along with. I kind of go up and down, but in 21 years we've never had a cross word, not one argument. That's because of him. If you can't get along with Pat Summerall, you can't get along with anyone."

Madden loved broadcasting football, telling his stories, and working with Pat. But there were things about a broadcast he didn't want anything to do with, like reading promos on the air, for example.

"I've never said I was a television guy," Madden said. "I've never passed myself off as a broadcaster. I'm a football guy who does television. I went through school for 21 years being in recess, and Pat was the school."[9]

Looking back 22 years later, Pat's son, Jay Summerall, held no ill feelings toward Fox.

"He battled his whole life," Jay said of his father. "He was always a competitor. He didn't want to go. I don't think they [Fox] did anything unusual. They thought it was time for him to move on. Hell, even Bill Belichick couldn't get a job [for over a year]."[10]

Fox wanted to pair Madden with Joe Buck after that 2002 season, which was to be John's final contract season with Fox. John, however, wanted to leave and go to *Monday Night Football*, where he would work with Al Michaels. Fox didn't stand in his way and, by not doing so, saved Madden's $8 million salary.

In 1975, when Michaels was a young play-by-play broadcaster with CBS, he was assigned to do an Oakland Raiders game. In the book *You Are Looking Live!*, Michaels described his first meeting with Madden.

"On the Friday before the game I drive across the Bay to Oakland to talk with John Madden, who was the Raiders' coach," Michaels said. "It was the first time I'm meeting him, and it turns out he was a big baseball fan, and we wind up talking in his office for 45 minutes, and he tells me how one day he wants to buy an RV and drive across the country like *Travels with Charley*. That was my first interaction with John, and right off the bat we clicked.

"Thirty years later [at NBC] it was fantastic."

CHAPTER FOURTEEN

SAYING GOOD-BYE TO PAT

PAT SUMMERALL AND JOHN MADDEN'S FIRST SUPER BOWL TOGETHER was in 1982, when the 49ers edged the Cincinnati Bengals, 26–21. Pat opened that broadcast saying, "Super Bowl XVI. What a build-up. We've been here all week, and I feel like running down and playing." Twenty years later, they did their eighth and final Super Bowl together, Super Bowl XXXVI, with New England beating the St. Louis Rams with a last-second field goal.

When it was over, Fox gave the two a chance to say good-bye. Pat spoke first: "We've been a team," he said, "and I'm proud of that fact. We've been a winning team."

Then Madden responded: "You are a treasure, and you are to be treasured. You are the spirit of the NFL. Those memories will be with us forever, and they can never take them away."[1]

While Madden, who was 66, was moving on to ABC to do *Monday Night Football* with Al Michaels, Pat wasn't quite ready to retire. And looking back at all those great games Summerall called, with and before John Madden, the one thing he loved was the opening tease for every game. Once you heard his voice, you knew it was an important game.

Joan Vitrano, an associate director with CBS Sports since 1978, worked four Super Bowls (XII, XIV, XVI, and XVIII) with Pat Summerall, and countless other big games with him as part of the "A" broadcast team. But what she remembers most is his voice.

"His voice gave everyone chills," she said. "Nobody had a voice like Pat Summerall. Pat loved voicing over the opening teases. He took a lot of pride in the process. I'd get the [written] teases, and then I'd find pictures to match the script. When he added his voice, it gave everyone chills. Even when he just read a promo like *Murder, She Wrote.*"

Those short, video-packed openings of each game were usually written by the producers, with an emphasis on getting the viewer excited. But with Summerall doing them, he added a sense of drama. "He reminded us of John Facenda," Vitrano said, recalling the Philadelphia television newscaster who voiced the dramatic NFL Films "frozen tundra" videos of Vince Lombardi's Packers.[2]

When Pat and John said their good-byes at the conclusion of Super Bowl XXXVI that February Sunday in 2002, it was emotional. But Pat wasn't ready to sit in the backyard with the dogs, as Madden did in 1978. Summerall only knew one thing: the routine of getting ready for a football game. His whole life, that is all he knew, and if he quit, he knew he'd miss football terribly. So Fox kept him on with analyst Brian Baldinger that first year, doing mostly Cowboys games from Dallas, so he wouldn't have far to travel. The voice was still great, but the mind wasn't quite as sharp, and the next two years the game opportunities became fewer and fewer. He did a Cotton Bowl one year and a few other things for others that Fox allowed until his body started to give way.

In 2004, despite not having taken a drop of alcohol for a dozen years—since The Intervention in 1992—his body kept breaking down from all the previous alcohol damage. He was told by doctors that if he didn't get a liver transplant he would die. Pat married Cheri Burns in 1996, and they were together until his death. She explains what happened in 2004:

"The liver just kept getting worse and worse, which is why he needed a transplant. It was pretty evident because he just kept getting sicker and sicker. They were doing transfusions that were supposed to last a month, and they'd only last about a week.

"The liver was just failing. We had hoped we could do it [the liver transplant] here in Dallas. Mickey Mantle had his done at Baylor in Dallas, and they got a black eye. They took some flak for giving Mickey the liver because he had cancer and then died. When Pat met with those doctors, they said, 'We can't put another high-profile celebrity in the program.'

"A doctor who was a good friend in Dallas said, 'I think you should call Mayo [Clinic] in Jacksonville.' They set it up for him to be tested to see if he was a candidate for their program. The testing was rigorous, and traveling was incredibly difficult for Pat. We got to Jacksonville, but he was in no shape to take a commercial flight home.

"Then Jerry Jones called and said: 'We know where you are. We know what's going on, and I'm going to send my plane to pick you up in the morning.' That plane flew us back to Dallas, and Pat went right into the hospital here [to recover]. While [he was] in the hospital, Mayo called and said, 'We've got good news and bad news. The good news is he qualified for our program. The bad news is, he's so critically ill, you're at the top of the list.'

"They sent an air ambulance, and we left that evening and went straight to Mayo. It was a young boy from Arkansas, Pine Bluff, 13 years old, who had an aneurysm in class. They put him on life support, and that's the liver we got. Pat was in the ICU from heaven for the surgery. And when he recovered, while still groggy, he tried to get up and said, 'I've got to get down to Butler Cabin.'"

It was a reference to the cabin at the Masters, where Pat had conducted so many interviews through the years.

"The liver transplant gave him another nine years," Cheri said. "I'll tell you—God has a plan."[3]

Unfortunately, those nine years weren't easy for Pat. He had contracted progressive supranuclear palsy, a neurological disorder that affects the brain and can cause problems with movement, balance, vision, speech, and swallowing. The doctors felt it was probably affecting him as far back as when he was still working with Madden. It caused him to be off balance, to at times shuffle his feet while walking, and eventually it caused him to trip and fall in his house and break his hip.

This was the second week of April 2013. It was Masters week, and instead of enjoying the tournament on TV, Pat was in the hospital getting a hip replacement.

"He did fine with it [the hip replacement]," said Cheri. "His first day he had no problem doing his rehab in the morning. Then he was setting up for his second session in the afternoon. When he tried to push himself up, he collapsed and had an embolism and died of a blood clot."[4] He was 82.

Pat Summerall was a giant, a titan in the world of football. He was the voice of the NFL, the voice of autumn. Everyone who ever knew him sent their respects, and so many who were close to him came to Dallas for the private service. Through the years after they did their last game together, John always stayed in touch with Pat. They spoke often. Pat was always glad to hear John's voice.

The memorial service was at Prestonwood Baptist Church in Plano, Texas, just outside of Dallas, on April 20, 2013, exactly one week after his death. Thousands of friends and fans who loved Pat Summerall attended the service.

According to the Associated Press's April 20, 2013, coverage: "The memorial service was powered by a group of church singers and a choir more than 300 strong, and NFL Hall of Fame players including former Cowboys quarterbacks Roger Staubach and Troy Aikman, ex–Dallas running back Emmitt Smith and former wide receiver Michael Irvin. Fullback Daryl Johnston was among other past Cowboy players who also attended along with Cowboys owner Jerry Jones and Coach Jason Garrett."[5]

Among the many tributes were these, from Jim Nantz, Jerry Jones, and NBC broadcaster Mike Tirico.

> **Jim Nantz:** "He is CBS Sports. I always thought he could work here until he was 75 or 80 years old. He's been a much larger influence on my career than I think he realizes. There will be a piece of Pat Summerall on the air as long as I do golf for this network."
>
> **Jerry Jones:** "Pat was the NFL's narrator for generations, with a voice that was powerful, eloquent, and distinctive. His presence at an NFL game elevated that event to a higher level. He was royalty in the broadcast booth. Humility and kindness were his closest companions. He was a trusted friend and confidant, and for all of his immense talents as a professional, he was an even better person."
>
> **Mike Tirico:** "He was the gold standard in so many ways. Summerall had a way to say more with less. When the moment got

bigger, whether it was the NFL, the Masters, the U.S. Open, he had the way to set the tone but never got in the way of the event."

"The night before the service," said Cheri, "John took the bus and came into town. He called me."

Cheri Summerall: "John, thank you so much for speaking tomorrow."
Silence.
Cheri: "What's wrong, John?"
John: "I didn't know I was supposed to speak."
Cheri: "Oh my, I thought someone had asked you. I'm so sorry. I was hoping you would."
John: "I'd be honored to do it."[6]

At the funeral, Lance Barrow was one of the first to speak. Barrow was a sophomore at Abilene Christian University when he first became Summerall's spotter on the golf tour in 1976, and he later replaced Frank Chirkinian as the director of the PGA coverage for CBS Sports. "He was as kind to me as anyone he knew," Barrow said, "and when he spoke to me, he made me feel like I was the only one in the room."[7]

Both of Pat's sons, Kyle and Jay, also spoke. "He never looked back," Kyle said. "That's a testament to his toughness and determination, but most of all the faith he found and the amazing grace which carried him through the rest of his days."[8]

Jay Summerall, Pat's older son, also made some very heartwarming remarks:

"He was a great man, and yet a modest, unassuming one. An American from the Greatest Generation, he was every bit its product and prototype. He respected authority, got to work early, worked hard, spoke softly, never boasted, took responsibility, and unfailingly helped others in need. He was tough as nails, too. I only saw him lose one fight in his life, to alcohol, and he eventually triumphed over that. It took its toll, though.

We lost some of his life to it, and we lost a great role model this week in part because of it.

"He excelled professionally, to say the least, as an athlete and as a broadcaster without peer. I think he was a Renaissance man among broadcasters. He covered football, tennis, golf, basketball, and a host of other sports including some boxing. He would do anything for CBS and go wherever they asked him, and one time they called him to do Winter Olympics, and worse than that it was in France."

Jay Summerall then spoke about a place that his father hated to go to—a place that had everyone laughing:

"He also did French Open tennis. Some people would have relished a chance to go to Paris to cover tennis. John Madden's laughing. He knows what I'm going to say. He [Pat] didn't like France. The hotel rooms weren't big enough. The dinner plates weren't big enough. The people didn't speak English, and they didn't bathe often enough for him. [Laughter.] He liked his big house in Lake City or South Lake, with easy access to DFW [the Dallas Fort Worth International Airport] and Las Colinas Country Club and the Dallas Cowboys [where he had so many friends]."

"There was no big shot in him," Jay Summerall continued. "He never said no when friends asked him to speak or make an appearance at a charity golf tournament. He answered his fan mail. He sent autographed pictures. He came to my kids' school and spoke to fourth-, fifth-, and sixth-grade classes. He became an ambassador for Betty Ford and helped countless people get free of addiction. He visited the grave of the Arkansas boy whose liver kept him alive for a decade, and he stayed in touch with that family. He was great like that."[9]

Sandy Montag, who was both Pat's and John's agent: "Pat had health issues. He and John stayed in touch. Pat was particularly close with the Cowboys, living down there. He had a great relationship with Jerry Jones and Rich Dalrymple [senior vice president of public relations and communications] and Troy [Aikman]. He stayed active in the Dallas community.

"I sat next to John at the funeral. He's given 1,000 speeches in his life, and I've never seen him as emotional or nervous as he was before that eulogy for Pat. It hit him hard. Al Davis passing [just 18 months before] and Pat passing really hit him hard. It had a profound impact on him."[10]

CBS and Fox producer Bob Stenner, who also attended the service: "When John spoke at Pat's funeral, there was genuine caring there. I remember standing outside the hotel and John couldn't tie his tie, so I tied it for him.

"When he spoke, it was beautiful. He had that way of . . . I don't know to this day if he had written it out beforehand or if he just spoke from his heart. It appeared he spoke from his heart, and it was obvious he was very emotional. The things he said, you wish you could have—that's how eloquent he was."[11]

John Madden was the final eulogist. This was his touching, emotional good-bye to his partner of 21 years, in full:

"I got up this morning and I thought. 'Pat, I need you.' I couldn't get my tie tied and my top button buttoned. You know, Pat Summerall was there for every need I ever had.

"There were voices before Pat Summerall, and there'll be voices after, but he was the voice of the NFL.

"If there ever was a book written about good guys, he'd be the star of that book, because that's what Pat was. He was a card-carrying great guy, and he showed it all the time, and not just to special people. . . . To me, he was John Wayne. He was the toughest, quietest guy I've ever known. On TV he was Walter Cronkite, because you just felt the comfort being there with him.

"Standing next to him for 22 years, I felt that great comfort, and I saw all the things he did for people. And you could feel how special he was.

"I got the first feeling even before I started. The first year I worked with Pat full time was in 1981. The year 1979 was my first year in television. I had just gotten out of coaching, and I didn't know anything about television. I didn't know where you go, I had never been in a booth, I didn't know [laughing] you put the headset on and if you put the mic in front or the back of your head—I didn't know those things.

"So I signed a one-year contract to do four or five games, and one of those games—it could have been my second or third game—was with

Pat. You know, sometimes you think of all the places you don't belong. This is a place I didn't belong. I wasn't ready for that. Tom Brookshier, his great partner, had a family wedding that weekend, so they put me with Pat. And Pat treated me so well. And the biggest thing was, he treated me with respect. I didn't know when we were in commercial, I didn't know when we were on the air—but he didn't look down. He didn't grab your arm and say, 'I'm gonna help you.' He didn't have to say, 'I'm gonna help you.' He just damn did it.

"That was my third game, and I didn't know if I'd ever do another game after that or if I'd ever do another game with Pat. But I came away from there with one thought: This guy is really a good guy, and if I get nothing else out of this, I've got that. And then two years later we started working together. Twenty-two great years. Never had an argument. Never had a fight. I was always happy to see him.

"The thing that I miss most about being out of television is Thanksgiving. We had 22 straight Thanksgivings [together]. Most people talk about Thanksgiving, and they say it's family. How is it being away from your family? And we said for years, and these aren't idle words, 'This is our family.' I know Pat's up there saying, 'John, I told you, brevity, brevity, brevity. I told you.' [Looking up, laughing]. This is one more time I'm gonna talk over you.

"Twenty-two Thanksgivings. Twenty-two years of family, and we would say this is our family. Pat and I are family. Bob Stenner, Sandy Grossman, Lance Barrow, Richie Zyontz—for 22 years that was our family. That's as real as you can get. That's not talk, those aren't words . . .

"My first good-bye with Pat was at CBS. And we were together at CBS, and we lost football, and then we had our last telecast, which was tough because we didn't know what was gonna happen. Then we both went to Fox, and we had our last broadcast at Fox was Super Bowl XXXVI. Our last good-bye. [Voice cracking]. This is the third good-bye. It's the toughest. Good-bye, Pat. Rest in peace. I love you."[12]

Chapter Fifteen
AN ALL MADDEN FAREWELL

EVERY YEAR, ON THE SATURDAY BEFORE THE SUPER BOWL, A PANEL OF writers and broadcasters discuss and then vote on who will be admitted into the Pro Football Hall of Fame. A nominee must garner 80 percent of the vote or more to be admitted. In 1985, in John Madden's first year of eligibility, he became one of 15 finalists whom the 39 voters considered.

There was every reason he should have been a finalist. In the history of the NFL, Madden was the third fastest to accumulate 100 victories. Madden was so proud of that feat that he wore an all-diamond ring in the shape of the number 100. He also had the highest winning percentage (.659) of any coach who completed 10 seasons. Madden never had a losing season, and he reached the AFC conference finals in 7 of those 10 years, winning the Super Bowl in 1977.

But 1985 came and went without Madden getting voted in. There's no telling what could have turned voters against him. Perhaps it was his 1-6 record in AFC championship games. Perhaps it was the constant rumors that Al Davis was calling the shots in Oakland, or simply dislike for Al Davis himself, for his role in the war with the NFL in the early '60s. Then 1986 came without Madden even becoming a finalist for the Hall.

Madden had already seen two of his players enter the Hall: center Jim Otto in 1980 and quarterback-kicker George Blanda in 1981. Then, in 1987, his great guard Gene Upshaw was admitted. In 1988, his great wide receiver Fred Biletnikoff got in, and in 1989, Art Shell did too. In 1990, the great linebacker Ted Hendricks (known as the Mad Stork) was admitted, and in 1992, on the seventh try as a finalist, even Al Davis got in. In 2002, the ninth Raider, tight end Dave Casper, was enshrined.

All of those great players who were coached by Madden had their greatness recognized, but not a whisper of a vote for Madden himself. After that he just forgot about it and concentrated on being the best broadcaster he could be. For 20 years after he was nearly voted into the Hall in 1985, Madden had racked up Emmy after Emmy for his contribution behind a microphone.

By 2006, Madden was working for his fourth network, NBC, after 13 years with CBS, 8 with Fox, and 4 with ESPN. The NFL certainly was aware of what he had done to popularize its game. But the question remained: Could those 39 voters locked in a conference room be convinced? In 2006, for the first time in over two decades, Madden's name was on the list of finalists.

The voting process for the Pro Football Hall of Fame is unusual. Each finalist is assigned one voter, who knows that nominee's qualifications well, to argue that nominee's case for admittance before the entire body of voters. Ira Miller of *The San Francisco Chronicle* was assigned to Madden's case, which was strange indeed because in the '80s, Miller was one of the voters who felt Madden shouldn't get in. But this time, Miller looked at Madden's qualifications with fresh eyes and made a terrific discovery.

When Miller examined Madden's coaching record against some of the great coaches already in the Hall of Fame, he discovered that Madden had a winning record against every single one of them, including Chuck Noll (Steelers), Don Shula (Dolphins), Hank Stram (Chiefs), George Allen (Redskins), Tom Landry (Cowboys), Weeb Ewbank (Jets), Sid Gillman (Chargers), and Bud Grant (Vikings). In total, his record against those Hall of Fame coaches was 27-13-2.

When Miller spelled out that Madden scorecard to the voters, it became next to impossible not to vote for him.

Knowing he once again had a chance to get in, he thought that if he was selected, he would get a call from the NFL. Rich Eisen was going to announce the new members of the Hall at 2 p.m. on the NFL Network. One-thirty and one-forty-five came and went without John getting a call.

"Oh well," he thought. He watched with *Sunday Night Football* producer Fred Gaudelli and family members in a small room.

Someone asked him, Madden recalled, "'Do you want me to turn it down or off?' I said, 'I didn't make it, but let's watch it to see who did make it.'" Eisen announced the names in alphabetical order. First came Troy Aikman, then the New York Giants' great linebacker Harry Carson. "And next he said, 'John Madden.'"

Madden froze. He wanted to treasure that moment forever. "You go from believing you had a shot of going in," he said, "all the way down to no, you didn't make it, to now you're in the Hall of Fame.

"[When he heard his name announced] I didn't come down or anything, for 24 hours. I don't remember what happened. I just had tingles all over me. I've never been so emotional for so long. I mean the feeling didn't go away."[1]

Madden during Hall of Fame week surrounded by his former CBS colleagues. From left: Janis Delson, Mike Arnold, Sandy Grossman, Richie Zyontz (kneeling), Joan Vitrano, Bob Stenner (and ex-wife Jill), Mike Frank, and Rich Russo. COURTESY OF RICHIE ZYONTZ

The Madden Cruiser left Pleasanton five days before the Saturday induction ceremonies (August 5, 2006) and arrived three days later after going through nine states. That left Madden enough time to attend parties and see everyone. Throngs of friends and former colleagues from CBS, Fox, and ESPN traveled to Canton to be with John for his induction.

"He chartered a plane to bring 300 of his friends from Oakland there," said former CBS and Fox colleague Janis Delson. "And he went out to the airport to meet the plane. We gave him a shirt pre-stained with ketchup. That got a rousing applause."[2]

In 1992, Al Davis had asked Madden to do the formal introduction of Davis as a new member of the Hall of Fame. Madden returned the favor, 14 years later, asking Al to introduce him. Davis, now in his 70s, wore all black with a silver tie. Raiders colors, of course.

"Nine Raider legends, nine are in the Hall," Davis began, emphasizing the mistake the voters made by waiting so long to induct Madden. And then he listed them all. "We have waited patiently for some 25 years for John to join us as enshrined in this Hall of Fame.

"Today is a day when our heroes of the past become the legends of the future.... Time never really stops for the great ones. We wrap them in a cloak of immortality and remember what great people they were.

"John Madden, the chill goes through my body as I hear the roar and think of those special people, but seeing you, John, down on the sidelines prowling those sidelines, yelling at officials, that flaming red hair, those arms moving left and right, screaming at Raider players, and most of all winning football games. But that is fantasy. Fantasy isn't the answer here today. But what is not fantasy is you coming up to this podium to be enshrined in the Pro Football Hall of Fame. Ladies and gentlemen, the great John Madden."[3]

Madden stepped up to the podium and began by thanking Davis. "To have Al Davis here is something special. I mean if it weren't for Al, I wouldn't be here. He was the guy who gave me an opportunity. He was the guy who hired me 40 years ago, brought me into pro football. He was the guy that made me a head coach when I was 32 years old. I had two years pro coaching experience.

An All Madden Farewell

"Who the heck names a guy 32 years old as a head coach? Al Davis did. But he not only named me as head coach, he stood behind me and helped me and he provided me with players, with great players. As he was saying, nine of those players are in the Hall of Fame. I mean those are the type of players he provided me with.

"He stood behind me not only the 10 years I was a head coach, but he stood behind me for the last 40 years.... I remember that I had the opportunity to induct him into the Hall of Fame. At the time, I said, talking about loyalty, what a guy Al Davis was. I said, he's the guy, you know, if you had anything happen, you had one phone call, who would you make that phone call to? I said it would be Al Davis."

And then that laugh of Madden's that was so familiar crept into his speech.

"You have to stay with me a moment on this one," he said. "This is a little goofy here. You're going to say, 'There is old Madden being goofy again.' But, I started thinking about this after I got voted into the Hall of Fame. The more I think about it, the more I think it's true, and I believe it.

"Here is the deal. I think over in the Hall of Fame, that during the day, the people go through, they look at everything. At night, there's a time when they all leave.... Then there's just the workers. The workers start to leave. It gets down to just one person. That person turns out the lights and locks the door. [Then] I believe that the busts talk to each other. I can't wait for that conversation. I really can't wait. Vince Lombardi, Knute Rockne, Reggie [White], Walter Payton, all my ex-players, we'll be there forever and ever talking about whatever. That's what I believe. That's what I think is going to happen, and no one's ever going to talk me out of that."

And then Madden remembered what his father, who had died in 1960, had told him, which stayed with him the rest of his life.

"I was playing in summer baseball on three or four different teams," he said. "I told my dad I'm going to drop a couple of these because I want to get a job to make some money. My dad said, 'I'll give you a couple bucks, go caddie, make a few loops. You'll be okay.' He said, 'Don't work. Once you start to work, you're going to be working the rest of your life.'

"It's been a great road from Madden's Lot in Daly City. John Robinson, John, who would have believed this, huh? This is amazing. Jefferson High School with my first real coach, Joe McGrath. Then Roy Hughes at Cal Poly. My roommate Pat is here. My college roommate. Philadelphia Eagles, Norm Van Brocklin had a great influence on me. Hancock College with Al Balder. Then to San Diego State with a great coach that someday will be in here, Don Coryell. He had a real influence on my coaching. Joe Gibbs was on that staff, too.

"I just want to say in closing that it's been a great ride. I want to thank everyone who has been along for any part of it. Speaking of great rides, I was lucky enough to be carried off the field when we won Super Bowl XI. I was told it took like five or six guys to lift me up, then they dropped me. But that's okay, because that was me and that was then. You carry him off for a while, boom, you dump him on the ground. But it was the happiest moment of my life.

Surrounded by his sons, Mike (left) and Joe, John shares a family hug after his Hall of Fame induction. COURTESY OF MIKE MADDEN

"Today feels like the second time of my life that I'm being carried off on the shoulders of others. Yet, instead of off the field, it's into the Hall of Fame. Instead of five or six guys, I ride on the shoulders of hundreds of friends, coaches, players, colleagues, family. I just say this, thank you all very much. This has been the sweetest ride of them all. Thank you."[4]

About a year or so later, Madden's agent Sandy Montag noticed a slight change in John.

"He loved to travel," said Montag, "but during his last season one morning he called me. I asked, 'Where are you?' He said, 'I'm in Nebraska.' Then later that day he called again, and I asked again, and he said, 'I'm still in fucking Nebraska.'

"It was the first time I got off the phone thinking, something's different. Later toward the end of the regular season, he said to me in confidence, 'We have the Super Bowl, and I'm thinking of retiring.' I wasn't surprised because I felt something. But I told him: 'You have the playoffs, you have the Super Bowl. Let's do that, let's enjoy that and don't say anything until we talk after that. You might feel differently. Take some time after.'

"The next month he said, 'I haven't changed my mind, I want to retire. I'm gonna call Dick [Ebersol].' It was a tough conversation. Dick was surprised. It was a lucrative contract with two years left on it."

Ebersol asked Madden if he and Montag could fly up to San Francisco and spend some time with John in Pleasanton to discuss it. Ebersol obviously wanted to talk John out of retiring.

"We went to Pleasanton," said Montag. "We had dinner, spent a great day with John. Dick said to John, 'Maybe you work half the season.' John said: 'Look, Dick, that's it. When I retired as a coach, I said I'm never going to coach another game, and now I'm saying I'm never gonna broadcast another game the rest of my life.' It was sad, it was emotional. But it was in his best interests to do that."

"So, when John retired," Montag said, "he did some radio and some commercials. There was no health issue when John hung it up, but before he died, he had a triple bypass [in 2015]. After he had the surgery, he was fine. At the end, he had trouble with his hips and his knees. His football injuries caught up with him, and he wasn't as mobile as he'd like.

"When he retired, Virginia didn't really know he would, and at one point Virginia called me about a month after he retired. She said, 'I don't know what you guys are doing, but the game plan of him being home 24 hours a day—when did this come about? I suggest you find him something to do.'

"So I called [NFL commissioner Roger] Goodell, and we discussed John being part of the NFL going forward. Goodell asked him to be a special assistant to the commissioner, and also asked him to be co-chair of the players' safety committee, which reported to the competition committee. Through that, he continued to have an unpaid role with the NFL to just give something back. It was a way of staying involved. It was important for John to stay connected."

"He was himself to the very end," Montag continued. "Richie [Zyontz] brought up the idea [of the *All Madden* documentary], and I was the one guy against the idea. For 40 years, I was protective of his image, and I still am. That last year of his life, he didn't look like what people remembered. They hadn't seen him for a long time. At 85 years old, you look different. But we all agreed we'd do it [the documentary], and it ended up being fantastic.

"John watched it on Christmas Day, and our last text exchange after it was kind of a good-bye. He said it was great and that everyone loved it, and he wrote me, 'Thank you for everything you did to make it happen.' I wrote him back. It was an emotional exchange. He died three days later. He had hundreds of text messages from all over the world.

"In my own way, through that text exchange, I was telling him what he's meant to my life, and my career—was me saying good-bye."[5]

―――

Of all the young guys who worked with John, beginning in 1982, Richie Zyontz was by far the closest to him. They were best friends, but it was almost like a father-and-son relationship through the years. And John not only introduced Richie to his wife-to-be, but he also hosted their wedding at his home in Pleasanton.

"I probably saw John more than anybody toward the end," said Zyontz. "I felt that you've got to honor people before they're gone. So, I had this idea [the *All Madden* documentary], and I wanted to do it. When I got in touch with Fox Sports head Eric Shanks, he didn't even blink. He said, 'Great idea.' He had just hired Tom Rinaldi [from ESPN], a brilliant journalist, and he put this project together using Tom as the single-voice narrator of the show. It was a perfect fit.

"We went through names of people who should be in the show. I wanted to stay involved in the project because John trusted me. We went with [his agent Sandy] Montag to visit John and lay out what it would look like. Then we brought in Joel Santos to produce the documentary who worked with Rinaldi putting it together. We ran by John people he'd like to be involved, players he liked.

"Fox turned the soundstage John had built in his backyard into this beautiful stage and backdrop. And John was the last person interviewed. [They interviewed people all over the country during that summer.] That last day, when we interviewed John, we picked up speed as we went along. Tom Rinaldi asked the questions, and John was able to look right into the camera lens and see Tom's face while being interviewed. It was a cool technique these guys came up with.

"It was so meaningful to him. Joel and Tom had this great idea to show John, even before his interview, clips from some of the people who were on the show. He sat in a chair and saw people like Joe Montana and Lawrence Taylor, and I can just see his face lighting up.

"We worried about his endurance. He hadn't done any interviews for 10 years. His mind never wavered. His mind was sharp, except physically he was a wreck.

"John's ailments: hearing—they had a hearing device [not a hearing aid] that was on the table. That he hung in there and was amenable to diving into every topic. Matt Millen and Willie Yarbrough [the Madden Cruiser driver] were people John wanted there. We'd take breaks and go over and talk to John. It was just a joyous day [July 7, 2021] taping.

"He slowed down, he moved slow. He went to regular checkups, and he was always a picture of health into his 70s. Full head of hair. It just started to hit him like a ton of bricks toward the end."[6]

The *All Madden* documentary was broadcast by Fox on Christmas to rave reviews. John Madden watched it live with his family and friends alongside him at his home.

That week Richie and John shared these final text messages about the documentary:

December 23

John: "What have you heard [about it]?"

Richie: "People are saying it's damn well done."

John: "But what do you say?"

December 25

Richie: "Merry Christmas to you and yours."

John (ignoring): "Did you see the whole show?"

Richie: "Yes, it's excellent."

Madden: "Thanks for everything you did to make this happen."

Richie: "I wish it could have been an hour longer. This is a far cry from an All-Madden [Team] shoot with four doughnuts and fatty chicken."

December 26

Richie to John: "Happy anniversary. Say hello to Virginia."

John (ignoring good wishes): "Thanks. Everyone says it should have been longer." (It was 90 minutes long.)

Richie: "I felt that way. No one said it was too long. All the Maddens done good."

"Nobody had the feeling he was going to die soon," said Zyontz. "He had a guy named Jim Otten that was helping out the family. He was driving John to a routine doctor's appointment, and he died in the car on the way."

That was December 28, just two days after John and Virginia's 62nd anniversary.

"The family held a private service," Zyontz recalled, "at a Catholic church in Oakland, Cathedral of Christ the Light. June [Richie's wife, for whom Madden was the matchmaker] and I went to the small service. She was devastated."[7]

The eulogies were the best reviews Madden ever received.

NFL commissioner **Roger Goodell** said that Madden "*was* football," adding, "There will never be another John Madden, and we will forever be indebted to him for all he did to make football and the NFL what it is today."

Dick Ebersol, the former president of NBC Sports, said, "There hasn't been anybody like him [Madden] before, and I guarantee you, there will never be anyone like him again."

Jerry Jones: "When I bought the Cowboys, we were 1-15 that first year, and I couldn't have been more depressed. Then I got a call from John and Al Davis. They were so optimistic and so reassuring that we were on the right track. They told me how competitive we had been. I'll never forget that call. When John got his bus, we used to have 40-yard bus races with my bus in our parking lot. And one time when just the two of us were ordering barbecue, I ordered some extra for the middle [of the table]. John loved that. He said he thought he was the only one who ordered extra for the middle."

Even 95-year-old **Vin Scully** had some kind words regarding his time with Madden: "He taught me so much," Scully told the Associated Press. "Eventually he met his true partner, and that would be Pat Summerall. The coach was kind of garrulous and full of beans. Pat was kind of understated and quiet, and as a former football player, he knew exactly how it felt and what it was like, and they made a perfect partnership. And I was so happy that I had spent a little time with John."[8]

Zyontz recalled one of the last times he saw Madden:

A couple of months before John died, I got to visit John at the hotel the family owns in Pleasanton, called the Rose Hotel. That was the meeting place. We'd sit in the lobby and talk for a couple of hours. Toward the end of his life, I'd visit him by myself. We'd sit for a couple of hours and tell stories. When it was time to go, you know John's not a hugger, so we shook hands. The parking lot to the hotel is right by the back door. John had his walker, and he was slowly making his way and I was very carefully helping him without showing him that I was trying to help him, to his big white pickup truck. I put the walker in the back of the truck and then he gets in. I walk about 30 feet to my car and I'm about to get into my car, and all of a sudden, he yells out, "Richie!" So I literally run the 30 feet to the truck to see what's wrong. I was palpitating. I was worried. And he just goes, in a soft voice, "Thanks for coming."[9]

Afterword

In 1977, the likeable Bill Riordan was managing the career of tennis great Jimmy Connors. That year he promoted and sold a series of matches to CBS featuring Connors against other top players. The matches were promoted as "winner-take-all" matches, with the winner of each match alleged to get all the prize money. The matches, which aired Sundays during the winter, were very popular, but a mini-scandal ensued when it was revealed that the losers got paid too.

Despite the bad publicity, Riordan remained well-liked among CBS Sports executives. In 1981, he was asked by a business associate to see if he could get that man's daughter a job at CBS Sports. Her name was Diana Rollnick, and she had just graduated from UCLA. Riordan called Kevin O'Malley, who agreed to meet her despite CBS having an overall job freeze at the time. O'Malley liked her and then sent her to meet executive Kay Wight, hoping she could do something. Kay then sent her to meet another executive, but no one mentioned anything about a job freeze. Eventually, Diana realized it was time to look elsewhere.

Riordan and I had a love for Thoroughbred racing in common, and we had enjoyed several lunch "meetings" at Belmont Park when he called asking for help. "I really screwed up," he said. "I promised a friend I'd get his daughter a job at CBS Sports and I didn't realize there was a job freeze there. She's now working at a talent agency and doesn't really know anyone in New York. Would you please take her to Runyon's and introduce her to some of our friends."

It turned out that Diana and I got along famously. She was from the Bay Area and was a big fan of the 49ers, who were on their way to the Super Bowl that year. It wasn't quite a whirlwind romance, but it certainly was fun. She met me for the Super Bowl in Detroit and we dined with *Saturday Night Live* head writer Jim Downey the night before the game. Downey was there because I had arranged with SNL producer Dick Ebersol for John Madden to host the show the week following the game. Around that time, Diana and I were also joined by Ebersol and his wife, film and TV star Susan Saint James, for an evening of tennis and a late-night snack at Elaine's, a Manhattan celebrity haunt. It was Ebersol who got us in.

Over the next few years, we also enjoyed a number of dinners with Madden and Jimmy the Greek. One day a few years later, Diana and I were walking along Central Park West in Manhattan when we bumped into John. He had just purchased his new apartment at The Dakota and, like a kid with a new toy, insisted that we come over to see it. That's how I remember John: joyful and fun to be with. I never thought that would be the last time I'd see him in person.

Diana and I were married in 1984, shortly after I left CBS Sports for a job on Wall Street. I am saddened that I lost touch with John during those years, but I always felt I could reach him if I needed to—that he would always be my friend. The years flew by, Diana and I had twins, and I always felt like we'd see John again someday. Then in 2021, when I heard that Fox was doing the *All Madden* documentary, I sat down and wrote him a letter. Nearly 40 years had passed by, but I was certain he'd write me back or call. I mailed the letter on December 17, right before the show aired on Christmas Day. He died three days later. The show was so wonderful, and it was so great to see him on it, even at age 85, and then so sad to lose him, and realize that my letter may never have reached him.

In a way, this book is my way of saying good-bye to John. And as for Diana, she is the "Diana" to whom this book is dedicated.

Rich Podolsky, March 2025

Acknowledgments

WHEN I SET OUT TO WRITE THIS BOOK, THE IDEA STEMMED FROM CONversations with my friend Janis Delson, a former executive at both CBS Sports and Fox Sports. Her thoughts and recollections were invaluable. Two others were also incredibly helpful. First is Sandy Montag, who represented both Pat Summerall and John Madden, and was Madden's close friend for decades. The other is Richie Zyontz, who more than 40 years ago began as Madden's broadcast associate and became his close friend. Richie and his wife June also provided some great photos from their wedding at the Madden house. Without their help and guidance, this book would have never happened.

I also need to thank Joe Buck and Troy Aikman, who gave their time to be interviewed and provided material that became the forewords for this book. Joe's recollections of his dad with Pat and Troy's of his close friendship with John made for great forewords.

This book could not have been achieved without the help of my personal editor, Mike Sisak, whom I first met in 1970 (see the author's note), and my editors from Lyons Press, Rick Rinehart and production editor Nicole Myers.

Besides Janis and Richie, I need to thank Ed Goren and David Hill from Fox Sports for their openness and willingness to discuss difficult decisions, Van Gordon Sauter and Peter Lund for discussing important events from their executive perch at CBS Sports, and former CBS Sports colleagues who were also an enormous support system. They include Joan Vitrano and Mike Frank for the anecdotes and photos provided, Bob Stenner, Tom O'Neill, Ted Shaker, Bill Fitts, Ellen Beckwith, Dick Stockton, Gary Bender, Lesley Visser, Rich Nelson, Hal Trencher, Lance

Barrow, Bob Fishman, Jay Rosenstein, George Rothweiler, George Schweitzer, Lou D'Ermilio (also Fox), Mary Kouw, and Adrian Stubbs.

Others who contributed their time and a helping hand were John's sons, Mike and Joe Madden; Pat's widow, Cheri Summerall; and Pat's son, Jay Summerall. Also Ray Didinger, Mike Weisman, Richard Sandomir, Terry Stewart, John Kelly, and Dave Sims, and from the Dallas Cowboys, Tad Carper and Jerry Jones. And, of course, thanks go out to Jim Nantz, Al Michaels, Bob Costas, and Tony Kornheiser for their comments regarding Madden and Summerall and the stories in this book.

And my thanks go out to Terry O'Neil for making it all possible.

Notes

Chapter 1: Will the Real John Madden Please Stand Up

1. "Hey, Wait a Minute! I Want to Talk," *Sports Illustrated*, September 1, 1983.
2. Author interview with Gary Bender, May 7, 2024.
3. Author interview with Mike Weisman, May 8, 2024.
4. Author interview with Jim Cross, May 1, 2025.
5. Bryan Burwell, *Madden: A Biography* (Chicago: Triumph Books, 2011).
6. Author email exchange with Bob Costas, June 22, 2024.
7. Burwell, *Madden*.
8. Author interview with Bob Fishman, May 9, 2024.
9. Pat Summerall, *Summerall: On and Off the Air* (Nashville, TN: Thomas Nelson, 2008).
10. Author interview with Kevin O'Malley, May 29, 2024.
11. Terry O'Neil, *The Game Behind the Game: High Pressure, High Stakes in Television Sports* (New York: HarperCollins, 1989).
12. Author interview with Jay Rosenstein, June 5, 2024.
13. Author interview with Sandy Montag. All Sandy Montag interviews were conducted from August to October 2024.

Chapter 2: Summerall: Right Place, Right Time

1. Pat Summerall, *Summerall: On and Off the Air* (Nashville, TN: Thomas Nelson, 2008).
2. Summerall, *On and Off the Air*.
3. Author interviews with Cheri Summerall from July to August 2024.
4. Summerall, *On and Off the Air*.
5. Pat Summerall and Michael Levin, *Giants: What I Learned about Life from Vince Lombardi and Tom Landry* (New York: Wiley, 2010).
6. Summerall, *On and Off the Air*.
7. "The Voice Is Familiar . . . But Pat Summerall, Who Will Broadcast His 11th Super Bowl on Sunday, Is a Hard Guy to Figure," *Sports Illustrated*, January 26, 1987.
8. Summerall, *On and Off the Air*.
9. Summerall, *On and Off the Air*.

Chapter 3: Masterclass by the Dutchman
1. Peter Richmond, *Game for Life: John Madden* (New York: Random House, 2019).
2. Bryan Burwell, *Madden: A Biography* (Chicago: Triumph Books, 2011).
3. Richmond, *Game for Life*.
4. Burwell, *Madden*.
5. Richmond, *Game for Life*.
6. Larry Peña, *Cal Poly Magazine*, Fall 2022.
7. Peña, *Cal Poly Magazine*, Fall 2022.
8. Richmond, *Game for Life*.

Chapter 4: It's "Super Summerall"
1. Bryan Burwell, *Madden: A Biography* (Chicago: Triumph Books, 2011).
2. Rich Podolsky, *You Are Looking Live! How the NFL Today Revolutionized Sports Broadcasting* (Guilford, CT: Lyons Press, 2021).
3. Author interview with Ellen Beckwith, July 24, 2024.
4. Pat Summerall, *Summerall: On and Off the Air* (Nashville, TN: Thomas Nelson, 2008).
5. Bill Lyon, *When the Clock Runs Out: 20 NFL Greats Share Their Stories of Hardship and Triumph* (Chicago: Triumph Books, 1999).
6. Summerall, *On and Off the Air*.
7. David Halberstam, SportsBroadcastJournal.com, January 21, 2020.
8. Summerall, *On and Off the Air*.
9. Summerall, *On and Off the Air*.
10. *New York Times*, October 18, 1966.
11. Summerall, *On and Off the Air*.
12. Summerall, *On and Off the Air*.
13. Author interview with Bill Fitts, May 14, 2024.
14. Summerall, *On and Off the Air*.
15. Bryan Burwell, *Madden: A Biography* (Chicago: Triumph Books, 2011).
16. Summerall, *On and Off the Air*.
17. Author interview with Joe Buck, August 29, 2024.
18. Lyon, *When the Clock Runs Out*.

Chapter 5: Madden and Summerall Rise to New Heights
1. Bryan Burwell, *Madden: A Biography* (Chicago: Triumph Books, 2011).
2. *All Madden*, Fox Sports Special, December 25, 2023.
3. Burwell, *Madden*.
4. Larry Peña, *Cal Poly Magazine*, Fall 2022.
5. Burwell, *Madden*.
6. Burwell, *Madden*.
7. *All Madden* documentary, Fox Sports, December 15, 2021.
8. *All Madden* documentary.
9. Author interview with Mike Frank. All Mike Frank interviews were conducted from July through October 2024.

Notes

10. *All Madden* documentary.
11. Raiders.com.
12. Raiders.com.
13. Burwell, *Madden*.
14. *All Madden* documentary.
15. *All Madden* documentary.
16. Peter Richmond, *Game for Life: John Madden* (New York: Random House, 2019).
17. Burwell, *Madden*.
18. "The Voice Is Familiar . . . But Pat Summerall, Who Will Broadcast His 11th Super Bowl on Sunday, Is a Hard Guy to Figure," *Sports Illustrated*, January 26, 1987.
19. Steve Tignor, Tennis.com, April 6, 2013.

Chapter 6: The Rise and Fall of Brookshier— and Summerall

1. Bill Lyon, *When the Clock Runs Out: 20 NFL Greats Share Their Stories of Hardship and Triumph* (Chicago: Triumph Books, 1999).
2. Lyon, *When the Clock Runs Out*.
3. Author interview with Ray Didinger, July 12, 2024.
4. Author interview with Ray Didinger, July 12, 2024.
5. ClassicSportsMedia.blogspot.com.
6. Lyon, *When the Clock Runs Out*.
7. Lyon, *When the Clock Runs Out*.
8. Author interviews with Bob Stenner from May to October 2024.
9. Author interviews with Bob Stenner.
10. Pat Summerall, *Summerall: On and Off the Air* (Nashville, TN: Thomas Nelson, 2008).
11. Author interviews with Bob Stenner.
12. Terry O'Neil, *The Game Behind the Game: High Pressure, High Stakes in Television Sports* (New York: HarperCollins, 1989).
13. Author interviews with Ted Shaker from May to October 2024.
14. Summerall, *On and Off the Air*.

Chapter 7: For John Madden, 1980 "Tasted Great!"

1. Author interview with Gary Bender, May 7, 2024.
2. Author interview with Joe and Mike Madden, July 4, 2024, and July 5, 2024.
3. Brandon Wenerd, BroBible.com, 2016.
4. Author interviews with Richie Zyontz from May to October 2024.
5. "John Madden Made Light Beer Legitimate," *USA Today*, December 28, 2021.
6. Bryan Burwell, *Madden: A Biography* (Chicago: Triumph Books, 2011).
7. Author interview with Gary Bender, May 8, 2024.
8. Author interview with Rich Nelson, July 23, 2024.
9. Author interview with Gary Bender, May 8, 2024.

Chapter 8: The Contest: Would It Be Summerall or Scully?

1. Terry O'Neil, *The Game Behind the Game: High Pressure, High Stakes in Television Sports* (New York: HarperCollins, 1989).
2. "There's Only One Way Up," *Sports Illustrated*, September 8, 1980.
3. Author interview with Van Gordon Sauter, May 23, 2024.
4. Author interview with Richie Zyontz, May 30, 2024.
5. Author interview with Van Gordon Sauter.
6. O'Neil, *The Game Behind the Game*.
7. Author interview with Kevin O'Malley.
8. Author interview with Richie Zyontz.
9. Author interview with Mike Madden.
10. O'Neil, *The Game Behind the Game*.
11. O'Neil, *The Game Behind the Game*.
12. Author interview with Kevin O'Malley.
13. O'Neil, *The Game Behind the Game*.
14. Author interview with Van Gordon Sauter.
15. O'Neil, *The Game Behind the Game*.
16. JoeMontanasRightArm.com, August 9, 2022.
17. *Dallas Morning News*, September 30, 2016.
18. Author interview with Van Gordon Sauter.
19. "Another Win for Napoleon," *Sports Illustrated*, January 30, 1984.
20. Author interview with Dick Stockton, May 31, 2024. All Dick Stockton interviews were conducted from May to September 2024.
21. Author interviews with Bob Stenner.
22. O'Neil, *The Game Behind the Game*.
23. O'Neil, *The Game Behind the Game*.

Chapter 9: What Made Them Great

1. Author interview with Dick Stockton.
2. Author interview with Richie Zyontz.
3. Author interviews with Ed Goren from May to September 2024.
4. Author interview with Richard Sandomir, email exchange, July 15, 2024. All Richard Sandomir interviews were conducted from July to August 2024.
5. Author interview with Dick Stockton.
6. Author interview with Jim Nantz.
7. Terry O'Neil, *The Game Behind the Game: High Pressure, High Stakes in Television Sports* (New York: HarperCollins, 1989).
8. O'Neil, *The Game Behind the Game*.
9. Author interview with Joan Vitrano, June 28, 2024.
10. Richard Sandomir, *New York Times*, January 18, 1984.
11. Author interview with George Rothweiler, May 17, 2024.

Notes

12. Raiders.com.
13. Author interviews with Ted Shaker.
14. O'Neil, *The Game Behind the Game*
15. O'Neil, *The Game Behind the Game*.
16. Author interview with Jim Downey, November 12, 2024.
17. Author's previous conversations with O'Neil.
18. Author interview with Hal Trencher, June 14, 2024.
19. Author interview with Mike Frank.
20. Author interviews with Bob Stenner.
21. Author interview with Mike Arnold, June 27, 2024.
22. Author interviews with Janis Delson and Ted Shaker. Author interviews with Janis Delson from February to October 2024 and also via email exchange.
23. Fox Sports 1998 charity dinner for birth defects.
24. Fox Sports 1998 charity dinner.
25. Raiders.com.
26. Author interview with George Rothweiler, May 17, 2024.

Chapter 10: The Train, the Bus, the Game, the All-Madden Team, and the Matchmaker

1. Author interview with Sandy Montag.
2. Author interview with Sandy Montag.
3. Author interview with Sandy Montag.
4. Peter King, *Sports Illustrated*, January 30, 2015.
5. Author interview with Sandy Montag.
6. Lesley Visser column in SportsBroadcastJournal.com, January 31, 2021.
7. Author interviews with Janis Delson.
8. Author interview with Troy Aikman, August 18, 2024.
9. "The Coppell Deli's Stubbs Sandwich Might Kill," *Dallas Observer*, February 13, 2012.
10. Author interviews with Janis Delson.
11. Author interview with Mike Arnold.
12. Author interview with Joan Vitrano, June 28, 2024.
13. Author interview with Joan Vitrano, June 28, 2024.
14. Author interviews with Janis Delson.
15. O'Neil, *The Game Behind the Game*.
16. *USA Today*, November 28, 2024.
17. Author interview with Mike Frank.
18. Author interview with Richie Zyontz.
19. Author interview with June Zyontz.
20. Email exchange with Janis Delson.

Chapter 11: Disaster: How CBS Lost the NFL Contract

1. "CBS Has Won the World Series . . . Now It Could Lose Its Shirt," *New York Times*, July 23, 1989.
2. "This Changes Everything," *Sports Illustrated*, July 9, 2012.
3. *Baltimore Sun*, "CBS' Dream Season Turned to Nightmare," September 30, 2021.
4. "This Changes Everything."
5. "This Changes Everything."
6. Rich Podolsky, *You Are Looking Live! How the NFL Today Revolutionized Sports Broadcasting* (Guilford, CT: Lyons Press, 2021).
7. Author interview with Jerry Jones, September 5, 2024.
8. Author interview with Peter Lund.
9. "The Great NFL Heist: How Fox Paid for and Changed Football Forever," The Ringer, December 13, 2018.
10. Author interview with Jerry Jones.
11. Author interview with Sandy Montag.
12. Kara Swisher, *Burn Book: A Tech Love Story* (New York: Simon and Schuster, 2024).
13. "The Great NFL Heist."
14. Author interview with Sandy Montag.
15. "The Voice Is Familiar . . . But Pat Summerall, Who Will Broadcast His 11th Super Bowl on Sunday, Is a Hard Guy to Figure," *Sports Illustrated*, January 26, 1987.
16. Author interviews with Bob Stenner.
17. Author interview with Dick Stockton.
18. Author interview with Richie Zyontz.
19. Author interview with Ed Goren.
20. Author interview with Mike Arnold.
21. Author interview with Mike Frank.
22. Author interviews with Janis Delson.
23. Author interviews with Janis Delson.

Chapter 12: The Intervention

1. Author interviews with Cheri Summerall.
2. Pat Summerall, *Summerall: On and Off the Air* (Nashville, TN: Thomas Nelson, 2008).
3. Author interviews with Janis Delson.
4. Author interview with Richie Zyontz.
5. Author interviews with Bob Stenner.
6. Author interviews with Ted Shaker.
7. Author interview with Mike Arnold.
8. Author interviews with Ted Shaker.
9. Author interviews with Bob Stenner.
10. Author interviews with Ted Shaker.
11. Author interviews with Ted Shaker.
12. Author interview with Chuck Milton, June 1, 2024.
13. Author interviews with Janis Delson.
14. Author interviews with Janis Delson.
15. Author interview with Peter Lund.

Notes

16. *New York Times*, January 27, 1992.
17. Author interview with Peter Lund.
18. Author interview with Ed Goren.

Chapter 13: It Was the Perfect Marriage—Until It Wasn't

1. Author interview with David Hill. All David Hill interviews were conducted from June to July 2024, through email exchange.
2. Author interview with David Hill.
3. Author interview with Ed Goren.
4. Author interview with David Hill.
5. Author interview with David Hill.
6. Author interview with Ed Goren.
7. Author interview with David Hill.
8. Author interviews with Cheri Summerall.
9. *Los Angeles Times*, January 25, 2002.
10. Author interview with Jay Summerall.

Chapter 14: Saying Good-Bye to Pat

1. Madden and Summerall quotes from CBS Super Bowl broadcast.
2. Author interview with Joan Vitrano.
3. Author interviews with Cheri Summerall.
4. Author interviews with Cheri Summerall.
5. "Pat Summerall Remembered as 'Voice of the NFL,'" NFL.com, April 20, 2013, https://www.nfl.com/news/pat-summerall-remembered-as-voice-of-the-nfl-0ap1000000162146.
6. Author interviews with Cheri Summerall.
7. From recording of Pat Summerall memorial service.
8. Pat Summerall memorial service.
9. Pat Summerall memorial service.
10. Author interview with Sandy Montag.
11. Author interviews with Bob Stenner.
12. John Madden at Pat Summerall memorial service.

Chapter 15: An All Madden Farewell

1. Author interview with Mike Madden.
2. Author interviews with Janis Delson.
3. Al Davis speech from NFL Hall of Fame transcript.
4. Madden speech from Hall of Fame transcript.
5. Author interview with Sandy Montag.
6. Author interview with Richie Zyontz.
7. Author interview with Richie Zyontz.
8. Associated Press quotes from Goodell, Ebersol, Jones, and Scully.
9. Author interview with Richie Zyontz.

Index

Page numbers in italic indicate images.

Aikman, Troy, xxvii, 131
Albertville Winter Olympics, 155
All-California Collegiate Athletic Association, 25
Allen, George, 9–10
All Madden (documentary), 130, 194–96
All-Madden Team, 98, 134–36, *136*, 149, 153, 160
Alston, Walter, 48
Alworth, Lance, 45
Amdur, Neil, 108
Arledge, Roone, 141
Arnold, Mike, 117–18, *123*, 133, 135–36, 153, 160
The Athletic, 129
Atkinson, George, 55
Austrian, Neil, 146–48

Bain, Bill, 134
Baltimore Colts, 47, 49
Banaszak, Pete, 51
Barrow, Lance, 183
basketball broadcasts, 142–43
Beathard, Bobby, 25
Beckwith, Ellen, 32
Beman, Deane, 163–64
Bender, Gary, 2, 71–73, 80–81
Betty Ford Clinic, 165–68
Beverly Wilshire Hotel, 9–11
Bleier, Rocky, 85–86
Bornstein, Steve, 146

Bradshaw, Terry, 49, 152
Brady, Tom, 111
Brendle, Bill, 33, 157–58
"broacast associate" positions, 87–88
Brookshier, Tom: background, 59–61; early broadcasting jobs, 61–63; end of Summerall partnership, xxv, 86, 89–91, 103–4; Musburger and, 99; personality, 61, 64; Summerall's relationship with, 41–42, 63–68, 69, 157–60; in "The Intervention," 164–65; on *This Week in the NFL*, 63–65; University of Louisville remarks, 69
Brown, Jimmy, 60, 62–63
Buck, Joe, xxvii, 37–41, 154–55, 176–77
bus trips, 126–28, 130, 162, 190, 195

California State Polytechnic University, 25, 79
cameras and cameramen, 96–97, 109–10
Cartwright, Gary, 64
Casper, Dave, 48
CBS Sports: baseball contracts, 141–42, 146; CBS Chalkboard, 97, 112–16, 121; early history of NFL broadcasts, xxiv–xxvii; losing contracts, 142–43, 151–55; spending sprees, 141–43; Summerall's early days with, 37–41. *See also specific CBS broadcasters and executives*
Cervantes, June, 137–38, *139*

championship broadcasts, xxiv. *See also* Super Bowls
Chirkinian, Frank, 55–56, 150, 161, 161–62, 164, 183
Christman, Paul, xxv
Chuy's restaurant, 130
Clark, Dwight, 114
claustrophobia, 2, 78–80, 126, 128
College of San Mateo, 24–25
Conerly, Charlie, 19, 20–21
Cook, Beano, 33
Cope, Myron, 49
Coryell, Don, 29, 43–44, 192
Cosell, Howard, xxvi–xxvii, 34–35, 173
Costas, Bob, 4–6, 55
"Counter Trey," 113–14
Cross, Irv, 61, 99–100
Culpepper, Chuck, 56
Culverhouse, Hugh, 163–64

Dailey, Bob, 40
Dallas Cowboys, 92, 95, 131, 144–45
Daly City, 23
Dangerfield, Rodney, 76, 78
Davis, Al, 44–46, 47–48, 73–78, 190–91
Delson, Janis, 93, 99, 118, 130–32, 137–38, 153–55, 190
Denver Broncos, 52–53
Didinger, Ray, 60
Dolph, Jack, 39
Downey, Jim, 115
DuMont Network, xxiii, xxiv–xxv, 39

Ebersol, Dick, 193, 197
Eisen, Rich, 188–89
Emmy Awards, 1, 84, 110, 116, 118–19, 169, 188
Enberg, Dick, 173

Fields, Virginia, 25–26, 28–29
Fighting Back (O'Neil), 85–86
Fishman, Bob, 7
Fitts, Bill, 39, 40
food stops, 130–33

football video games, 128–29
"Fox Box," 170
Fox network: Grossman at, 152, 153, 169; Madden at, 148–49, *149*, *150*; new hires for Fox Sports, 169–70; NFL contract, 144–48; Stenner signing with, 169; Summerall at, *149*, 149–50
Frank, Barry, 2–4, 148–49, 151–52
Frank, Mike, 49–50, 153, 159

The Game Behind the Game (O'Neil), 88, 100, 101, 158
game preparation, xxvii–xxviii, 108–12, 117
Gaudelli, Fred, 189
Gibbs, Joe, 43
Gifford, Frank, xxvi–xxvii, 22, 61
Gillman, Sid, 46
Goodell, Roger, 194, 197
Goren, Ed, 106, 153, 154, 166, 168, 169–73
Governali, Paul, 45
Gowdy, Curt, xxv
Grange, Red, xxiv
Grays Harbor College, 25
Green Bay Packers, 46–47
Green Bay Power Sweep, 45
Grimm, Russ, 113–14
Gross, Herb, 10–11
Grossman, Sandy: CBS Chalkboard and, 113; concern about Summerall's drinking, 159–61, 166–67; at Fox network, 152, 153, 169; importance of, 107

Harrington, Jim, 93
Harris, Franco, 49
Hawkins, Trip, 128–29
Healey, Joe, *3*
"Heidi" game, 47
Hey, Wait a Minute (I Wrote a Book) (Madden), 79
Hill, David, 145, 169–75

Index

Hookstratten, Ed, 88–89
Howell, Jim Lee, 18

"I" formation offense, 29
Immaculate Reception call, 49–50, *50*
interruptible foldback earpiece, 40
Isaacs, Stan, 67

Jackson, Keith, xxvi–xxvii
The Jack Sterling Show, 35–37
Jacobs, Kathy, 18
Jacoby, Joe, 113–14
Jones, Jerry, 144–45, 146–47, 181, 182, 197
Jordan, Michael, 142–43

Kansas City, 48–49
Kelley, Steve, 173–74
Kennedy, Ray, 126
Kennedy's assassination, 33
King, Peter, 127–28
Krieger, George, 153

Lamonica, Daryle, 48
Landers, Barry, 34–35
Landry, Tom, 19, 32
Layne, Bobby, 16–18, 158
Lenz, Bob, 75
Lombardi, Vince, 19–20, 28, 40, 45–47
Lubell, Ron, 71
lunches in New York, 32–33, 40–41
Lund, Peter, 100, 145–48, 160, 163–68
Lyon, Bill, 39, 64

MacPhail, Bill, 32–33, 37–39, 61, 158
Madden, John: *All Madden* (documentary), 130, 194–96; All-Madden Team, 98, 134–36, *136*, 149, 160; autobiography, 79; awards and tributes, 1, 116, 118–19, 169, 188, 197; claustrophobia and fears, 2–3, 8, 55, 78–80, 125–26, 155; death, 196–97; as Eagles player, 25, 26–28; favorite food stops, 130–33; health issues, 1, 53, 195;

as matchmaker, 136–38, *139*; in Miller Lite commercials, 11, 73–74, 87; personality, 4, 80, 86–87, 88, 132–33; turduckens for Thanksgiving, 133–35; video game, 128–29; youth and college years, 23–26, 28. *See also* Madden as broadcaster; Madden as coach; Madden Cruiser; Madden family
Madden as broadcaster: auditions, 4–9; Bender paired with, 72–73; CBS and NBC negotiations, 3–4; at Fox network, 148–49, *149*, *150*; Maddenisms, 120–21; retirement, 193–94; style and talents, 68, 80, 86–87, 88, 104, 132; on Summerall, 119–20, 171–72, 176, 179, 184–86; teaching perspective, 111–12. *See also* partnership of Madden and Summerall; partnership success; Pro Football Hall of Fame
Madden as coach: at Alan Hancock College, 29; learning the job, 27–28; Lombardi and, 46; with Raiders, 2–3, 47–51; retirement, 1–2, *54*, 54–55; at San Diego State, 43–44; Stringley and, 53–54; style and talents, 48, 51–52; at Super Bowl XI, 52, *52*
Madden Cruiser, 126–28, 130, 164, 190, 195
Madden family: hosting Zyontz's backyard wedding, 138, *139*; Joe, *54*, 74, *192*; Mike, *54*, 55, 74, 92, *192*; Summerall as part of, 186; *Time Out* (boat) trips, 80–81; Virginia, 2, 25–26, 28–29, *54*, 74, *74*, 194
Madden NFL (video game), 128–29
Major League Baseball, 141–42
Mantle, Mickey, 34, 162, 180
Manuche, Mike, 40–41
Mara, Wellington, 32
Martindale, Wink, 22, 36
Marty Glickman Award, 125
Martzke, Rudy, 153, 154
McCann Erikson advertising agency, 75

McCarthy, Clem, xxiii
McKay, John, 29
McKenna, Jim, 87–88
Meredith, "Dandy" Don, xxvi–xxvii
Miami Dolphins, 49
Michaels, Al, 177
Millen, Matt, 111–12, 130
Miller, Ira, 188
Miller Lite commercials, 11, 73–74, 87
Milton, Charles "Chuck," III, 7, 64–65, 72, 93, *123*, 166
Minnesota Vikings, 51
Monday Night Football, xxvi
Montag, Sandy: as agent, 11, 148–50; on Madden retiring, 193–94; receiving Marty Glickman Award, 125; at Summerall funeral, 184–85; traveling with Madden, 125–27, *127*, 128–29, 132
Montana, Joe, 110–11, 128
Murder, She Wrote promos, 116–17
Murdoch, Rupert, 144–50, *150*
Musburger, Brent, 9–10, 84, 98–101
Mushnick, Phil, 100, 175–76

Nantz, Jim, 107–8, 182
Nathanson, Ted, 4
NBA broadcasts, 142–43
NBC broadcasts, xxiv
Nelson, Rich, 79–80, 159
Nettleship, Johnny, 79
New England Patriots, 51–52, *52*, 53
New York Giants, 18–20, *21*, 114
New York Jets, 47
The NFL Today, 84

Oakland Raiders, 2–3, 46–51, 177
Ohlmeyer, Don, 4
Olympics coverage, 157
O'Malley, Kevin, 9–11, 86, 89
O'Neil, Terry: All-Madden Team and, 134–36, *136*; background, 85–86; changing culture of broadcasts, xxvii, 108–12; contributing to Madden's success, 96–98; departing from CBS, 98; hiring Madden, 87–89; increasing camaraderie, 121–24, *122*, *123*; at NBC, 142; partnership of Madden and Summerall and, 89–94, 98, 103–4; personality, 95–96; restricting alcohol on game day, 159, 160; volunteering to talk to Scully, 95–96. *See also* Telestrator (CBS Chalkboard)

Parker, Buddy, 17
partnership of Madden and Summerall: beginnings of, 89–94; camaraderie of, 121–24, *122*, *123*; CBS Chalkboard, 112–16, 121; executives voting for, 93–96; first pairing together, 89–92; game preparation, xxvii–xxviii, 108–12, 117; humanity of, 116–17; love and respect in, 117–18; Musburger eavesdropping on, 98–101; O'Neil and, 89–94, 98, 103–4; Summerall's unselfishness, 103–8. *See also* partnership success
partnership success: Goren on, 106; Nantz on, 107–8; Sandomir on, 106–7; Stockton on, 104; Zyontz on, 104–5
Pearl, Mike, 98–99
Philadelphia Eagles, 59–61
Pilson, Neal, 141–42, 147, 152, 150–61, 166
Pinchbeck, Val, 108, 153–54
Pittsburgh Steelers, 49, 51
Pro Football Hall of Fame: Eisen announcing winners, 188–89; Madden induction, *189*, 190–93, *192*; voting process, 187–88
progressive supranuclear palsy (PSP), 174, 181

Rand, Sally, 37
Rauch, John, 45, 46, 47–48
Reiffel, Leonard, 112
Richmond, Peter, 53
Riggins, John, 113–14

Index

Rinaldi, Tom, 195
Robinson, John, 9, 23–24, 29
Rosen, Bob, 71, 89, 153
Rosenstein, Jay, 11, 147
Rote, Kyle, 31, 35
Rothweiler, George "Hulk," 110
Rozelle, Pete, xxvi, 9–11, 32, 164
Rupp, Adolph, 15

Sambuca restaurant, 133
San Diego Chargers, 43, 45–46
San Diego State, 43–44
Sandomir, Richard, 56, 106–7, 161, 172
San Francisco 49ers, 95, 110, 114
Santos, Joel, 195
Saturday Night Live, 74, 115, 117–18
Sauter, Van Gordon: with author, *85*; background, 83–85; hiring O'Neil, 85–86; splitting up Summerall and Brookshier, 68–69, 86, 159; views on Madden, 71, 86–88, 98; views on Scully, 88–89, 94
Schenkel, Chris, xxiv–xxv, 31, 33–34
Scott, Ray, xxiv, xxv, xxvi, 39
Scully, Vin, 88–92, 94, 197
Shaker, Ted, 68, 112, 159–61
Shanks, Eric, 195
Shaw, Buck, 60–61
Sky Sports, 170
Smith, Frank, 10
Snell, Matt, 75
Snyder, Tom, 77
Sports Broadcasting Hall of Fame, 171
Stabler, Kenny, 51
Stanton, Frank, 35
Stenner, Bob: and CBS Chalkboard, 114; Fox network signing, 169; Madden pointing out Immaculate Reception phone to, 49–50; Summerall's drinking and, 64, 67, 159, 166–67; at Summerall's funeral, 185; views on CBS losing NFL, 151–52; views on Madden and Summerall partnership, 117; views on O'Neil, 96, 136

Stephens, Jackson T. "Jack," 16
Sterling, Jack, 35–36
Stern, Bill, xxiii
Stern, David, 152
Stewart, Larry, 171, 175–76
Stingley, Darryl, 53–54
St. Louis Cardinals, 92
Stockton, Dick, 96, 104, 107, 152
Stram, Hank, 9–10, 95
Stringer, Howard, 145–46
Stubbs sandwich, 130–31
Stydahar, Joe, 18
Summerall, Pat: autobiography, 14; awards and tributes, 118–19, 169, 182–86; with Cardinals, 18, 31–32; death, 181–82; drinking excessively, 157–63, 167–68; as emotional, 163–64; farming investments, 18; with Giants, 18–20, *21*; health issues, 160–61, 171, 174, 180–82; with Lions, 16–18; on Madden, 119, 179; not ready to retire, 171–76, 180–81; slippage in performance, 171; sobriety of, 168; teaching jobs, 17, 18; as tennis player and broadcaster, 14–15, 55, 56–57; "The Intervention," 163–68, 181; youth and college years, 13–16, 17, 158. *See also* partnership of Madden and Summerall; Summerall as broadcaster; Summerall family
Summerall as broadcaster: as CBS Sports analyst, 37–41; Fox network and, 147–48, *149*, 149–50; for golf, 55–56, 150–51; on *The Jack Sterling Show*, 35–37; Madden auditioning with, 7–8; *Murder, She Wrote* promos, 116–17; Schenkel teamed with, xxvi; Scott teamed with, xxv; style and talents, 33, 39, 55–56, 89, 103, 104, 179–80, 184; *This Week in the NFL*, 61, 63–65. *See also* Brookshier, Tom; partnership of Madden and Summerall; partnership success

215

Summerall family: Augusta Georgia "Aunt Georgia," 13–14, 16, 22; Cheri (Burns), 157–58, *167*, 174, 181–82, 183; Jay, 163, 176, 183–84; Kathy (Jacobs), 18, 34, 164; Kyle, 183; Susan, 165–66

Summerall: On and Off the Air, 14–15

Super Bowls: I, 40, 46; II, 46–47; III, 47; VI, 62; VIII, 40; X, xxv; XI, 51–52, *52*; XII, xxv, 66–67; XIV, xxv, 9, 67–69; XVI, 109–10, 113, 114–16, 179; XVII, 44, 89; XVIII, 98, 109; XXXVI, 179

"Super Summerall" poster, 37, *38*

The Superteams (TV show), 2–3

Swearingen, Fred, 49

Tagliabue, Paul, 145–48
Telestrator (CBS Chalkboard), 97, 112–16, 121
Thanksgivings, 133–34, 135, 186
This Week in the NFL, 41–42
Thomas, Duane, 62–63
Tignor, Steve, 56–57
Time Out (boat), 80–81
Tirico, Mike, 182–83
Tisch, Larry, 141–42, 144–48, 154
"Tom Brady rule," 111
Toomay, Pat, 52, 54
touch football series, 121–24, *122*, *123*
Tour de France, 84–85
Trabert, Tony, 56
Trencher, Hal, 116–17
Trimble, Jim, 59
turduckens, 107, 133–34, 135

University of Arkansas, 15–16
University of Louisville promos, 69
Upshaw, Gene, 1

Van Brocklin, Norm, 27–28
Venturi, Ken, 56
Vermeil, Dick, 69
video games, 128–29
Villapiano, Phil, 121
Visser, Lesley, 130, 148
Vitrano, Joan, 78, 109, 133, 179–80

Walsh, Bill, 52, 114
Washington Redskins, 44, 113–14, 161
Waters, Charley, 69
WCBS Radio, 20–22, 33–35
Weisman, Mike, 4
Wiles, Susan, 165–66
Wismer, Harry, xxiv
Wussler, Bob, 40–41, 71, 84

You Are Looking Live! (Podolsky), xxvi, 99, 177

Zyontz, Richie: and *All Madden* documentary, 194–96; background, 83; last visit with Madden, 198; on Madden and Summerall, 86–87, 89, 104–5, *105*, 159; Madden as matchmaker for, 136–38, *139*, 194; Madden's relationship with, 133, 137, 194–97; on Miller Lite commercial, 76; views on CBS losing NFL contract, 152–53